Your Ultimate
LIFE
MANAGEMENT
SYSTEM

Your Ultimate LIFE MANAGEMENT SYSTEM

How Jesus's Inaugural Address
(The Sermon on the Mount)
Can Change Your Life

David L. Johnston

HIGHERLIFE
PUBLISHING & MARKETING
Oviedo, FL

Published by HigherLife Development Services, Inc.
 PO Box 623307
 Oviedo, Florida 32762
 (407) 563-4806
 www.ahigherlife.com

ISBN: 978-1-954533-78-3 (Paperback)
ISBN: 978-1-954533-79-0 (Ebook)

Printed in the United States of America.

10 9 8 7 6 5 4 3 2 1

Contents

Introduction

B efore turning the pages of *Your Ultimate Life Management System*, before reading the thoughts and statements, before studying the biblical and historical context, begin with a realization of these three facts:

- Nobody is smarter than God.

- Nobody cares more about your well-being than God.

- That's why He came here—to show you His care.

Many normal concepts in life are contradicted and repudiated, but do not allow that to discourage you or deter you from seeking His will for your life. Open your heart and mind to receive that which surpasses normal understanding. Follow, without compromise, His life management principles, as outlined in this book, and you will excel in this life—and the next.

These principles are found in what I call "Jesus's Inaugural Address"—the first teaching He gave publicly, early in His ministry. His profound Sermon on the Mount is chronicled in chapters 5–7 of the Gospel of Matthew. The teachings Jesus delivered in this teaching are often referred to as "the Ethics of the Kingdom." They embody the basic standard of Christian righteousness and, in essence, provide a blueprint for how to conduct our lives, even today.

It was Jesus's first, or inaugural, address. *Inaugural* means a change of management, the beginning of something new. In this case, it is the blueprint for a new life—an ultimate life management system.

As you read *Your Ultimate Life Management System*, listen as Jesus talks. Like any inaugural address, with a speech marking the beginning of a new administration, Jesus's inaugural address is no exception. It is more eloquent than the soliloquies of Shakespeare, more life-changing than Lincoln at Gettysburg, and more inspiring than the addresses of John Fitzgerald Kennedy, Ronald Wilson Reagan, Franklin Delano Roosevelt, General Douglas MacArthur, or Martin Luther King, Jr.

Most people recognize it as the Sermon on the Mount. This, the greatest speech in human history, is where He outlines the blessing, the principles, the policies, the procedures, and the budget provisions for His never-ending kingdom.

Every inaugural address has its audience. Historically, the audience is made up of both like-minded people and those who are virulently opposed to the speaker's message. The crowds who listened to Jesus were a mixed multitude with a variety of motives, hopes, and responses, yet all were eager to hear the One who spoke with authority. Jesus was just as willing and eager to teach and engage. This was His life.

The Scriptures describe the gathering: *"And there followed him great multitudes of people from Galilee, and from Decapolis, and from Jerusalem, and from Judaea, and from beyond Jordan"* (Matthew 4:25).

He Is

The first and most important thing you must know about God is that *He is*. Do you believe He is? Only a fool can look at a work of art and say there is no artist or look at a book and say there is no author. *"The fool hath said in his heart, There is no God"* (Psalm 14:1).

Likewise, we cannot look at creation and say there is no Creator. C. S. Lewis said, "We may ignore, but we can nowhere evade the presence of God. The world is crowded with Him. He walks everywhere incognito."

God Is a Blesser

God not only exists; He is a blesser. A blesser is one who guards, guides, protects, and provides great advantages:

Introduction

"He that cometh to God must believe that he is, and he is a rewarder of them that diligently seek him." (Hebrews 11:6)

How can we know that God is, indeed, a blesser? It's simply a matter of history.

God blessed the earth:

*"For the earth which drinketh in the rain that cometh oft upon it, and bringeth forth herbs meet for them by whom it is dressed, **receiveth blessing from God.**"* (Hebrews 6:7, bold emphasis mine)

Is it not beautiful? In Psalm 33:5, David writes, *"The earth is full of the goodness of the Lord."* Then, Psalm 104:24 states, *"The earth is full of thy riches."* Isaiah 6:3 states, *"The whole earth is full of His glory."* Every tree, flower, vegetable, and fruit—every plant—is not only the work of His hand; it is also the beneficiary of the blessing of His hand.

He blessed the animals, the fish of the sea, the fowls of the air, and the beasts of the field:

"And God created great whales, and every living creature that moveth, which the waters brought forth abundantly, after their kind, and every winged fowl after his kind: and God saw that it was good.

***God blessed them**, saying, Be fruitful, and multiply, and fill the waters in the seas, and let fowl multiply in the earth."* (Genesis 1:21–22, bold emphasis mine)

How magnificent! God made each of the creatures—every bug, bird, and insect *ad infinitum*! He created more than 350,000 species, designing each of them to be unique:

- Elephants stand on their feet for forty years; eat 200-400 pounds of vegetation per day; have molars that are 12 inches long and four inches wide; pregnancies that last two years; and hearts that weigh 45 pounds. They communicate at frequencies from 14 to 35 hertz, which is below the hearing range of the human ear.

- Giraffes are six feet tall at birth and have tongues 20 inches long.

- Termites can live up to 30 years.

- Woodpeckers can peck 20 times a second without suffering any brain damage.

- Bees flap their wings at 300 times per second.

- Tuna swim constantly and at an average speed of nine miles per hour.

- Seals often swim for eight months and travel as far as 6,000 miles without touching land.

- Flamingos can eat only when their heads are upside-down.

- Frogs must close their eyes to swallow.

- Pigs can run a mile in 7.5 minutes.

- Rabbits talk to each other by thumping their feet.

- Fleas can jump higher than 12 inches, which is comparable to a human being leaping over the Washington Monument.

- Earthworms have neither eyes nor ears.

- Ants have five noses and never sleep.

- Ducks frequently swim while sleeping.

- All polar bears are lefties.

- Hummingbirds weigh less than a penny.

- Pigeons' have feathers that weigh more than their bones.

- Cows chew 18 hours a day.

- Adult moths never eat.

- Horses can look forward with one eye and backward with the other.

Can you imagine such creativity? It's almost never ending:

- Whales and dolphins fall only half asleep. The two hemispheres of their brains take turns sleeping; the half of the brain that is awake can make sure they continue going to the surface to breathe.

- Blue whales can weigh up to 300,000 pounds and can whistle at 188 decibels. (Humans experience ear pain starting at 125 decibels and suffer hearing-tissue damage at 180 decibels.)

- Adult kangaroos can jump 30 feet in one hop, but they are only one inch long when born.

- Electric eels can release up to 650 volts.

- Mockingbirds can imitate any sound.

- Ostriches' eyes are bigger than their brains.

- Owls can't move their eyes.

- Some insects have blood that is yellow.

- The fastest pace at which snails can move is 3/100th of a mile per hour.

- Tigers' skin is striped, as well as their fur.

- A lion's roar can be heard five miles away.

Why did God create such diversity? Are these simply animal decorations for the planet? No. He blessed the animal kingdom with such diversity so they could bless us. Each of these creations has a built-in design to teach us something:

> *"But ask now the beasts, and they shall teach thee;*
> *and the fowls of the air, and they shall tell thee:*
> *Or speak to the earth, and it shall teach thee: and*
> *the fishes of the sea shall declare unto thee.*

> *Who knoweth not in all these that the hand of the*
> *LORD hath wrought this?*
>
> *In whose hand is the soul of every living thing, and*
> *the breath of all mankind."*   (Job 12:7–10)

God blessed the earth, the animals, the fish, and the fowl to be a blessing.

He blessed mankind:

> *"So God created man in his own image, in the*
> *image of God created he him; male and female*
> *created he them.*
>
> ***And God blessed them.* . . . "**
>
> (Genesis 1:27–28a, bold emphasis mine)

Imagine creating mankind in "His own image!" What a blessing it is to be made, not equal with God, but in the likeness of God. We are in the same category as God. Only beings in the same category as each other can fellowship. For example, it is impossible for humans to have genuine and deep fellowship with a cow. There isn't anything wrong with the cow *per se*, but because the cow is in a different category, true fellowship isn't possible.

However, God made mankind to fellowship with Him. God's intention is for our relationship with Him to last forever!

God blessed marriage. Male and female is God's idea. Marriage is God's idea. It is significant that God made for Adam one woman, not ten. Similarly, God made for Adam a *woman*, not another man. Then God set the terms for all future marriages:

> *"Therefore shall a man leave his father and his*
> *mother, and shall cleave unto his wife: and **they***
> *shall be **one** flesh."* (Genesis 2:24, bold emphasis mine)

The word "they" in Genesis 2:24 denotes *one man* and *one woman*.

His Blessing Is Available for Everyone

God blesses everyone—Christians and non-Christians alike:

> *"He maketh his sun to rise on the evil and on the*
> *good, and sendeth rain on the just and on the*
> *unjust."* (Matthew 5:45)

He doesn't say He is just going to give sun to the good guys or withhold rain from the bad guys. In fact, Luke 6:35 says, *"He is kind unto the unthankful and to the evil."* In Psalm 145:9, David exhorts, *"The LORD is good to all: and his tender mercies are over all his works."* God is a blesser, and His blessings abound to everyone. God, who is love, understands that if anyone is going to follow Him, it will be because they realize that God is good.

God doesn't want you to be damaged. He wants you up, not down. He wants you helped, not hindered. He wants you healed, not hurt. He wants you moving forward, not backward. He is for you, not against you. He wants you blessed, not cursed.

True Fellowship with God
Requires Redemption

Genuine fellowship requires more than just being in the same category. It requires likeness of character, and that likeness can be achieved only by redemption. Light and darkness cannot coexist, good and evil cannot coexist, and right and wrong cannot fellowship (see 2 Corinthians 6:14).

Mankind has departed from the high and holy ways of God and must bring himself back—otherwise, fellowship cannot happen. This way back is called *redemption*, and this wonderful being of God, who loves us immensely and desires our fellowship, has fully provided it for us. However, we must desire this relationship with God. Otherwise, we will continue pursuing our own ways, which are contradictory to His:

> *"All we like sheep have gone astray; we have*
> *turned everyone to his own way."* (Isaiah 53:6)

This "going our own way" is what the Scriptures describe as *iniquity*, which is wickedness and akin to narcissism. Our selfish, egocentric usurpation of God's proper place in our lives becomes the driving force for sins of every sort.

This brings us to the biggest blessing available to mankind: allowing God to change us from selfishness to love. Love is the essential core of God's nature. It is the opposite of selfishness. According to God, love is the operating system of every soul. Love takes the risk out of empowerment.

Why would God eternalize selfishness and empower it to contaminate every part of the universe? He would not! That would be like a judge freeing willful, deliberate criminals back into society to continue killing, raping, and kidnapping. Such evil must be terminated, confined, or restricted. Similarly, narcissism must be terminated, confined, or restricted. Only love can be trusted. Here's the big blessing for mankind:

> *"God, having raised up his Son Jesus, sent him to bless you, in turning away every one of you from his iniquities."* (Acts 3:26)

Jesus came to turn us away from selfishness and toward love, which is the proof of a genuine Christian. Going to church doesn't make you a Christian any more than going into a pig pen would make you a pig or having athlete's foot would make you an athlete. Jesus Christ came to do something about this human predicament and to establish a new way of living. He shows us a different path from the wayward, selfish narcissistic path mankind has taken.

This new way of living is precisely what Jesus defined—it is the ultimate life management system for us to follow.

From Obstacles to Blessings

Yes, God is a blesser, but we face many obstacles to receiving His blessings. Our contemporary culture tries to convince the unsuspecting that evil is good and good is evil:

"Woe unto them that call evil good, and good evil;
that put darkness for light, and light for darkness;
that put bitter for sweet, and sweet for bitter! Woe
unto them that are wise in their own eyes, and
prudent in their own sight!" (Isaiah 5:20–21)

Unbelief or a distorted and inadequate concept of God will also block blessing. Here's why:

"He that cometh to God must believe that he is,
and that he is a rewarder of them that diligently
seek him." (Hebrews 11:6 NASB)

Blessing is the purpose of Calvary. The Apostle Paul said it this way: "*I shall come in the fulness of the blessing of the gospel of Christ*" (Romans 15:29). Calvary changed the destiny of mankind forever. No wonder the same apostle said, "*For I am not ashamed of the gospel of Christ: for it is the power of God unto salvation to everyone that believeth...*" (Romans 1:16).

For centuries now, lives have been changed by this power—from drunkenness to sobriety, from sinner to saint, from harlotry to dignity, and from bondage to freedom. Shackles are broken. Chains fall off. Satan is defeated. Hell is kept out of the lives of men, women, and children. Good deeds are done.

Blessedness was and is the message and mission of Jesus. This is the primary content of Jesus's inaugural address and the subject of this book.

"And seeing the multitudes, he went up into a
mountain: and when he was set, his disciples came
unto him:
And he opened his mouth, and taught them, saying,
Blessed...." (Matthew 5:1–3)

"And it came to pass, when Jesus had ended
these sayings, the people were astonished at his
doctrine." (Matthew 7:28)

You are His audience. Accept *your ultimate life management system*. Believe it. Receive it. Live it. Your life and the lives of all those around you will be blessed beyond your imagination.

Chapter 1

The Must-Have of Reliable Life Guidance

Jesus's First Sermon Is His Guide for Our Lives

O verlooking the Sea of Galilee, in what we know now as northeast Israel, people gathered to listen to Jesus deliver His first public speech. The location was of no special importance. It did not receive the name Mount of the Beatitudes until long after this event took place. People came from all over the country—from regions as far south as Jerusalem and as far east as the Jordan River.

By this time, Jesus's fame had spread across the nation. He routinely drew crowds in the tens of thousands. Although history did not record how many attended this significant event, known as the Sermon on the Mount, the Bible routinely records gatherings in which this great teacher taught and fed five thousand men, not counting the women and children.

This momentous speech, which was Jesus's first known as the Sermon on the Mount, was significant for several reasons. In it, Jesus taught his followers the Lord's Prayer, told them several parables, and cited the Beatitudes (e.g., *"Blessed are they who are meek."*)

This sermon is Jesus's longest description of how His followers should conduct themselves to serve as members of God's kingdom. (Please note that the word "kingdom" can connotate a political establishment. In this book, and in general, when I use the word "kingdom" or the phrase "God's kingdom," I am not referring to a political establishment but rather to a new grouping of persons under the ultimate management system He outlined for His followers.)

In this epic sermon, Jesus presented His standard for Christians to exemplify the love and selflessness that Jesus Himself displayed.

Jesus's Immense Audience

In addition to recognizing this sermon as a turning point in Jesus's role as a teacher, we must try to grasp the immensity of His audience. This was not simply a multitude, but a plurality of multitudes. Whenever Jesus saw a crowd, something powerful and compassionate stirred within Him:

> *"But when he saw the multitudes, he was moved*
> *with compassion on them, because they fainted,*
> *and were scattered abroad, as sheep having no*
> *shepherd."* (Matthew 9:36)

Crowds gathered with intensity and fervor whenever Jesus came. They were willing to travel. They were willing to forgo food, even for days. Yet He was not willing for them to go away hungry and faint, either in body or soul. Whenever He saw a great audience, a great crowd, a great multitude, He was always moved. His heart held great tenderness for their need:

> *"Then Jesus called his disciples unto him, and said,*
> *'I have compassion on the multitude, because they*
> *continue with me now three days, and have nothing*
> *to eat: and I will not send them away fasting, lest*
> *they faint in the way.'"* (Matthew 15:32)

Who Were the People in the Crowd?

It is reasonable to conclude that all His disciples were in attendance. There were also people from every walk of life: the educated and the illiterate, the prostitutes and the demon possessed, the wealthy and the poor, and the young and the old came to hear the address.

At that time, Judaism was divided into four main camps, or groups, that provided the religious context in which the meeting took place: the Pharisees, Sadducees, Essenes, and Zealots.

The Pharisees believed holiness was found in keeping the law of Moses and rabbinical traditions, already well established at that time. These law-keeping traditionalists found their identity in historic Judaism. The Orthodox sects of today claim to be descendants of this group.

The Sadducees, the liberal branch of Judaism, were much like liberal Jews today. They suspended rules and regulations to fit their lifestyles and modes of thinking. To this day, the liberal branch of Judaism scraps Mosaic Law to live a faith based on their ever-changing, personal comfort.

The Essenes believed the only way to be holy was to remove themselves. They left Jerusalem and neighboring cities and moved into the wilderness. Living as isolationists and nomads, the Essenes dug themselves into the mountains and hid away. The Qumran community, related to the Dead Sea Scrolls, left evidence of the lives of the Essenes.

Last, the Zealots were in favor of political revolution. These social activists worked and fought for political reform. The Zealots, with their desire to dethrone Rome, used the fortress of Masada, southeast of Jerusalem on the Dead Sea, as a refuge from Rome. This ancient stronghold is near the former cities of Sodom and Gomorra.

To this day, if you stand at the top of Masada, you can look down and see the ruins and ashes of Sodom. As the Zealots became active against Rome, they were pursued by the Roman army, which built a ramp up to their fortress. Rather than be captured and enslaved by Rome, the Zealots committed mass suicide. Masada is their grave.

This mixed multitude came from the four corners of Palestine. The general population (who had refused to join any of the religious groups) gathered alongside the disciples and the Pharisees, Sadducees, Essenes, and Zealots. All these diverse groups concentrated around Jesus on the mountain.

Getting a Sense of the Setting

Consider an earlier scene with Moses on Mount Sinai. As thunder boomed and lightning flashed all around him, Moses brought the ten commandments and the law to the Jewish people. God and Moses looked down to see the children of Israel, led by Aaron, worshiping the golden calf.

Now the scene was set on another mountain, the one that would be called the Mount of Beatitudes. There was no thunder and no coldness, but a beautiful day with blue skies and a feeling of expectation, void of wrath:

> *"And seeing the multitudes, he went up into a mountain: and when he was set, his disciples came unto him."*
> (Matthew 5:1)

Jesus was ready to teach. He was ready to engage people from every walk of life and every religious sect. He sat down, just as Jewish Rabbis do today, to teach students. He had the chair. He was the chairman. He looked upon His audience with compassion.

The Timeliness of the Teaching: Seven Themes

Jesus picked a specific time, place, and audience to reveal the ultimate life management system. Before we look at each point in detail, let's look at seven overarching themes that are important to understand:

1. His words showed why a new way was necessary.
The King had arrived to begin His new administration.

He would be establishing a completely new set of ideas for a new kingdom. Although He had drawn the masses before through His miraculous healings, this was Jesus's first public teaching. His compassion and power had gained their attention, and now many were ready to hear anything He had to say. People came with their own backgrounds, motives, and expectations. He was there to meet them.

The Old Testament ended with the possibility of a curse upon the land and its people, but the New Testament opens with a blessing. Jesus came to institute new concepts, new ways of thinking, new ways of believing, and new ways of receiving. Repeatedly, He said, "*You have heard that it was said by them of old... but I am telling you it is a new day now*" (see Matthew 5:21–22, 27–28, 31–34, 38–39, 43–44). He outlined a new set of principles and new way of life.

2. **His address deals with underlying attitudes instead of conduct.** Many in the audience were accustomed to teachings about outward conduct, but this was a new message. Jesus came to deal with the underlying attitudes that produce outward conduct. He went for the heart. How should people respond when persecuted? What about when spoken against falsely, or lied to, or misrepresented? What were they to think and do when individual adversaries or entire organizations were set against them? What are *we* to think and do? In His new kingdom, His new grouping of people, it all starts on the inside because that is where His kingdom resides—within us.

3. **He reveals the greatest insight into the mind of God.** These official words of Jesus reveal His heart and mind so everyone would know His will. When you know what is in the mind of Christ, you know what is in the mind of God His Father. There is nothing "un-Christlike" about the Father or the Holy Spirit. All

three agree because their characters are identical. In Jesus dwelt the fullness of the godhead in bodily form. The world had already existed, mankind had already traversed the earth for about three thousand years, and the King Himself was about to explain, in great detail, what was on His mind.

He reveals His thoughts because He desires that we think like Him. We cannot think like Him without knowing His thoughts:

> *"Let this mind be in you, which was also in Christ Jesus."*   (Philippians 2:5)

This was not a lecture given by an idealist, a psychologist, or a historian. This was God-made-flesh speaking His mind. Up until this point, people were taught that only a select few could know the mind of God. Jesus came to change that. *All* could know. *We* could know. Jesus was voicing His ultimate life management system for them. And for us. That is what makes this address so important.

4. **Jesus taught that there is the only way to true happiness: to be *blessed*.** The Amplified Bible elaborates on the word "blessed"—happy, to be envied, and spiritually prosperous, with life joy and satisfaction in God's favor and salvation, regardless of outward conditions. Blessed means happy. Blessed means you are to be envied. It means you are spiritually prosperous. You are full of life joy. What a great phrase that is! Filled with satisfaction, knowing that you are living in God's favor and are salvaged.

We are to be enviably happy? Yes, regardless of outward conditions, with a genuine sense of internal joy. The world has its system for the pursuit of happiness. We are told to acquire the next thing, then the next thing, in a never-ending chase to obtain things to make us happy. Yet, how can a spiritual need be met with something physical? It cannot. The world is caught up in pursuits of happiness that can never satisfy. Then the King of Glory comes to tell us the way of genuine and lasting happiness.

Solomon should have been happy, right? Look at what he had. He was born into royalty. He had silver sitting around like rocks. He lived in the best city on the planet, Jerusalem. He had the best food. He had more women than can be imagined. He had everything except happiness. What did this king, this teacher, this preacher have to say?

> *"Vanity of vanities, saith the Preacher, vanity of vanities; all is vanity."* (Ecclesiastes 1:2)

Solomon, with all his worldly possessions, never obtained an internal, genuine consciousness of joy. Jesus came to tell us, in His address, how to get happiness. No wonder the exclamation was made in Matthew 12:42: *"Behold, a greater than Solomon is here."*

5. **Jesus's address teaches us what truly pleases God.** Because of the Sermon on the Mount, we learn what truly pleases the heart of God. We learn how the children of the Father live in heaven. We learn the principles of the kingdom.

6. **Jesus's powerful speech strikes to the heart of the matter.** The Sermon on the Mount, or the inaugural address of Jesus, is designed to get to the heart of all things. It does not focus on the outside but on the inside, where attitudes and motives reside.

Luke 11:39–40 says, *"And the Lord said unto him, Now do ye Pharisees make clean the outside of the cup and the platter; but your inward part is full of ravening and wickedness. Ye fools, did not he that made that which is without make that which is within also?"*

When the Lord Jesus dealt with the Pharisees, the most religious and legalistic of the Jews, He rebuked them for cleaning only the outside of the cups and platters. However, on the inside, their hearts remained desperately wicked. They had developed their external lives with exacting observance, yet the real problems dwelled within their hearts.

Here came the King to introduce a whole new set of ideas—straight from His mind—that were contrary to the thinking of everyone around Him. His thoughts were so revolutionary that some may have wondered if He had lost His mind. Our culture influences us so much that His truth, which is so juxtaposed, so opposite, seems almost offensive. How can happiness come from poverty of spirit? How can happiness come from mourning? How can happiness come from meekness?

Nine times in the first few verses of Matthew 5, Jesus tells us how to be blessed. If these new ideas are not difficult enough, we now hear that we can be happy when persecuted. It does not make sense. Jesus boldly claimed that no matter what the outside circumstances of life may be, that believers could live in blessedness and happiness.

7. **Jesus taught the principles of the kingdom of God.** (Again, please keep in mind that God's kingdom is not a political establishment but rather a new grouping of persons under His ultimate management system.) It is essential to understand the laws and principles of any earthly kingdom to successfully live and operate in that kingdom. Likewise, it helps us know if we are operating within God's kingdom and how to change if we are not:

> *"But seek ye first the kingdom of God, and his righteousness; and all these things shall be added unto you."* (Matthew 6:33)

Jesus Challenges Us through Paradoxes

Jesus offers the ultimate life management system, as He described in the Sermon on the Mount, to lead us to reach true and lasting happiness, regardless of circumstances. This is the happiness reported in Scripture, a joy that cannot be taken from us. Jesus says He came to give us joy that is full and leaves no room for sadness.

Jesus challenges us through paradoxes. How is it that the negative can produce the positive? How can we be happy when all the circumstances around us do not appear to be blessings? *"And He opened his mouth, and taught them, saying, blessed..."* (see Matthew 5:2–3).

He began to explain how blessedness, happiness, is the way of His kingdom. He came to reveal greater dimensions of blessings from God than we ever had before. He told us we could be blessed in everything we do. He created the earth and blessed it. He made the animals and blessed them. He formed mankind, breathed into him the breath of life, and blessed him. Male and female, He blessed. He is a blesser. He blesses everything. He blesses in life and in death. He blesses and bestows genuine happiness.

Jesus came to plant happiness into our thinking. He opened His mouth and taught them to blessed—happy and envied:

> *"And it came to pass, when Jesus had ended these sayings, the people were astonished at his doctrine."* (Matthew 7:28)

We have no idea how long this first address lasted. We don't know if the audience sat all day, if He paused to let His words sink into their hearts, or if they whispered to each other as they listened. All we know is that the masses were completely astonished! The Message Bible describes it like this:

> *"When Jesus concluded his address, the crowd burst into applause. They had never heard teaching like this."* (Matthew 7:28–29 MSG)

9

This message is as true today as it was on the day Jesus delivered it. It is the Father's will that we all walk in the reality of God's blessings. As exciting as this message is for believers, there is more. In Matthew 5, Jesus starts a transition. He begins to speak of salt and light:

> *"Ye are the salt of the earth; but if the salt has lost his savor, wherewith shall it be salted? it is thenceforth good for nothing, but to be cast out, and to be trodden under foot of men.*
>
> *Ye are the light of the world. A city that is set on a hill cannot be hid.*
>
> *Neither do men light a candle, and put it under a bushel, but on a candlestick; and it giveth light unto all that are in the house."*   (Matthew 5:13–15)

We cannot be the salt of the earth or the light of the world until we have mastered the first twelve verses of Matthew 5. It is a progression. The King of all ages, of all worlds, who came to represent His Father and the Blessed Holy Spirit came to impart concepts and a new way of thinking. Only by following His teachings can we go forth as His ambassadors—blessed, happy, and full of light.

Chapter 2

How Attitudes Determine Outcomes

Blessed Are the Beatitudes

When I was eighteen, I attended a camp meeting in Ontario, Canada. On Wednesday evening, I went forward to become a Christian. I prayed at the altar, but nothing happened.

The next morning, I hopped into my rickety old 1952 Chevrolet and drove out of the camp to see some young ladies in the same province. I saw my parents and told them I'd given up on my pursuit of God—of happiness.

Then, when I was twenty-two miles away in a little town called Brighton, I heard an audible voice come out of heaven: "David, if you go back to the camp tonight, I'll meet you at the altar at the conclusion of the service."

Well, this was mind-blowing. My dad had told me about supernatural stuff like that. At once, I turned my car around and drove back.

My parents happened to be walking around the campsite when I pulled in, so I stopped by to say hello. They asked me if I had decided not to take my trip anymore, and I told them I'd changed my mind and had come back to get saved. They thought I was making fun of them, like I had many times before. That night, a preacher from Texas spoke. His text was Matthew 5:6, which said, *"Blessed are they which do hunger and thirst after righteousness: for they shall be filled."*

The moment he gave the altar call, I ran to the altar. I reached the altar spot closest to where I'd been sitting. I had sat only four or five rows back because I had a date with God at the altar that night. For more than three hours, I was only vaguely aware of my surroundings as indescribable happiness flooded my thirsty soul, quenching me in an instant. When I came back to my senses, the place was empty, except for a small bare lightbulb hanging over the exit. That Scripture is the one God used to change my life.

On Tuesday night, two days before my divine encounter, I had spent some time at the campgrounds, making friends with the camp "cop." He wasn't a real policeman but a pastor doing camp security duties. I thought that if I became his friend, I would be exempt from keeping the ten-o'clock-lights-out curfew. He was a nice guy, and hanging out with him was fun. I decided to open my heart to him.

I said, "Ah, I tried to find God."

"Really? Where have you looked?" he asked.

"Well, I have read Barclay and Descartes and have also talked to my dad a lot."

"If you want to find God, go where God is—at the altar," he advised. "He will meet you there. Go to the altar in the meeting place over there, and you'll find Him."

That's why I went to the altar on Wednesday night. However, when I went back the next night, I met God, just as the "policeman" had said. I found true happiness that day, and my life has never been the same since that encounter with God at the altar.

In the wee hours of the morning, I walked out of the tabernacle and went to the shore of Lake Ontario. Sitting on an old railroad tie, I stared at the lovely sky for several hours. I became aware that the God who placed all those stars in the sky now lived in my heart.

At about six-thirty in the morning, I found my way to my parents' cottage. When I opened the door, they came over and hugged me. We sat down at the breakfast table, and I looked them in the eyes and asked for their forgiveness. A lot of tears were shed that morning as reconciliation took place. For the next ten days, my soul was enraptured by celestial glory because I had entered the kingdom of heaven.

The Only Way to Lasting Happiness: Blessed Are the Poor in Spirit

Happiness. It's the joyful state that has eluded mankind for centuries. From philosophers to psychologists, from clergy to laity, from sages to fools, from academics to comedians, from kings to paupers, people have fiercely debated the big question: What makes people happy? Aristotle, one of the greatest thinkers in the history of Western philosophy, spent a whopping twenty-seven pages of his ninth treatise book trying to define happiness. His conclusion? Happiness depends on us. Amazingly, Thomas Aquinas, the popular medieval theologian, agreed with him!

For most people, the source of happiness is hard to define. Jesus—not the philosopher or the theologian, but God in the flesh—gives us the details of the way to lasting happiness. That is why God Himself made sure that the way to genuine blessedness was item number one in His Son's inaugural address.

Jesus didn't leave us baffled about this crucial question that has stumped minds for so long. Happiness is the subject of the first "be-attitude." It explains the only way to genuine and lasting happiness. God wants us to be happy so much that He made "living blessed" the number one item in His Son's inaugural address.

The Kingdom of Heaven— Seven Vivid Metaphors

Before we get into the nitty-gritty of the kingdom of heaven, it's important to point out one truth: poverty of spirit is the only route that'll take you there. In Matthew 13, Jesus gives us seven parables about the kingdom of heaven:

1. Like a seed sown by a farmer that produces a bumper harvest, the kingdom of heaven brings forth abundant blessings (see Matthew 13:24).

2. Like a minuscule mustard seed that grows into a huge tree, the kingdom of heaven produces gigantic blessings (see Matthew 13:31–32).

3. Like expansive yeast that leavens the whole dough, the kingdom of heaven brings ever-increasing blessings, which engulf a believer's life (see Matthew 13:33).

4. Like a fisherman's net that catches all kinds of fish, the kingdom of heaven brings all sorts of people into everlasting happiness (see Matthew 13:47–50).

5. Like a housemaster who brings out old and new treasure out of his storeroom, the kingdom of heaven oozes blessings from its limitless divine stores (see Matthew 13:52).

6. Like an ecstatic man who discovers hidden treasure, the kingdom of heaven imparts rapturous joy (see Matthew 13:44).

7. Like a man who foregoes everything to buy a precious pearl, the kingdom of heaven can only be accessed by those who sacrifice everything for its sake (see Matthew 13:45–46).

What, then, is the kingdom of heaven? Why would you want to be poor in spirit, so you might inherit it? The kingdom of heaven is the greatest treasure anybody could ever have anywhere at any time. Not only is it desirable; it's jam-packed with joys of every kind. If you are in the kingdom of heaven, you have the best of everything that exists now and throughout eternity. No wonder the Scriptures say, *"Thou wilt shew me the path of life: in thy presence is fulness of joy; at thy right hand there are pleasures for evermore"* (Psalm 16:11).

Because the kingdom of heaven is the greatest of all pleasures, it calls for the greatest commitment. Mark 8:36–37 puts it this way, *"For what shall it profit a man, if he shall gain the whole world, and lose his own soul? Or what shall a man give in exchange for his soul?"* God's kingdom is so valuable that, once you get it, nothing else matters. Nothing on the planet comes close to the value and joy of being in the kingdom.

How to Enter the Kingdom of Heaven

God's desire is for broken humanity to find hope, healing, and joy in the kingdom (again, not a political establishment, but rather a new grouping of persons under His ultimate life management system). He wants you blessed and perpetually ecstatic, even if you're being persecuted. The first characteristic Jesus describes of kingdom dwellers is that they are *poor in spirit.*

Being poor in spirit does *not* mean being in a state of financial or physical poverty. It's poor in spirit, not poor in your pocketbook. If all that was required to enter the kingdom was financial poverty, then a lot of people would be in the kingdom. Instead, being poor in spirit means to have a humble and contrite spirit.

First, God declares, *"For all those things hath mine hand made, and all those things have been, saith the LORD: but to this man will I look, even to him that is poor and of a contrite spirit, and trembleth at my word"* (Isaiah 66:2). God is searching for people who are poor in spirit and tremble at His Word. Proud people do not tremble at the Word of God. Self-sufficient people don't care about the Bible, but those who are poor in spirit do. Poverty of spirit opens a new vista for mankind:

> *"The sacrifices of God are a broken spirit: a*
> *broken and a contrite heart, O God, thou wilt not*
> *despise."*   (Psalm 51:17)

Psalm 34:18 says, *"The LORD is nigh unto them that are of a broken heart; and saveth such as be of a contrite spirit."* God is close to the brokenhearted. What a proclamation! Anyone, whether president or pauper, who wants to come into God's kingdom must enter the same way. You must lose your life to find it. This was Paul's testimony—that death brings life (see Galatians 2:20).

In Luke 18:9–14, Jesus uses the parable of the Pharisee and the Publican to illustrate how few are willing to take the route of brokenness and of an impoverished spirit. At its core, the problem with the Pharisee's prayer was that he was putting himself before God. In fact, he is described as "praying with himself," so his prayer didn't go anywhere but to his own ears.

This idea of "enthroning oneself" is still just as popular today. Self-improvement is not just a buzzword; it is a massive, multibillion-dollar industry that is bent on producing self-confident and self-reliant people. The world says you should believe in yourself, build your ego, get ahead, and be above everybody else. God comes along and says, no, it's the other way around. The way up is actually down. A humble heart that is willing to die to self and to joyfully serve others characterizes being poor in spirit.

Jesus's concluding remarks are clear: everyone who exalts himself shall be abased, while everyone who humbles himself shall be exalted. Becoming poor in spirit is the way to happiness and promotion.

How to Become "Poor in Spirit"

Thankfully, the Scriptures, as always, point out clear steps to take to become spiritually destitute and to attain happiness.

First, we must desire God more than anything else. The kingdom of God is not for casual seekers—you must desire Him more than anything or anyone—even more than life itself. Hebrews 11:6 says it this way: *"For he that cometh to God must believe that he is, and that he is a rewarder of them that diligently seek Him."*

You'll find God only if you passionately pursue Him, and He will draw close to you. My search for God led me to philosophy books and, ultimately, to the altar at a camp meeting where I met Him. This is a universal truth: if somebody genuinely wants to find God, they will.

God made these serious declarations:

*"And ye shall seek me, and find me, when ye shall
search for me with all your heart.
And I will be found of you saith the* LORD*..."*

(Jeremiah 29:13–14)

*"Draw nigh to God, and he will draw nigh to
you...."*   (James 4:8)

In our pursuit to become poor in spirit, we must not only draw near to God; we must also let go of all our sin. Because of our sin, we cannot possibly reach a holy God. The good news is that Jesus bridged the gap between sin and God through the cross so you and I can reach Him, in spite of our sinfulness. To truly desire God more than anything else includes letting go of all forms of sin.

James 4:8–9 says, *"Cleanse your hands, ye sinners; and purify your hearts, ye double minded. Be afflicted, and mourn, and weep: let your laughter be turned to mourning, and your joy to heaviness."* If you are holding onto a known sin, you'll never find God. To find Him, be brokenhearted, humble yourself, and ruthlessly deal with sin in your life.

Likewise, it is important to check the motives of your heart. Unlike man, who focuses on outward appearance, God looks at the heart. To receive blessings from Him and partake of all the joys of heaven, you must get your motives right. Purity of heart leads to spiritual poverty. Also, be single-minded in your pursuit of God. James 1:7–8 says a double-minded man will not receive anything from God and that he is unstable in all his ways.

Pursuing God takes a clear and focused heart. But we must also allow emptying and brokenness to occur. In contemporary American Christianity, we don't hear much about the process of emptying oneself to experience the fullness of Christ. Too many have bought into the self-improvement movement that preaches self-exaltation and self-gratification. Drugs, alcohol, or the acquisition of material things can never satisfy the ego. Happiness has *nothing* to do with arranging the stuff around you. Happiness is a mental, emotional, and spiritual condition inside

17

you. God's route to success is the opposite of what most modern-day philosophers teach. He urges us to stop pumping up our egos and instead mourn and surrender our own will to His perfect one. Of course, to do all this, humility is essential.

Humility is simply a DIY attitude adjustment. According to Webster's dictionary, *humility* is "a modest or low view of one's own importance." It is something you can teach yourself to do, and it is far better to humble yourself than to have God do it for you! If you humble yourself, He will lift you up. That's a firm promise from His Word. James 4:10 says, *"Humble yourselves in the sight of the Lord, and he shall lift you up."*

How high is He going to take you? How full is He going to fill you? The answer, my friend, is that He's going to take you into the kingdom of heaven. He's going to take you to the highest level, to an intoxication of joy, which is enduring, unlike the fleeting joy you feel when you feed your ego.

Jesus's way to happiness is a condition produced in us; it doesn't require praise or kudos. Because it's an internal, completely fulfilling condition, it doesn't require anything from anybody. No one can knock it out of you, no matter what they say or do. You become indomitable. You don't need to try to lift yourself up again because He will lift you up. You don't have to push and shove to get promotions. You don't have to do what everybody else does to get payoffs.

You're in the kingdom now. And in the kingdom, promotion does not come from the east or from the west, from the south or from the north. It comes from the Lord (see Psalm 75:6). When He lifts you up, nobody can put you down. If you lift yourself up with some conniving scheme that you carried out, you can fall quickly, especially with a disposition of ego and pride. For pride, the Scripture says, comes before destruction and a haughty spirit before a fall (see Proverbs 16:18). Not so for the poor in spirit, because they're lifted up by God.

Likewise, when God is the one lifting you up, there is no need to speak evil of others to make yourself look better. God calls this "slander." It is not a kingdom activity. People should have nothing to fear from us. Instead, they should be the benefactors of our love and our prayers because the poor in spirit see through a different lens. Instead of competing with our ridiculers, we feel compassion toward them. The poor in spirit return good for evil. They bless their enemies, but the proud cannot.

When you become poor in spirit, you're no longer competing, so you easily admit your weaknesses. You have no more cover-ups in your life. Transparency is not easy for the egotistic and the proud.

Throughout the Bible, we see examples of people who accepted their failings and were elevated as a result. Think about the stories of Jacob, Isaiah, Gideon, Peter, and Paul.

Jacob wrestled all night with an angel and ended up with a dislocated hip. He was beaten in an uncommon wrestling match. Imagine standing toe to toe with an angel. He didn't stand a chance, did he? What happened after he lost the fight and admitted his helplessness? God blessed him. *"And Jacob asked him, and said, Tell me, I pray thee, thy name. And he said, Wherefore is it that thou dost ask after my name? And he blessed him there"* (Genesis 32:29).

The prophet Isaiah mourned about his sinfulness. Because of Isaiah's humility, God sent an angel to touch his lips, take away his narcissism, and transform him. *"Then said I, Woe is me! for I am undone; because I am a man of unclean lips, and I dwell in the midst of a people of unclean lips: for mine eyes have seen the King, the LORD of hosts"* (Isaiah 6:5).

Gideon also could acknowledge his insufficiency. He became poor in spirit because he admitted his weaknesses. *"And he said unto him, Oh my Lord, wherewith shall I save Israel? behold, my family is poor in Manasseh, and I am the least in my father's house"* (Judges 6:15). In response, an angel reassured Gideon that the Lord was with him and that he was a mighty man of valor. Gideon was not weak anymore, but was made strong through God. Paul said, *"For when I am weak, then am I strong"* (2 Corinthians 12:10).

Peter was once a cocky loudmouth. He was the kind of guy who swam the farthest or climbed the highest. He had to outdo everyone. He was always talking out of turn and jockeying for first place. It was only after witnessing the miraculous catch of fish that Peter became broken and threw himself at Jesus's feet. *"When Simon Peter saw it, he fell down at Jesus' knees, saying, 'Depart from me; for I am a sinful man, O Lord'"* (Luke 5:8).

When you become broken, you're at the threshold of the kingdom of God.

Paul, once a persecutor of the faith, became one of the humblest men in the entire Bible. *"I am become a fool in glorying; ye have compelled me: for I ought to have been commended of you: for in nothing am I behind the very chiefest apostles, though I be nothing"* (2 Corinthians 12:11). Paul says, "I'm nothing." Out of that nothingness, he wrote fourteen of the twenty-seven New Testament books.

Being poor in spirit means to be without ego, pride, resources, selfishness, and self-reliance. This is big news: being poor in spirit is the beginning of the kingdom of heaven. It is not the end of you. It is the end of the unconditioned, undisciplined, unbroken, unyielding ego. Jesus asserts that until you get ego out of the way, you can never be happy. We can find happiness only through surrender and spiritual poverty.

Evidence of Being "Poor in Spirit"

The moment you embrace spiritual poverty, grace kicks in. *You will thank God for His grace.* Heaven showers you with bountiful blessings triggered by your inward posture of total dependence on God:

> *"God resisteth the proud, but giveth grace unto the humble."*
> (James 4:6)

Ego wants all the credit and all the glory for self. Ego says, *"I'm everything, I don't need God. I don't need anybody."* People go on, ruled for a lifetime by narcissism/iniquity and insatiable egos that can never find lasting happiness. Humility is the gateway to God's grace, His favor, eternal joy, and our souls are transformed by God's goodness.

Another benchmark of being poor in spirit is that *you will view everything as a gift from God*. Pompousness, arrogance, and ego vanish as you realize everything you have is a gift from above. First Corinthians 4:7 says, *"For who maketh thee to differ from another? and what hast thou that thou didst not receive? now if thou didst receive it, why dost thou glory, as if thou hadst not received it?"*

God has freely given you every talent, every mental capacity, and every divine endowment you have so you will use them for His glory and for the good of others. Knowing this, all kinds of dynamics kick in. When people think they did something all by themselves, they will not be grateful to God or anyone else. They get all the credit. They bask in the glory of their accomplishments. Pride-motivated, ego-driven, and chest-thumping people spend their entire lives striving as if they must prove something to somebody. It is not the same for those who, in humility, realize they owe everything to God. They lead serene lives filled with gratitude to God and other people.

Once your ego is out of the way, trying to one-up others becomes a thing of the past. Streams of God-given joy cannot flow freely if ego is clogging the course. Only when you get rid of self is heaven's joy released.

"Being poor in spirit is the end of iniquity, the Bible's word for narcissism. A good angel, Lucifer, chose to be a narcissist. He was the "anointed cherub," in heaven and had access to the whole universe. And then it happened, "Thou wast perfect in all thy ways from the day thou wast created, 'til iniquity was found in thee" (See Ezekiel 28:14-15). Iniquity (narcissism) turned a good angel into the devil.

Consequently, Lucifer was cast down, restricted, confined, and could no longer have access to the universe. If God gave eternal life and supernatural capabilities to narcissists the whole universe would become a war zone. Imagine that! God will only give eternal life to those that will do good and give up being self-ruled, living by the philosophy of evil and Satan.

Ego is blind. It doesn't see anything good in other people because it's too busy looking at itself. It's always competing, contending, and jostling for recognition. The merits and contributions of other people are not seen. If they are seen, they're ignored.

When you attain spiritual destitution, things change drastically because you look at things from a totally different standpoint. You will now be able to see the goodness in others. Now that your ego is gone, you can see what God has put in others and encourage them. You can also mercifully look past people's faults and see their deepest needs instead. The ego is no longer the critical binocular tainting your vision. You have new eyes that perceive the goodness in others.

Being poor in spirit also means *you will pray a lot*! If you acknowledge that you're nothing and God is everything, it follows that you'll pray a lot as you lean on Him.

You will be desperate to stay connected to Him because you know that once you disconnect, everything will fall apart.

Indeed, in Him, we move, live, and have our being (see Acts 17:28).

Maybe the biggest piece of evidence of being poor in spirit is that you will be very happy. How do you react emotionally and mentally to this Scripture?

"For without me ye can do nothing."   (John 15:5)

What is your reaction to those seven words? Maybe it's this: "Why does Jesus put that in my face—w*ithout Him I can do nothing!?"*

Or are you able to say, *"I can do all things through Christ which strengtheneth me"* (Philippians 4:13)? John the Baptist, of whom Jesus said there is no greater man in Israel, understood this. He said, *"He must increase, but I must decrease"* (John 3:30). That may be a hard pill to swallow—until you understand the heart of God behind it.

Here's the exciting news: when you decrease and become poor in spirit, He *will* lift you up. He does it for your own promotion, empowerment, and happiness. Indeed, the lives of those who are poor in spirit are characterized by unparalleled joy.

Chapter 3

How Negatives Are Turned into Positives

Blessed Are They Who Mourn

When I was a kid, we use to walk the railroad tracks, which were just five inches off the railroad tie. One time, my buddies and I were walking the track across the train trestle with a drop-off of more than 150 feet.

Imagine yourself on the track closer to the edge of the trestle. Let's say you stumbled and were falling toward the edge of that precipice, but your buddy pulled you back. He didn't just save you from the five-inch trip-off from the track to the tie, but from a 150-foot drop. He really saved you!

The world treats sin like a fall from the five-inch track when really, the drop is much more severe. No sin, no mourning, and no comfort. The only ones who can be rid of the guilt of sin and receive the comfort of forgiveness are those who recognize and mourn over their sin.

Jesus continues His inaugural address in Matthew 5:4 with the idea that those who mourn will be blessed. He's progressing toward a crescendo, which began as He described the poor in spirit as happy.

First, we enter into the kingdom of heaven by being poor in spirit, and then we mourn. From there He says we're blessed to be meek, merciful, and pure in heart; to make peace; and to be persecuted. It may seem natural for blessings to follow the meek, merciful, the pure in heart, and those who make peace, but first we must deal with a contradiction. The way to be happy is to be sad:

> *"Blessed are they that mourn: for they shall be comforted."*
> (Matthew 5:4)

Four Causes of Mourning

To understand Matthew 5:4, it helps to understand the many causes of mourning. Here are four:

1. **We mourn when we lose a loved one.** This mourning, although followed by comfort, is not the one Jesus spoke of in His address. It gives believers hope that they will have a futuristic reunion with the departed loved one in the Lord:

   > *"But I would not have you to be ignorant, brethren, concerning them which are asleep, that ye sorrow not even as others which have no hope."*
   > (1 Thessalonians 4:13)

   We have hope that our wonderful God will end all those things that now grieve our hearts, minds, and bodies. He has an answer for that kind of mourning:

   > *"And God shall wipe away all tears from their eyes; and there shall be no more death, neither sorrow, nor crying, neither shall there be any more pain: for the former things are passed away."*
   > (Revelation 21:4)

2. **We mourn when we are disappointed.** For example, people often let us down—they don't always show up or do as they promised. Even those we love the most may not seem to come through:

> *"Then when Mary was come where Jesus was, and saw him, she fell down at his feet, saying unto him, Lord, if thou hadst been here, my brother had not died."* (John 11:32)

There are things in this life that will wear us down, repeated circumstances and concerns that cause us to become weary and full of sorrow. Like the Israelites traveling through the wilderness, we can become discouraged and mourn. Numbers 21:4 says, *"And the soul of the people was much discouraged because of the way."*

Yet Jesus said to bring this kind of weariness to Him. He will give us rest from our burdens and lighten our loads. Matthew 11:28–29 says, *"Come unto me, all ye that labour and are heavy laden, and I will give you rest. Take my yolk upon you, and learn of me; for I am meek and lowly in heart: and ye shall find rest unto your souls."*

3. **We mourn over world conditions.** Many of us carry the weight of what is happening in America and around the globe. We grieve the escalation of our nation's demise and that of others. We look forward to the day when God will make all things as He intended. In fact, all of creation longs for that day:

> *"For we know that the whole of creation groaneth and travaileth in pain together until now.*
> *And not only they, but ourselves also, which have the firstfruits of the Spirit, even we ourselves groan within ourselves, waiting for*

the adoption, to wit, the redemption of our
body."   (Romans 8:22–23)

4. **We also mourn over our sins.** Jesus spoke of this type of mourning in His inaugural address. This is the kind of mourning that results in the greatest comfort. Let's take a closer look at His promise of comfort.

There are two categories of sorrow. One guarantees eternal benefit and the other eternal destruction. One brings a change of mind that prompts repentance, and the other leaves a feeling of regret without remedy. We need not shy away from godly sorrow; it's the kind that preserves life: *"For godly sorrow worketh repentance to salvation not to be repented of: but the sorrow of the world worketh death"* (2 Corinthians 7:10).

Mourning over our sin brings everlasting comfort. Happy are they who mourn over sin, for they shall receive forgiveness. God, in His mercy, forgives, cleanses, heals, and restores the person who grieves over his or her sin. Such a mourner is blessed!

"Blessed is he whose transgression is forgiven,
whose sin is covered."   (Psalm 32:1)

Imagine being completely forgiven when we should be judged and sentenced for our behavior. Imagine being legitimately justified, proven innocent, and set free without penalty. How blessed is that! Blessed is he whose transgression is forgiven. It's gone. It's out of the way. Our sin is covered. That is happiness beyond measure and comfort beyond compare!

King David spoke of a time when he did *not* mourn over his sins. David broke his silence over his sin. He acknowledged his iniquity (narcissism) before God and stopped hiding. When he confessed his transgression, God forgave him. Blessed are they who mourn over

their sins and acknowledge their sin and iniquity
because the Lord forgives:

> *"When I kept silence, my bones waxed old*
> *through my roaring all the day long.*
>
> *For day and night thy hand was heavy upon*
> *me: my moisture is turned into the drought of*
> *summer. Selah.*
>
> *I acknowledged my sin unto thee, and mine*
> *iniquity have I not hid. I said, I will confess*
> *my transgressions unto the LORD; and thou*
> *forgavest the iniquity of my sin. Selah.*
>
> *For this shall every one that is godly pray unto*
> *thee in a time when thou mayest be found:*
> *surely in the floods of great waters they shall*
> *not come nigh unto him."*   (Psalm 32:3–6)

We must ponder David's words. We cannot treat
them as a mere academic exercise or poetic read. *Selah*–
we must pause and think them over, allowing them to
sink in. If we cover up our sins and fail to acknowledge
them, they can damage our minds, emotions, bodies,
relationships, and anything else.

Do you want to be happy? Mourn over your sin. You
will be comforted. If we want to change our course, we
must do as David did and face our sins. God is waiting
to forgive. He is close to those who are contrite, those
who feel their sin and come before Him. When we feel
the greatness of our sin, there He is. He is close to us.

Jesus said He didn't come into the world to
condemn it, but to save it. Receive this vital truth:
when people deny their sinfulness, they go further
into sin. It becomes easier and easier to continue in it.
Their hearts become harder, and God seems farther and
farther away. But God is not the one who moved. Our
sins have moved us from Him, and His voice grows
dim and distant. We are no longer tender before Him.

27

However, God is willing to forgive. He longs to move in close to the contrite heart.

In Luke 15 is an example of what mourning our sin should look like through the story of the prodigal son. In this chapter, we see the son go astray and fail, but we also see him repent. Even more important, we see the father's response:

> *"With great determination and a desire to make things right, he headed home, saying, 'I will arise and go to my Father, and I will say unto him, Father I have sinned against heaven, and before thee,*
>
> *and I am no more worthy to be called thy son...'"*
> (Luke 15:18–19)

Yet he didn't make it all the way there before his father saw him in the distance and ran to greet him. That is exactly what God is like. Show me someone who mourns over their sins, and I'll show you someone who is close to God:

> *"He that covereth his sins shall not prosper: but whoso confesseth and forsaketh them shall have mercy."*
> (Proverbs 28:13)

Guilt Is a Gift from God

Guilt is to our souls as pain is to our bodies. What if you ran across a parking lot, in your bare feet, and cut your foot wide open on a piece of glass and felt no pain? You could suffer blood loss, infection, or even blood poisoning. Pain is good. God built pain into the human anatomy as a warning mechanism. When we cut our feet, we feel pain. We know we have a problem, and we know we must fix it. Guilt works the same way—we are aware that we've done something wrong.

A person who pushes guilt away consistently, rationalizes it, or blames someone else is ignoring the need to fix the problem. Karl Menninger's book *Whatever Became of Sin?* reflects on how our culture has virtually eliminated the concept of sin. Sin has become a mere "mistake." Our judicial system even legalizes sin in some instances. We face a cultural crisis where there is no longer an acknowledgment of sin. Therefore, there is no mourning, and there will be no comfort. There is no cleansing, no healing, no forgiveness, and no recovery, and, as a result, our culture is not sustainable.

I believe the greatest need in America, and around the world, is to be conscious and be convicted of sin. If we think lightly of sin, we will think lightly of the need for a Savior. If we see the greatness of sin, we will see the greatness of our Savior.

When we sin, we set dynamics into motion. We may think we're getting away with the sin with no consequences, but the truth is that destruction has begun for this life and the next. Mourners will stop their sin and mourn their actions. Happiness doesn't come from the mourning, but from God's response to the mourner. He forgives, cleanses, and removes our guilt forever.

Clearly, mourning is essential to receive God's blessing of comfort. The good news is, *we can learn how to become mourners*.

Five Ways Sin Erodes Our Fellowship with Him

Sin damages our fellowship with Him, and it creates distance between Him and us. Here are five biblically based facts about the devastating effects of sin in our lives:

1. **We can learn to hate sin by understanding its consequences.** Sin doesn't care what God says, and it doesn't care what the Bible says. *Sin causes us to trample God's laws.* A sinful nature says, "My own self-expression and self-fulfillment are all that are important." Sin's ego takes over God's position in our lives and is the essence out of which all sin flows. Ego is never satisfied. Feed it, and it wants something

more. It's always reaching, clutching, grasping, and grabbing.

2. **Sin slights God's love.** Sin mocks God's love. It says, "I don't need you, God. Get out of my life." Sin is an attempt to elevate the created over the Creator, and it breaks fellowship with the One who gave us life.

3. **Sin grieves the Holy Spirit.** The Scriptures tell us not to grieve the Holy Spirit: *"Whereby ye are sealed unto the day of redemption"* (see Ephesians 4:30). The Spirit will not always strive with men.

4. **Sin damages our glory.** Romans 3 tells us that all have sinned and come short of the glory of God. We are created in His image. No other part of creation compares with mankind, but sin damages our glory. The psalmist declared, *"What is man that thou art mindful of him? and the son of man, that thou visitest him? ...and hast crowned him with glory and honor"* (Psalm 8:4–5).

   He has made us in the same category as Himself! As previously stated, He has crowned us with glory. If we want to fellowship with God, we must be in *His* category. That's how He designed us. If His image in us gets tarnished, tainted, damaged, and damned, we will lose our glory. We will lose our dignity. We lose our position in the universe.

5. **Sin changes us from the image of God to that of a beast.** We fall short, and we move from the image of God to the image of a beast. We are no longer capable of fellowship with God. Beloved, we must learn to hate sin. It removes us from fellowship with God.

Six Steps for Becoming a True Mourner

Now that we've discussed the devastating effects of sin and how it prevents us from mourning and being comforted, let's look at six steps for becoming a true mourner:

1. **Resist an "evil imagination."** The industrialized church has lost track of what sin is. Our pulpits aim to make people laugh instead of weep. This spills over into our daily lives, where Christians can be entertained by the story line of a movie, magazine, or book that focuses on evil. We begin to take pleasure in sinful things. *Never think lightly of, or be entertained by, sinful acts*:

   > *"That they all might be damned who*
   > *believed not the truth, but had pleasure in*
   > *unrighteousness."* (2 Thessalonians 2:12)

   We cannot allow outside entertainment by the very thing that causes us to mourn; neither can we allow evil, on the inside, to entertain our minds. The Bible calls this "evil imaginations." Our imaginations allow us to receive joy from evil desires and thoughts in our minds, instead of going out to perform our sins. In our culture, what was once appalling and disgraceful is now acceptable. This acceptance of sin has infiltrated our minds and emotions. We are conditioned to accept evil as the status quo. This does not promote the mourning that results in comfort.

2. **Look to the cross to become a true mourner.** Jesus's ultimate sacrifice on the cross reminds us of when God did His best and man did his worst. At the cross, we are reminded about the price of our sin—the very blood of God:

   > *"He is despised and rejected of men; a man*
   > *of sorrows, and acquainted with grief: and*
   > *we hid as it were our faces from him; he was*
   > *despised, and we esteemed him not.*
   > *Surely he hath borne our griefs, and carried*
   > *our sorrows: yet we did esteem him stricken,*
   > *smitten of God, and afflicted.*

> *But he was wounded for our transgressions,*
> *he was bruised for our iniquities: the*
> *chastisement of our peace was upon him; and*
> *with his stripes we are healed."* (Isaiah 53:3–5)

3. **Study the Scriptures.** Numbers 32:23 give us this warning, *"But if ye will not do so, behold, ye have sinned against the* LORD: *and be sure your sin will find you out."*

Unfortunately, there is little contemporary preaching about this. Maybe you remember the song "Give Me That Old Time Religion." The song speaks of a faith that taught the truth about sin and the sinner and called us to mourn. If we listened to the old way, we would find the good path, walk in it, and find rest for our souls. Instead, we often seek a way of pleasure apart from God's commands:

> *"Were they ashamed when they committed*
> *abomination? nay, they were not at all*
> *ashamed, neither could they blush: therefore*
> *they shall fall among them that fall: in the*
> *time of their visitation they shall be cast down,*
> *saith the* LORD.*"* (Jeremiah 8:12)

Like Judah, most no longer blush over their sins. Don't let this be true of you. We cannot mock God. Our shameless sinning reaps dire consequences. The Scriptures remind us of the damaging consequences of sin and beseech us to learn to mourn, "Oh my sin, my sin, O God."

> *"Be not deceived; God is not mocked: for*
> *whatsoever a man soweth, that shall he also*
> *reap."* (Galatians 6:7)

4. **Eliminate any hindrances to realizing sin.** Stop justifying and excusing; stop blaming and rationalizing. The greatest problem with sin is its deceptiveness. We have trusted in our own ways and the worldly ways around us. We have plowed wickedness. We must work hard to eliminate the hindrances that block our view of sin in our lives:

> *"Sow to yourselves in righteousness, reap in mercy; break up your fallow ground: for it is time to seek the LORD, till he come and rain righteousness upon you.*
>
> *Ye have plowed wickedness, ye have reaped iniquity; ye have eaten the fruit of lies: because thou didst trust in thy way, in the multitude of thy mighty men."* (Hosea 10:12–13)

5. **Avoid allowing your heart to become hardened.** Great men are those whose hearts are soft, gentle, sensitive, and compassionate. Watch out for your heart:

> *"Take heed, brethren, lest there be in any of you an evil heart of unbelief, in departing from the living God.*
>
> *But exhort one another daily, while it is called To day; lest any of you be hardened through the deceitfulness of sin."* (Hebrews 3:12–13)

An evil, unbelieving heart will cause us to depart from the living God. We must encourage each other daily or we will become hardened through the deceitfulness of sin. When we first became Christians, we were done with sin. We wanted nothing more to do with it. We saw it for what it was: evil, gross, and despicable.

But as time went by, unholy, outside influences and our culture infiltrated our thinking. Gradually, the sins we had once detested became commonplace in our lives. Throughout history, however, revival has risen from the hearts of those who recognized their sin. Complacent sinners became mourners, ushering in comfort for themselves as each, in turn, began to mourn. Their mourning produces comfort and gladness.

There are four comforters: Jesus, the Holy Spirit, Scripture, and followers of Christ. When we separate ourselves from fellowship, we are in danger. The Bible tells us to assemble together. To do so can produce unchecked hardening of our hearts.

6. **Mourn until the comfort comes.** Blessed are they who mourn sufficiently over their sins, for they shall be comforted. If we confess our sins as mourners do, He is faithful and just to forgive us our sins and to cleanse us from all unrighteousness. We can go to church and be religious, but that will not change the condition of our hearts. We must mourn and endure the pain of confession and repentance. It is promised, eventually, that joy will replace sorrow:

> *"For his anger endureth but a moment; in his favour is life: weeping may endure for a night, but joy cometh in the morning."* (Psalm 30:5)

> *"Thou hast turned for me my mourning into dancing: thou hast put off my sackcloth, and girded me with gladness."* (Psalm 30:11)

Three Signs Our Mourning Is Complete

When our mourning is complete, and God's forgiveness and cleansing have done their work, we will know. Here are three signs:

1. **First, our guilt is removed.** When we mourn our sin and are forgiven, there is no longer any condemnation. Hallelujah!

   "Verily, verily, I say unto you, He that heareth my word, and believeth on him that sent me, hath everlasting life, and shall not come into condemnation; but is passed from death unto life."
   (John 5:24)

   "There is therefore now no condemnation to them which are in Christ Jesus, who walk not after the flesh, but after the Spirit."
   (Romans 8:1)

   What freedom after mourning! Jesus came to take our guilt so we could pass from death to life. That is true and lasting comfort.

2. **We can truly feel we are among the beloved.** God has made us acceptable! The Pharisees hid their sins and pretended to be acceptable, yet they were self-deceived. The man who called out for God's mercy, on his sinful estate, went away justified. Through the blood of Jesus, we receive forgiveness of sins according to the riches of His grace.

3. **We are also at peace with God.** Part of the comfort is peace with God! We mourn until comfort comes and receive His peace that surpasses all understanding. We know we don't deserve it. We know the sins that sent us into mourning, but still Jesus keeps His Word. Blessed are those who mourn over their sins because they will receive the comfort of forgiveness, acceptance, and peace in their hearts forever.

Mourners are sensitive to sin, and they weep over it. Mourners also know the joy of forgiveness.

If you have not been mourning yet need to, go to God. Earnestly begin this process. If you have been mourning, receive God's forgiveness. He desires people who are sin-sensitive. He wants people who will not allow their hearts and minds to dwell on things that are contrary to His Word. Go to Him and receive your comfort. You will be forgiven.

Weeping endures for the night, but joy—real and lasting—comes in the morning!

Chapter 4

The Power of Controlled Strength

Blessed Are the Meek

The Good News—the Gospel—is for the meek, those with their strength under control. Generally, the proud will not respond to the Gospel because they think they have no need. While the haughty *can* get the Good News, first they must receive the bad. All must mourn their sin, as we learned in the previous chapter from Matthew 5:4: *"Blessed are they that mourn for they shall be comforted."* To gain comfort, we must do the mourning, and to mourn, we must humble ourselves. Then we can move forward in meekness.

Jesus continued His inaugural address, saying, *"Blessed are the meek; for they shall inherit the earth"* (Matthew 5:5). His ideas were new and no doubt captivating to His audience. He had already talked about the poor in spirit and those who mourn; then, He brought up the meek and their inheritance. Everyone likes to hear his or her name connected to an inheritance, but what was this prerequisite of meekness, and what did it mean to inherit the earth?

> *"The Spirit of the Lord God is upon me; because the Lord hath anointed me to preach good tidings*

*unto the meek; he hath sent me to bind up the
brokenhearted, to proclaim liberty to the captives,
and the opening of the prison to them that are
bound."*   (Isaiah 61:1)

God chose to save the meek of the earth. He wants to salvage
and redeem them; He wants to help and provide backing for them:

*"Thou didst cause judgment to be heard from
heaven; the earth feared, and was still,*

*When God arose to judgment, to save all the meek
of the earth. Selah."*   (Psalm 76:8–9)

Why God Takes Pleasure in the Meek

God takes pleasure in the meek because they recognize their
need for Him. The person who thinks he has it all together cannot
be saved. He does not see his need for God. He doesn't think he
needs help or forgiveness. He is committed to destructive forces
and to pleasing himself. He must come to the end of himself,
as echoed in the old song, "Amazing Grace": "'Twas grace that
taught my heart to fear and grace my fears relieved."

A simple definition of *meekness* is a humble and correct attitude
of our spirits toward others. People discern our spirits by more
than just what we say. They discern our spirits by how we respond
to them. A meek person interacts with others and responds with a
humble attitude, no matter how they are addressed.

Meekness does not incite. Meekness does not answer in anger.
Meekness is not weakness or the absence of backbone. Meekness
does not blurt; it is not brash, nor is it filled with indignation.

Meekness controls its responses. Meekness is quiet with
heroic, inner strength. Meekness weeps for the wrongdoer rather
than the wrongs received. Meekness is calm, in spite of emotional,
mental, spiritual, or physical storms. Meekness remains humble in
thought, word, and deed before God and man.

When we speak with meekness, we produce words with a positive effect. Jesus gave the perfect example of a meek response when, just before His death, His accusers reviled Him:

> *"Who, when he was reviled, reviled not again;*
> *when he suffered, he threatened not; but committed*
> *himself to him that judgeth righteously."*
>
> (1 Peter 2:23)

To *revile* means to speak against or to criticize in an angry manner. Though others reviled Him, He did not respond in kind. As He suffered, He did not threaten. He heard what they were saying, just as we hear those who criticize us. Yet the thoughts of the meek are far deeper than a surface, knee-jerk reaction. They do not give a quick and shallow response. A meek person commits himself to God. He knows God is in control; therefore, he doesn't need to defend himself or counterattack. He calmly trusts God to handle all outcomes. He is free to go forward, enjoying life.

The meek not only get the best out of life; they will inherit the earth:

> *"For yet a little while, and the wicked shall not be:*
> *yea, thou shalt diligently consider his place, and it*
> *shall not be.*
>
> *But the meek shall inherit the earth; and shall*
> *delight themselves in the abundance of peace."*
>
> (Psalm 37:10–11)

The wicked will be gone because their way is not sustainable. They self-destruct and have hundreds and thousands of ways to reach their destruction. The meek will inherit the earth, for they will delight themselves in the abundance of peace. It is the opposite for the wicked.

Jesus encouraged his followers, saying, *"Fear not, little flock; for it is your Father's good pleasure to give you the kingdom"* (Luke 12:32).

The kingdom of God belongs to the meek. They will get the very best from life. They will enjoy the transitory hours, days, weeks, months, and years at the highest level of fulfillment.

The meek enjoy an abundance of peace because peace is their perpetual condition. Their situation does not depend on what others say or do. They can extract the goodness from what they hear and respond in kind. They have no regrets and nothing to go back and fix:

> *"But the meek shall inherit the earth; and shall delight themselves in the abundance of peace."*
>
> (Psalm 37:11)

Because the Meek Are Teachable, They Can Make Good Decisions

God guides the meek in making their decisions. It's amazing that *El Shaddai*, the Lord God Almighty, commits to help the meek even in their daily decisions. The egotistical and proud are incapable of being taught, guided, and informed:

> *"The meek will he guide in judgment: and the meek will he teach his way.*
>
> *All the paths of the LORD are mercy and truth unto such as keep his covenant and his testimonies."*
>
> (Psalm 25:9–10)

The meek understand proper judgment, which includes God's mercy and truth.

With God's guidance and a teachable heart, it is easy to understand why *the meek are continuously being filled with joy.* Their joy is like a spring-fed pond, always receiving more:

> *"The meek also shall increase their joy in the LORD, and the poor among men shall rejoice in the Holy One of Israel."*   (Isaiah 29:19)

No matter what they encounter, the meek can rejoice in God. He teaches and leads them in mercy and truth, which enables them to respond with joy and to receive joy in return.

God Looks after the Meek and Personally Sustains Them

God wants to show His support to the meek. They are not perfect in the sense of never doing wrong, but they keep themselves perfect before God, in a right relationship.

God sees all, and we cannot escape His gaze. It is like the little girl who was asked in Sunday school, "Where is God?"

She answers, "Tell me where He ain't!"

God is busy looking for the meek:

> *"Great is our Lord, and of great power: his understanding is infinite.*
>
> *The LORD lifteth up the meek: he casteth the wicked down to the ground."* (Psalm 147:5–6)

Our society promotes self-sufficiency and self-focus. It teaches us how to out-maneuver, out-sell, and out-smart the other guy. It teaches us that we can formulate and fulfill our own destinies without God. The meek realize their need for God. He provides them with salvation, and they are joyful with His provision. They sing aloud! They are continuously filled with joy:

> *"For the LORD taketh pleasure in his people: he will beautify the meek with salvation.*
>
> *Let the saints be joyful in glory: let them sing aloud upon their beds."* (Psalm 149:4–5)

The Meek Have Emotional Tranquility

They will get the best from this earthly experience. They will live at the most joyful level because they know what it means to trust wholly in God. The meek have learned from the life of Jesus and emulate His meek and lowly heart:

> *"Come unto me, all ye that labour and are heavy laden, and I will give you rest.*
>
> *Take my yoke upon you, and learn of me; for I am meek and lowly in heart: and ye shall find rest unto your souls.*
>
> *For my yoke is easy, and my burden is light."*
>
> (Matthew 11:28–30)

A Meek and Quiet Spirit Is of Great Value and Radiates Inward Beauty

Peter says this when referring to godly women. However, such calm repose reflects the hidden nature of the heart, whether male or female. Meekness adorns. It's a valuable ornament in the eyes of God:

> *"But let it be the hidden man of the heart, in that which is not corruptible, even the ornament of a meek and quiet spirit, which is in the sight of God of great price."*   (1 Peter 3:4)

Meekness does not pretend it isn't hurt when others attack or that it didn't hear an insult. Yet it cannot be corrupted, defiled, or conquered. It genuinely sustains its composure, regardless of outward circumstances, people, and provocation.

What we believe about Jesus is the most important thing in our lives, and *the meek understand Christ's nature*. Some of the worst representations of Jesus came from those claiming to be His followers. An angry man, who claims to be a Christian, easily misrepresents our Savior. Did Jesus get angry? Yes, the Bible records such emotion a few times. Yet Jesus's anger was directed toward *unbelief*, not the *unbeliever*. He was moved with indignation toward the evil condition of their hardened hearts:

"And when he had looked round about on them
with anger, being grieved for the hardness of their
hearts, he saith unto the man, Stretch forth thine
hand. And he stretched it out: and his hand was
restored whole as the other."　　　　(Mark 3:5)

A meek person does the same. The sin angers Him, but not the sinner. His anger is toward what angers God. It is constructive. If we cannot grasp the meekness of Jesus, we will misrepresent Him, either with our words or with our lives. His daily walk showed us His humility and right attitude in spirit toward all. He came in meekness:

"Tell ye the daughter of Sion, Behold, thy King
cometh unto thee, meek, and sitting upon an ass,
and a colt the foal of an ass."　　　　(Matthew 21:5)

The Meek Qualify to Correct Others

This is because they approach others with a spirit of humility, with an aim for restoration. An egocentric person uses a prideful approach, and his heart is hypocritical, self-righteous, and holier than thou. His pride competes with the pride of the one he attempts to correct, which does not accomplish a beneficial result:

"Brethren, if a man be overtaken in a fault, ye
which are spiritual, restore such an one in the spirit
of meekness; considering thyself, lest thou also be
tempted."　　　　(Galatians 6:1)

The apostle Paul needed to admonish the early church. He gave them a choice when he asked if they'd like a rod or an expression of love and meekness. Note that love and meekness go hand in hand:

"What will ye? shall I come unto you with a rod, or
in love, and in the spirit of meekness?"
　　　　(1 Corinthians 4:21)

43

The Meek Know How to Lead Others

They follow Christ's example of leadership. Again, the apostle Paul, in speaking to God's people, alludes to a meek and gentle approach, like Christ's approach. Paul's meekness did not exclude boldness, but he was not brash. When a message is delivered in meekness, it takes effect. Paul combined his meekness with boldness to benefit those he led:

> *"Now I Paul myself beseech you by the meekness*
> *and gentleness of Christ, who in presence am base*
> *among you, but being absent am bold toward you."*
>
> (2 Corinthians 10:1)

When the meek give counsel, the chance of restoration is increased because their words and their delivery carry power. The meek tell others what is required to be rescued from the works of the enemy:

> *"And the servant of the Lord must not strive; but be*
> *gentle unto all men, apt to teach, patient,*
>
> *In meekness instructing those that oppose*
> *themselves; if God peradventure will give them*
> *repentance to the acknowledging of the truth;*
>
> *And that they may recover themselves out of the*
> *snare of the devil, who are taken captive by him at*
> *his will."*　　　　　　　　　　(2 Timothy 2:24–26)

The servant of the Lord knows striving against others will not work. Instead, he must be gentle to obtain the right result. He must be able to teach and apply what he knows to benefit the recipient.

The Scriptures Stir the Meek

The meek allow God's words to go down deep into their hearts. Other people may hear the words but do not allow them to permeate their spirits. Therefore, they do not receive the long-term benefit. The meek receive the Word that saves their souls. If your soul is saved, you become a doer, not just a hearer. Meekness allows the engrafting of the Word, so it becomes a real and lasting part of us:

> *"Wherefore lay apart all filthiness and superfluity*
> *of naughtiness, and receive with meekness the*
> *engrafted word, which is able to save your souls.*
> *But be ye doers of the word, and not hearers only,*
> *deceiving your own selves."*   (James 1:21–22)

The Word of God goes forth to achieve a specific result. To its sender, it does not return void. It always accomplishes the will of God. The Word of God, which is ready to respond to anything, makes life much easier:

> *"For as the rain cometh down, and the snow from*
> *heaven, and returneth not thither, but watereth the*
> *earth, and maketh it bring forth and bud, that it*
> *may give seed to the sower, and bread to the eater:*
> *So shall my word be that goeth forth out of my*
> *mouth: it shall not return unto me void, but it shall*
> *accomplish that which I please, and it shall prosper*
> *in the thing whereto I sent it."*   (Isaiah 55:10–11)

The Meek Have a Strong Testimony

A spirit of meekness helps believers properly represent Christ. The Good News of salvation is for everyone; delivering it in a spirit of meekness allows it to take hold inside the heart of the recipient:

> *"But sanctify the Lord God in your hearts: and be*
> *ready always to give an answer to every man that*
> *asketh you a reason of the hope that is in you with*
> *meekness and fear:*
> *Having a good conscience; that, whereas they*
> *speak evil of you, as of evildoers, they may*

*be ashamed that falsely accuse your good
conversation in Christ.* "   (1 Peter 3:15–16)

Five Ways to Develop Meekness

When it comes to character qualities, many think we either
have them or we don't. They think we were born meek, kind, or
gentle by nature or we weren't. If that were true, it could excuse
us from trying to cultivate Christ-like virtues. But character is
developed by choice, not chance. We must consciously determine
to strengthen it. Choice and development are what set us apart
from the animals.

Here are five ways to develop meekness:

1. Consciously Desire to Be Meek

Meekness will not drop out of the sky—*first, we
must consciously desire to be meek*. We must seek
meekness and righteousness, just as we seek the Lord:

> *"Seek ye the* LORD, *all ye meek of the earth,
> which have wrought his judgment; seek
> righteousness, seek meekness: it may be ye
> shall be hid in the day of the* LORD's *anger."*
>
> (Zephaniah 2:3)

2. Walk in the Fullness of the Holy Spirit

The Scriptures teach us that if we *walk in the
fullness of the Holy Spirit*, we will not fulfill the lusts
of the flesh. Meekness counteracts and contradicts our
temptations. When we walk in the fullness of the Holy
Spirit, we'll display the fruits of the spirit—one of
which is meekness. To return evil for evil is to operate
in the flesh, while responding with a humble and right
attitude is to walk in cooperation with the Spirit:

> *"But the fruit of the Spirit is love, joy, peace,
> longsuffering,*

gentleness, goodness, faith, meekness,
temperance: against such there is no law.
And they that are Christ's have crucified the
flesh with the affections and lusts."

(Galatians 5:22–24)

3. Put on the Clothes of Meekness

A third way to obtain the fruit of meekness is to "put on the clothes of meekness." The New Testament uses the example of "putting on clothes" when we want to take on something of value. Often, people dress the way they think, and they act accordingly.

For example, if you get up in the morning and stay in your pajamas until 11:00 a.m., you will most likely get little done. Pajamas make you think of rest and relaxation, not productivity, and you act accordingly. Likewise, if a person dresses seductively, he or she is thinking and feeling seductive and will act accordingly.

There is a philosophy behind our apparel. The first thing Adam and Eve did, after sinning in the garden, was to look for something to cover their naked bodies. They wanted clothing so they could cover themselves, after sinning.

To clothe oneself with meekness is to be dressed like Christ. Meekness looks good on everyone, inside and out, and enables us to walk in forgiveness. Forgiveness neutralizes the power others could gain over us, while bitterness perpetuates it. To be clothed in compassion, kindness, and meekness gives us a quiet, heroic inner strength:

"Therefore, as God's chosen ones, holy and
loved, clothe yourselves with compassion,
kindness, humility, meekness, and patience."

(Colossians 3:12)

4. Normalize Meekness in Your Walk with Him

God guides us throughout His Word. He is specific as to what we should do and what we should leave behind. In 1 Timothy 6, He directs us away from the love of money toward personal qualities that we should pursue. Meekness is included in His lineup:

> *"But thou, O man of God, flee these things;*
> *and follow after righteousness, godliness,*
> *faith, love, patience, meekness."*
>
> (1 Timothy 6:11)

Remember, meekness is our humble and right attitude toward others. As you *strive to normalize meekness in your walk with God*, you will find it enables you to respond, not react. A meek person can take a lot. He doesn't need to blast back at the first sign of enemy fire. He can forgive and keep his trust in God. When we leave all the possible outcomes to God's righteous judgment, we can forgive others and respond to them in love. We can keep our unity of Spirit and enjoy peace:

> *"I therefore, the prisoner of the Lord, beseech*
> *you that ye walk worthy of the vocation*
> *wherewith ye are called,*
>
> *With all lowliness and meekness, with*
> *longsuffering, forbearing one another in love;*
>
> *endeavoring to keep the unity of the Spirit in*
> *the bond of peace."* (Ephesians 4:1–3)

5. Demonstrate Meekness to Everyone, Always

Finally, make meekness a full-time walk by *demonstrating meekness to everyone, always*. Don't speak evil of anyone. Don't get in a brawl in your mind, your emotions, or physically. With meekness, there is no room to argue. We should remember when we were also foolish and disobedient, and this should help to strengthen our gentleness and meekness toward others:

> *"Put them in mind to be subject to*
> *principalities and powers, to obey magistrates,*
> *to be ready to every good work,*
>
> *to speak evil of no man, to be no brawlers, but*
> *gentle, shewing all meekness unto all men.*
>
> *For we ourselves also were sometimes foolish,*
> *disobedient, deceived, serving divers lusts and*
> *pleasures, living in malice and envy, hateful,*
> *and hating one another."* (Titus 3:1–3)

Blessed are the meek. They can respond to all men, at all times, in a spirit of humility and with a right attitude. They remain composed and at peace, receiving the greatest enjoyment of life! The meek follow the management system for life, demanding nothing in return. Yet they shall inherit the earth.

Chapter 5

The Pursuit of Right

Blessed Are Those Who
Hunger and Thirst after Righteousness

E very creature understands *thirst*. An animal may quench its thirst at a watering hole, at a bucket of collected rainwater, or, like an ant, from a drop of dew on a blossom. In some countries, people walk for miles and through dangers of all kinds to obtain something as basic as water. In America, we know very little about true hunger or thirst—if we missed our normal lunchtime, we think we are famished.

However, Jesus wants us to realize there is another form of hunger and thirst that is even more critical to our survival—righteousness. David said, *"As the heart panteth after the water brooks, so panteth my soul after thee, O God"* (Psalm 42:1). We must desire righteousness as much as we desire food and drink!

> *"Blessed are they which do hunger and thirst after*
> *righteousness: for they shall be filled."*
>
> (Matthew 5:6)

The whole point of Jesus's inaugural address is to create a kingdom of happy, blessed, and joyful people. The truths He shares, if we act on them, will bring maximum enjoyment and fulfillment to our lives. However, in our society, we suffer from a bad case of "culturized Christianity." Biblical principles have been compromised, and hedonistic practices of self-gratification and pleasure seeking are now common. Jesus, in His inaugural address, teaches the true route to lasting happiness, fulfillment, and blessing is through obedience. There is no other way. If we seek the blessings while bypassing the obedience, we forfeit true satisfaction in this life and endanger our position in the life to come. We must seek to be filled *His* way. It carries an eternal guarantee.

God is not stingy and will not withhold blessings from us. He desires to give to His children with a free and open hand. However, seeking His hand instead of His face will not quench our hunger and thirst. If we focus on the stuff He can give us instead of God Himself, we will never be satisfied. Just like the man who dreams of plentiful food and ample drink awakens to hunger, thirst, and starvation, we become the unsatisfied people who seek things other than the kingdom of God and His righteousness.

Hunger and Thirst for God and Righteousness Are a Normal Condition for Mankind

God has set eternity in every person's heart. Therefore, we have a different perspective than animals do. We can see the stars, and then we can contemplate them and develop a philosophy of life around them. Everyone's a theologian at some point, with an innate desire to know the Creator and the origins of our earth and beyond. We want to know what God is like. It's in everyone. There's an empty place in every human heart that only God can fill. If we don't find Him, that place remains barren and unsatisfied. David said in Psalm 63:1, "*O God, thou art my God; early will I seek thee: my soul thirsts for thee, my flesh longeth for thee in a dry and thirsty land, where no water is.*"

This is how we relate to God. We need Him as desperately as we need food and drink. Remember, people who come to God must first believe that God *is* and that He rewards people who diligently seek Him. Casual observers and seekers will not find Him. When people wrestle with what they see around them—the sun, moon, and stars—if they do not look to the Creator, they will be lost in their wonderings. God *can* be found, and He desires that we seek Him. All creation points to Him. When we think about His works and long after Him, we will find Him. "*I remember the days of old; I meditate on all thy works. I muse on the work of thy hands. I stretch forth my hands unto thee: my soul thirsteth after thee, as a thirsty land. Selah*" (Psalm 143:5-6).

It is a normal hunger to want to know our creator, to understand how the philosophy of life is settled, and to know what is right in every situation. It is intrinsically human to stretch our minds and hands toward Him.

Evil Influences Can Divert Our Hunger and Thirst for Him

People can lose their natural hunger and thirst for God because someone or something came along to get them off track. We must be careful with our children. We must guard them in every way possible to keep them on the path of God and away from evil influences. Some people will come into our lives, and those of our children's, who speak against the Lord:

> "*For the vile person will speak villany, and his
> heart will work iniquity, to practice hypocrisy, and
> to utter error against the* Lord, *to make empty the
> soul of the hungry, and he will cause the drink of
> the thirsty to fail.*"   (Isaiah 32:6)

Vile people will misrepresent the Lord. They want to put an end to our natural hunger and thirst for God. We can end up sidetracked and suffer all kinds of unproductive, negative, destructive, and sorrowful things in our lives. Then we become accustomed to these destructive thoughts and habits. Our brains get polluted. We believe what the seducer, the diverter, has told us. We get off track and don't know what's wrong:

> "*There is a way which seemeth right unto a man,
> but the end thereof are the ways of death.*

53

Even in laughter the heart is sorrowful; and the end of that mirth is heaviness."   (Proverbs 14:12–13)

What once seemed right leads to death. This is not just physical death, but also the death of our spirit, mind, and emotions. Our satisfaction, joy, and peace leave us. They're gone. Even behind our laughter is deep sorrow, and the result of our amusement is heaviness.

Our Hunger and Thirst Can Be for Wrong Things

We can hunger and thirst for power, prestige, or praise. We can desire possessions or seek pleasure and entertainment. To obtain the true and lasting life He provides, God desires for us to lose our carnal desires.

Our hunger and thirst cannot be filled by substitutes.

We *can* pursue substitutes to satisfy our hunger and thirst, but after the chase, we'll still be as empty as before. We'll receive no satisfaction. Why does this happen?

One reason is that we distance ourselves from God. Then we look for other things to fill a need only He can fill. There are seemingly limitless ways to attempt satisfaction outside Him. Yet it's like trying to grasp water that slips through our fingers. It's like using a broken pitcher to hold water for someone who desperately needs a drink. In our futile attempts, we try the same things over and again in the hope that eventually, we will satiate our needs:

"For my people have committed two evils; they have forsaken me the fountain of living waters, and hewed them out cisterns, broken cisterns, that can hold no water."   (Jeremiah 2:13)

Like the man dreaming of a fine banquet and plentiful drink, when he awakens, he's still starving and dying of thirst; so is the person who seeks the substitute rather than God. The same is true of the country, nation, and culture that fight against Mt. Zion, the place that bears God's name. We can pursue the things that do not bear His name or resemblance or go places that do not reflect His glorious presence, but they will not satisfy our hunger and thirst:

> *"It shall even be as when an hungry man dreameth,*
> *and, behold, he eateth; but he awaketh, and his*
> *soul is empty: or as when a thirsty man dreameth,*
> *and, behold, he drinketh; but he awaketh, and,*
> *behold, he is faint, and his soul hath appetite: so*
> *shall the multitude of all the nations be, that fight*
> *against Zion."* (Isaiah 29:8)

Jesus Offers the Only Way
to Quench Our Thirst

Jesus gives a guarantee for all who hunger and thirst after righteousness. He promises they will be blessed, happy, fulfilled, and content. They will have true peace and will not hunger or thirst: *"And Jesus said unto them, I am the bread of life: he that cometh to me shall never hunger; and he that believeth on me shall never thirst"* (John 6:35).

While traveling to Jerusalem with His disciples, Jesus stopped in Samaria. Typically, the Jews had no dealings with the people living there. The Samaritans had settled into Jewish territory because of a political move. They mingled with the Jews to some extent, through marriage and the adoption of various Jewish beliefs. However, they retained their pagan modes of thinking and worship, which sharply differed from the Torah of Moses and customs of the early rabbis.

Samaritans were considered half-breeds, and the Jews did not associate with them. Yet Jesus said He needed to go through Samaria. There was a woman there He needed to speak with. (By all rabbinical standards of the day, this was also a questionable act.) He found the woman at the public well and asked her to give Him a drink. He spoke with her about thirst, and He also told her things about herself she had kept secret. Then Jesus turned the conversation from physical thirst to eternal thirst. He explained to her the way of Living Water, the way of salvation, ending all thirst:

> *"Jesus answered and said unto her, Whosoever*
> *drinketh of this water shall thirst again:*
> *But whosoever drinketh of the water that I shall*
> *give him shall never thirst; but the water that*
> *I shall give him shall be in him a well of water*
> *springing up into everlasting life."*(John 4:13–14)

The Samaritan woman received His message and took it into the city. She gathered the men she had been with and told them about the man who told her everything she ever did and about His promise of living water. She knew Jesus had the answer to the thirst of mankind. It didn't matter how broken, troubled, sinful, or perverted their lives had become—Jesus had arrived to wipe those things away. In sin's place, He would freely give of the things that satisfy:

> *"Ho, everyone that thirsteth, come ye to the waters,*
> *and he that hath no money; come ye, buy, and eat;*
> *yea, come, buy wine and milk without money and*
> *without price.*
> *Wherefore do ye spend money for that which is not*
> *bread? and your labour for that which satisfieth*
> *not? hearken diligently unto me, and eat ye that*
> *which is good, and let your soul delight itself in*
> *fatness."*
> (Isaiah 55:1–2)

With Jesus, We Get It All

Jesus is ready to give, but not just a little or a one-time amount. He wants to fill us up and keep us filled. He desires that we be fully filled, fully content, and fully satisfied. Matthew 5:6 says, *"Blessed are they which do hunger and thirst after righteousness: for they shall be filled."*

How does He desire to fill us and are there conditions to receiving fulfillment? We know there is no cost in monetary terms. We know He desires our time, focus, and devotion, but how do we go about giving Him these things?

First, we seek the kingdom of God:

> *"But seek ye first the kingdom of God, and his righteousness; and all these things shall be added unto you."* (Matthew 6:33)

Once we seek His kingdom, He fills our longing and hungry souls with His goodness:

> *"For he satisfieth the longing soul, and filleth the hungry soul with goodness."* (Psalm 107:9)

The Scripture in 1 Corinthians 3:21 says it this way: *"Therefore let no man glory in men. For all things are yours."*

All things are ours as we actively seek them. Don't miss the word "do" in this section of Jesus's inaugural address. Blessed are they who "do" hunger and "do" thirst after righteousness. We are not filled because we once hungered and thirsted, yet we stopped. We aren't blessed because we *intend* to hunger and thirst someday. We are blessed as we actively and presently seek the things of God. *"Blessed are they that do hunger and thirst after righteousness: for they shall be filled"* (Matthew 5:6).

Seven Ways to Know if You Are Hungering and Thirsting after God

So what does this "doing" really look like, practically? How do we know if we're really hungering and thirsting after God and His righteousness? Here are seven ways to know:

1. **First, you will spend time in His presence.** Do you love to spend time with God? Do you look forward to time alone in His presence? That is the place of our deepest joy: *"Thou wilt shew me the path of life: in thy*

presence is fulness of joy; at thy right hand there are pleasures for evermore" (Psalm 16:11).

2. **Second, you simply love the words from His mouth.** True hunger and thirst are characterized by a love of Scripture. Although our relationship with God contains an academic component, it is still a relationship rooted in love. King Solomon talked about listening for the voice, and seeing the face, of his beloved. Do we yearn for God in this same way? *"O my dove, that art in the clefts of the rock, in the secret places of the stairs, let me see thy countenance, let me hear thy voice; for sweet is thy voice, and thy countenance is comely"* (Song of Solomon 2:14).

   Job also spoke of the importance of God's words above his necessary food. He had learned to value and prioritize God's place in his life: *"Neither have I gone back from the commandment of his lips; I have esteemed the words of his mouth more than my necessary food"* (Job 23:12).

   Jeremiah said God's words caused his heart to rejoice: *"Thy words were found, and I did eat them; and thy word was unto me the joy and rejoicing of mine heart: for I am called by thy name, O LORD God of hosts"* (Jeremiah 15:16).

3. **You keep in constant communication with Him.** Prayer isn't just a poetic exercise we do in the morning, at noon, at mealtimes, and before we go to sleep. It isn't just for Sundays or when something frightening or difficult comes our way. Prayer is constant communion with God. In 1 Thessalonians 5:17, we are advised to *"Pray without ceasing."*

4. **You are quick to obey His instruction.** It is good to obey His instruction, but how quickly are we to do so? Does it take us a day or two, or maybe even weeks, months, or years? *Procrastination is disobedience in slow motion.* When we hunger and thirst for God, we'll

be quick to carry out His will. In meekness, we will respond to God and man in the right attitude of spirit, being quick to do what is right.

5. **You have unswerving devotion to His interests.** Are we interested in what interests God? Love wants to keep connected and share the same interests. It believes in and pursues those things shared with the ones we love. We need to get our orders from His headquarters and follow His interests: *"Wherefore be ye not unwise, but understanding what the will of the Lord is"* (Ephesians 5:17).

6. **You will not compromise on what is right or righteous.** In Daniel 1, we see four young men ready to die rather than to compromise their beliefs. They would not defile themselves with the king's meat or wine; neither would they bow down to an idol when they heard the sound of pagan worship music. Their stand took them to the furnace, but they knew God could deliver them: *"Shadrach, Meshach, and Abednego, answered and said to the king, O Nebuchadnezzar, we are not careful to answer thee in this matter. If it be so, our God whom we serve is able to deliver us from the burning fiery furnace, and he will deliver us out of thine hand, O king. But if not, be it known unto thee, O king, that we will not serve thy gods, nor worship the golden image which thou hast set up"* (Daniel 3:16–18).

    What faith! They didn't bow. They didn't bend. We must do the same. If we love God, we will stand for what is right with zero tolerance for what is wrong. No compromise.

7. **Finally, if you hunger and thirst for God, you will be diligent.** You will have no spiritual complacency, no lethargy, and no casual interest. Instead, you'll have a genuine and active interest in God and His agenda. If we hunger and thirst for God and His righteousness, we'll have zeal. We'll be enthusiastic and diligent as

we seek Him. Hebrews 11:6 says it this way: *"But without faith it is impossible to please him: for he that cometh to God must believe that he is, and that he is a rewarder of them that diligently seek him."*

Three Ways to Separate Ourselves from Culturally Influenced Christianity

One of my heroes of the faith is William Booth, the founder of The Salvation Army. At the age of seventeen, he gathered a group of musicians and began preaching on the streets of England. He taught about the Fire and the Blood. Many challenged him—they threw things at him, spat in his face, and did all they could to discourage him. However, he had zeal. Within ten years, he had more than 25,000 trained officers preaching the Gospel throughout the world. They were trained to obey and take orders at a moment's notice. He had strict regulations for his officers that many of today's slothful, sloppy American Christians would challenge.

Do we obey God and diligently seek Him as the commander of our souls? Or do we approach Him and His ways in a casual and half-hearted manner?

A noted humorist was asked to account for his success in the theater and the failure of the church. He said, "The theater takes what is make-believe and acts it out on stage as if it's real. The church takes what is real and acts like it's make-believe."

This is the same problem we have today in the form of culturally influenced Christianity. We make it up, per our culture's values, and act it out, as we like.

Jesus said, in His inaugural address, we must first become poor in spirit so we can be welcomed into the kingdom. Then we mourn over our sins and receive comfort. Next, we learn meekness, which results in the greatest inheritance of joy we can have on this earth. When we hunger and thirst, He fills us. This is real. It is not an act. It is God's truth.

How do we separate from this American-made Christianity and increase our hunger and thirst for God and His righteousness? Here are three actions we must take to accomplish this:

1. **We must keep ourselves from idols.** We cannot let anything or anyone take the place of God in our lives. We cannot let anything or anyone become more interesting to us than God. We must not let anything or anyone occupy our thinking as it usurps the rightful place of God. Do not let anything compete for Him in your life. Increase your hunger for God by smashing your idols to the ground: *"Little children, keep yourselves from idols. Amen"* (1 John 5:21).

2. **We must take responsibility for our own spiritual condition.** It's amazing how many people take a *laissez faire* attitude when it comes to their spiritual well-being. They take no responsibility and don't intend to change. They are not active in their walks with God and are content with their complacency. They may not even realize they've become so cold or lukewarm, but they show they are no longer responsible, watchful, and active: *"Wherefore I put thee in remembrance that thou stir up the gift of God, which is in thee by the putting on of my hands"* (2 Timothy 1:6).

   Remaining stirred up takes zeal and commitment. It won't happen by laziness or neglect. We must purposefully evaluate and take charge of our own spiritual condition.

3. **We must remember the tremendous benefits of becoming hungry and thirsty for God.** When we eat a meal, our stomachs are filled. Likewise, when we pursue God, *we will be filled.* We'll be satisfied and satisfying, fulfilled and fulfilling. We get the best, both here and in the next life. We'll have no emptiness and no void and will feel no need to chase things that do not satisfy.

Moreover, *our children will be blessed.* I was rebellious in my teenage years, but my father was a pastor, and he and my mother knew how to pray. They were hungry and thirsty on my behalf, and they did not give up on me. My dad wouldn't compromise one inch with the enemy on anything. I was kept in church, even if I slept through the services. I watched my parents love God with all their hearts, with all their souls, with their strength, with their might, and with their minds. They had set a continual example before me, and I could not run for long.

Their diligence caused the Spirit of God and multiplied blessings to be poured onto my weary head, until I came into the right place with God. When I came to Jesus at the age of eighteen, I was not casual about it. The spirit came upon me, and I responded: *"For I will pour water upon him that is thirsty, and floods upon the dry ground: I will pour my spirit upon thy seed, and my blessing upon thine offspring: And they shall spring up as among the grass, as willows by the water courses"* (Isaiah 44:3–4).

Let's be diligent to hunger and thirst so our families can be filled from our overflow. God promises this will happen for our children if we, as their parents, stick with God. We cannot be casual in our relationship with Him. If our children begin to stray, we must run closer to God. If we want our children to grow in their faith, they must see our dedication. They will do as they have seen *us* do so. If they see us hungering and thirsting after righteousness, and being filled with it as a result, they will follow our lead.

God Rewards Those Who Thirst and Hunger after Him

When we hunger and thirst after God and His ways:

*"For he satisfieth the longing soul, and filleth the
hungry soul with goodness."*   (Psalm 107:9)

He also promises to give us *deliverance and direction.* When
we are hungry and thirsty, we can cry out to God. When we are in
trouble, He is there. He will deliver. He will lead us in the way we
should go. We are filled up and directed onward:

> *"They were hungry and thirsty, and their lives
> ebbed away.*
> *Then they cried out to the LORD in their trouble, and
> he delivered them from their distress.*
> *He led them by a straight way to a city where they
> could settle."*   (Psalm 107:5–7 NIV)

When we learn to delight ourselves in the Lord, we enjoy
fellowship with one another, we have a hopeful attitude, and we
live at a contented level. *Life becomes sweet—nothing is mundane.*
Yes, we will still encounter difficulties and trials, but we won't
stay discouraged. When we're hungry, we know we can keep
being filled and rise again in victory:

> *"Then shalt thou delight thyself in the LORD; and I
> will cause thee to ride upon the high places of the
> earth, and feed thee with the heritage of Jacob thy
> father: for the mouth of the LORD hath spoken it."*
>   (Isaiah 58:14)

Being spiritually hungry also means *we'll use our money
wisely.* We will stop buying things to bring joy and happiness but
instead get our satisfaction from the true giver of all:

> *"Wherefore do ye spend money for that which is
> not bread? and your labour for that which satisfieth
> not? hearken diligently unto me, and eat ye that
> which is good, and let your soul delight itself in
> fatness."*   (Isaiah 55:2)

When we humble ourselves, we will be comforted. When we learn the meekness of Jesus, we will inherit the earth. When we hunger and thirst, we will certainly be filled. Then we will ride upon the high places of the earth, not because we sought those places, but because we sought the Lord and He gave them to us.

To become great, we must become less.

Chapter 6

The Secret of How to Treat Others

Blessed Are the Merciful, for They Shall Obtain Mercy

Mercy does not reciprocate negative for negative, but instead gives undeserved favor. Mercy feeds our hungry enemy and gives him a drink. Mercy blesses him when he curses and loves when he hates. This is the same motivation as God's great mercy to us when He sent His Son. It comes from a heart and disposition of love. His love also created us in His image and is the same love that allows us to enter His kingdom.

As we move forward in Jesus's inaugural address, let's note the new way He presents cause and effect. We've seen that the poor in spirit are given the kingdom of heaven, that those who mourn will be comforted, and that the meek shall inherit the earth. We examined what it means to hunger and thirst for righteousness, and we saw that those who do so will be filled. As we come to the next segment of our Lord's address, there is a difference—this time, we get back exactly what we give.

Reciprocity:
We Must Give What We Expect to Receive

This concept in the Sermon on the Mount introduces God's law of *reciprocity*: *"Blessed are the merciful: for they shall obtain mercy"* (Matthew 5:7). If we want mercy, we must give it. If we want forgiveness, we must give that, too. In modern terms, reciprocity is often used in a negative sense, as in, "What goes around comes around."

Yet, in the kingdom of God, He wants us to understand both sides:

> *"With the merciful thou wilt shew thyself merciful;*
> *with an upright man thou wilt shew thyself upright;*
>
> *With the pure thou wilt shew thyself pure; and with*
> *the forward thou wilt shew thyself forward."*
>
> (Psalm 18:25–26)

The merciful will see God's mercy. The upright will see He is upright. The pure will see His purity. To the perverted, however, God will show Himself unacceptable. Grasping this law of reciprocity is crucial in obtaining mercy. I define *mercy* as a non-retaliating spirit that gives up all attempts at self-vindication, a spirit that does not return injury for injury, one that replaces evil with good and love in the place of hatred.

Mercy Is a Fundamental Disposition of God

Mercy is an unchangeable part of God's nature. He loves all the time. He is good all the time. His character never changes. Ephesians 2:4–5 says, *"But God, who is rich in mercy, for his great love wherewith he loved us, Even when we were dead in sins, hath quickened us together with Christ (by grace ye are saved)."*

God is rich in mercy that will never run out. His mercy comes from His love for us. Even when we were His enemy, He loved us and sent His son to die for us. Even when we were full of sin and rebellion, God so loved the world. Love leads to mercy, and mercy leads to forgiveness. What if, instead, we were given what we deserve? The soul that sins shall die. In other words, if God dealt with us according to our sins, we would die. His great mercy is unalterable:

"The LORD is merciful and gracious, slow to anger, and plenteous in mercy.

He will not always chide: neither will he keep his anger for ever.

He hath not dealt with us after our sins; nor rewarded us according to our iniquities.

For as the heaven is high above the earth, so great is his mercy toward them that fear him."

(Psalm 103:8–11)

Throughout time, people have refused to obey. They "hardened their necks" and preferred to return to sinful bondage rather than submit to God's loving authority. And what did God do?

"But they and our fathers dealt proudly, and hardened their necks, and hearkened not to thy commandments,

And refused to obey, neither were mindful of thy wonders that thou didst among them; but hardened their necks, and in their rebellion appointed a captain to return to their bondage: but thou art a God ready to pardon, gracious and merciful, slow to anger, and of great kindness, and forsookest them not."

(Nehemiah 9:16–17)

God does not give up on people. He is rich in mercy and forgiveness, springing from His heart of love. We sing the wonderful hymn "Great Is They Faithfulness," which speaks of His mercies, which are new every morning. Every morning, He is committed to show mercy toward us, with love and compassion; He is faithful even when we are not.

Jesus was the most merciful man who ever walked this earth. He fed the hungry and healed the sick. He delivered people from demons and pardoned the condemned. He was and is the visible image of the invisible God. There is nothing un-Jesus-like about God the Father, or un-Jesus-like about God the Holy Spirit. In Jesus dwells the fullness of the godhead. He is God embodied and visible among us. Jesus was the most merciful man who ever lived because He represented our merciful God.

What does mercy do? It forgives sin, iniquity, and all transgression. Yet by no means does God *clear* the guilty. We must qualify for His abundant mercy. He is merciful, gracious, and slow to anger, but mercy will not always wait. He will not hold back His anger forever. The prophet said *today* is the day, and this is the accepted time. This is the day of salvation. Mercy has a time limit. *This life* is that time. In death, we cannot expect to be met with His love, mercy, and forgiveness if in life we walked in full rebellion against Him.

He is always ready to forgive and will be plentiful in mercy for everyone who calls on His name. We need His mercy, and it's always there, but if we cover up our sin, we will not prosper. We learned earlier in this inaugural address that we must recognize our need. We must become poor in spirit to enter the kingdom of God. We must recognize our guilt and put aside all attempts at self-justification. If we confess and forsake our sins, we will receive His mercy.

God is merciful because it is His nature, and we are to emulate Him when dealing with others. Luke 6:36 says, *"Be ye therefore merciful, as your Father is merciful."*

We are to show mercy to others because God has shown mercy to us. And there is more: the merciful man is being kind to his own body, mind, emotions, and mental health when he shows mercy to others. How we treat others—with mercy or cruelty— will manifest itself in our physical bodies and affect our health and well-being. One of the best things we can do for ourselves is to walk in mercy:

> *"The merciful man doeth good to his own soul: but*
> *he that is cruel troubleth his own flesh.*

*The wicked worketh a deceitful work: but to him
that soweth righteousness shall be a sure reward.*

*As righteousness tendeth to life: so he that pursueth
evil pursueth it to his own death."*

(Proverbs 11:17–19)

Eight Benefits of Being Merciful

The following are eight ways we enrich our own lives when we are merciful to others:

1. **We get mercy in return!** If you have ever received forgiveness, then you know the power of forgiving others. Likewise, we must give mercy to receive it in turn. This is the law of reciprocity in practice. Psalm 18:25 says, *"With the merciful thou wilt shew thyself merciful...."* Be warned: if we have not shown mercy, we will also be judged without mercy. James 2:13 says, *"For he shall have judgment without mercy, that hath shewed no mercy; and mercy rejoiceth against judgment."*

2. **We please God by carrying out His instructions.** It's amazing when we realize we can bring pleasure to the God of the whole universe! Our thoughts, attitudes, and actions can bring Him pain or pleasure. This is one of the relational aspects between Him and us. Whenever we are merciful, we are doing what God wants. We have a disposition like His, and the fruit of our obedience is pleasing to Him. Micah 6:8 says, *"He hath shewed thee, O man, what is good; and what doth the LORD require of thee, but to do justly, and to love mercy, and to walk humbly with thy God?"*

3. **We receive life and honor from Him.** If we do what is right and grant others mercy, we will find life, righteousness, and honor. We have no honor if we are cruel, unforgiving, bitter, and without mercy. Jesus

was speaking in the context of the Roman Empire. The Romans saw mercy as a weakness or even a mental disorder. Jesus taught the mixed multitude an entirely new way of thinking. When we are merciful, we create a class that distinguishes us from others. We receive honor. Proverbs 21:21 says, *"He that followeth after righteousness and mercy findeth life, righteousness, and honour."*

4. **We have a sense of doing what is just and right.** The wicked will not only withhold from helping those in need; they also will not repay what they owe. The righteous one enjoys a sense of doing what is right. Psalm 37:21 states, *"The wicked borroweth, and payeth not again: but the righteous sheweth mercy, and giveth."*

5. **We gain satisfaction and joy.** We are happy when we are merciful. In the biblical account of the Good Samaritan, we see mercy at work. A Jewish man traveled down from Jericho and was attacked by thieves. They beat him, robbed him, and left him for dead on the side of the road. A priest came by, and then a Levite—neither of whom stopped to help. Next came a Samaritan. Historically, Jews and Samaritans had no dealings with each other, yet this Samaritan took pity on the wounded man, cleaned and bandaged his wounds, and put him on his donkey. He took the man to an inn and paid the people there to look after him. He told the innkeeper he'd come back and pay any further costs of helping the wounded man.

Do you think this Samaritan was happy as he went on with his business? He had helped a person who was truly in need. Jesus told this story to a lawyer to help answer the question, "Who is my neighbor?" Jesus taught that a neighbor is anyone with whom we cross paths. We are living in a generation of twisted, broken, fragmented, distorted, lonely, empty, and brokenhearted people. Many of them will become our "neighbors," even if for just a moment. When we stop and show mercy, we will always go forth rejoicing! Proverbs 14:21 says, *"He that hath mercy on the poor, happy is he."*

6. **We accurately represent God when we show mercy.** Jesus's followers were first referred to as "Christians" in Antioch. The term means "little-Christ" and was originally meant as a jeer against those who believed in Jesus. For believers, however, the term is a wonderful identification.

    When we show mercy, we are being little Christs, or Christ-like. We are in a position to accurately represent God. As His ambassadors of love, mercy, and forgiveness, we can attract others to Him: *"Now then we are ambassadors for Christ, as though God did beseech you by us: we pray you in Christ's stead, be ye reconciled to God"* (2 Corinthians 5:20).

7. **We prevent self-destructive actions when we offer mercy.** Satan comes to steal, kill, and destroy. Suicide rates are at an all-time high. Typically, when we think of killing ourselves, we think of it as an instant action. However, there are millions who are committing suicide on the installment plan. We do all kinds of self-destructive things that eventually rob us of life. God brings abundant life. Every piece of advice He gives us is for our health and well-being, not for our destruction or demise.

    The merciful person curbs and restricts these destructive forces by showing mercy and forgiveness, while a bitter person poisons himself. Destructive thoughts, words, and deeds create chemical and neurological changes in our bodies. An unmerciful person is bitter, unforgiving, and full of anger and resentment. This sets destructive forces at work that break down mind, body, emotions, and spirit.

Unfortunately, no doctor can offer medication to fix a spiritual problem. A merciful man, on the other hand, does good to his own soul.

8. **We become disciplined,** and mercy keeps us from making emotional errors. Emotions were never made to be a guidance system. They were given to provide us with the energy to follow through on intelligent, spiritual choices. Emotions should not rule us, but rather put the boost behind enacting good decisions. Unlike animals, we get to choose and reason. Therefore, we should not decide based on what we *feel*; instead, we should make decisions based on God's Word. Emotions can help us carry out what is right. We *decide* to show mercy, to attend church, to call that friend, or to help the needy. Then, as we follow through, we experience happiness, joy, and a sense of fulfillment.

Four Ways to Overcome Compassion Fatigue

Here are four strategies for overcoming:

1. **First, we must realize love comes in human-sized packages.** God loves the whole world. Jesus loves the whole world. You and I do not have the ability to love the whole world. Edward Everette Hale, American author, historian, and minister said, "I am only one, but I am one. I cannot do everything, but I can do something. The something I ought to do, I can do. And by the grace of God, I will."

God wants us to love one another, and then love will be perfected in us. We can make each person in our sphere of influence the object of our love, affection, and mercy. We may love the whole world in a sentimental way, but not in a practical, active, and focus-driven way. We simply don't have that ability. God has given each of us our own sphere of influence, and that is where we should show our compassion. We are human-sized, not God-sized: *"If we love one another, God dwelleth in us, and his love is perfected in us"* (1 John 4:12).

Focus your time and attention on the people and problems that exist within *your* world. This will combat compassion fatigue. Figure out who is in your world—who is in your inner circle, and then the next circle out, and the next? Demonstrate God's love to these groups of people. Do not neglect your sphere of influence by going out to places not intended for you.

Look again at the story of the Samaritan. He was going about his business when he saw someone in need in *his* path. He helped the needy person and continued onward. For a brief time, the injured man came into his inner circle, and then he left. Don't reach beyond those God has chosen to put into your life. When He does bring a new person, or people, in *your* path, show His compassion.

2. **Limit your exposure to guilt-inducing messages.** People will try to guilt us into action. Others may accuse us as people who lack compassion when we don't help their cause. The devil also tries to convince us to compare ourselves with those around us, saying, "You're not doing as much as he is to help the world." We can also become self-condemning by believing the words of others over Scripture. God says, however, there is no condemnation for those who belong to Christ and walk in the Spirit: *"There is therefore now no condemnation to them which are in Christ Jesus, who walk not after the flesh, but after the Spirit"* (Romans 8:1).

We have been set free from all guilt and all sin, past and present. As we listen to the right voice, God's voice, we will be free from the guilty persuasion of men. If we are full of guilt, we need a spiritual adjustment.

As a side note, be careful not to use guilt as a motivator for children. We can encourage them to do the right thing purely for the joy and benefits that follow. Jesus taught that the law was external. It can enforce outward actions without changing the heart. When we walk in inward love and obedience, we will produce the outward action, yet our motivation is positive. It springs from a willing heart. We shouldn't do the right things out of guilt, pressure, or strife. Instead, our motive should be love of the Father and the desire to do all things to glorify Him. Be careful, and limit yourselves and your children from guilt-inducing messages. Instead, "Do all to the glory of God" (1 Corinthians 10:31). And Philippians 2:3 says, *"Let nothing be done through strife or vainglory; but in lowliness of mind let each esteem other better than themselves."*

3. **When needs are great, combine resources.** The world is full of needs, and there are times when we should reach out. By combining our resources with others and with God, we can have a greater impact. This is where missions come in. Big projects and specific mission trips combine talent, finances, and time to have a greater impact than individual efforts alone: *"We then, as workers together with him..."* (2 Corinthians 6:1).

4. **Honor the Sabbath.** We all need a planned rest. We plan to work, so we must also plan to rest. If we don't take that break, we'll run out of energy and accomplish less in seven days than we can in six. People who genuinely love others carry a huge load and can quickly experience burnout. The Sabbath is a recovery point to help us recuperate and invigorate. In Mark 6:31, Jesus called to His disciples, saying, *"Come ye yourselves apart into a desert place, and rest a while."* Jesus knew the importance of solitary places for rest and rejuvenation. We, too, can come apart with Him

for rest or just be apart from the stress and pace of our busy world.

The Nature of Mercy

Once we learn to avoid compassion fatigue, we can begin to understand the nature of mercy. The following are three characteristics of mercy:

1. **Mercy is condemnation-free.** We are to respond to others in a kind and loving manner—not with insults or accusations. Jesus came not to condemn the world, but to save it. He was the most merciful man who ever was: *"For God sent not his son into the world to condemn the world; but that the world through him might be saved"* (John 3:17).

   The Bible records a situation in which a woman who had been caught in adultery was brought to Jesus. The men who brought her were ready to condemn her and put her to death by stoning. Jesus said the one who had no sin could throw the first stone. Then He stooped down and wrote something on the ground. We aren't sure what He wrote. But one by one, from the oldest to the youngest, each of her accusers walked away without tossing a single stone. Did He jot down a list of sins committed by these men? Maybe He wrote out the names of women with which these men had also committed adultery. Jesus looked around and saw that her accusers had left. In mercy, He told her that He did not condemn her, yet she must go and sin no more (see John 8:7–11).

   How do we react when someone in our world does the wrong thing? Do we start to condemn them, or do we shower them with mercy? Our response, whether to condemn or show mercy, will affect their lives. Our reaction should not be to criticize, accuse, or condemn, nor should we act religious or pious. As Jesus illustrated, those with sin are in no position to act as judges. We must respond to those around us, especially children, with mercy.

James 4:11–12 says, *"Speak not evil one of another, brethren. He that speaketh evil of his brother, and judgeth his brother, speaketh evil of the law, and judgeth the law: but if thou judge the law, thou art not a doer of the law, but a judge. There is one lawgiver, who is able to save and to destroy: who art thou that judgest another?"*

Judging people is up to God. We do not know which law to apply, and we do not fully understand another person's motivation. If we try to judge someone, we put ourselves above him or her and use the law as a weapon against that person. There is only one lawgiver, and that is God. He is the One who will save or destroy.

When we are merciful, we are tender and gentle. We should always be sensitive and more concerned about the offender's condition than our own, even if they have offended us. In chapter 5, we learned about meekness. If we act in meekness, we can tell another person what they need to resolve in a spirit of love and restoration. Meekness and mercy are constructive and redemptive toward others. Jesus desires a kingdom of merciful people who, in all their dealings, whether with their spouses, children, friends, coworkers, or those who come across their paths, are full of mercy.

Some people treat others with more mercy than they give themselves. Maybe they haven't received compassion from others and are more accustomed to criticism and judgment. The result can be self-condemnation. Healing can start in people only when they've been exposed to mercy. Another human being, like Jesus, who is gentle, tender, sensitive, and gracious, must enter their lives and reach out as He did.

When we are merciful, we do not retaliate. We remain calm and keep our peace. We don't give back what others may deserve; instead, we give better. We give mercy. We give love. What if the offender keeps on? We keep on also, in mercy.

2. **Mercy follows the example of Jesus.** Most of us have seen the letters "WWJD" ("what would Jesus do?"). Although this question is a great prompt, it is important that we know from Jesus's life what He *did* do. Books like *In His Steps* by Charles Monroe Sheldon give us a good picture of what our Lord did in many circumstances. However, nothing can replace studying the Word to learn *what Jesus did.*

   When we discipline our children, we should ask, "How would Jesus do it?" He would take that child up into His arms and do so with love and gentleness, not with anger. Disciplining our children without love is abuse. Mercy does not retaliate. True mercy will always follow the example of Jesus.

3. **Mercy fulfills our life mission to bless everyone.** In Genesis 12, God tells Abraham that He will bless him. We should see ourselves in the passage from verses 2–3:

   > *"And I will make of thee a great nation, and I will bless thee, and make thy name great; and thou shalt be a blessing:*
   > *And I will bless them that bless thee, and curse him that curseth thee: and in thee shall all families of the earth be blessed."*

   God blessed Abraham and his descendants. When others blessed them, God blessed those gracious people as well. What if someone cursed Abraham? Did God tell Abraham to curse them back? No. That was God's business. God blessed those who blessed Abraham and his descendants, and God cursed those who cursed Abraham and his descendants.

It's the same with us. God is watching. He knows whom to bless and whom to curse. He says vengeance belongs to Him, not to us. We can live our lives with sure and peaceful hearts, knowing He will fight our enemies and judge them on our behalf. We don't need to defend ourselves because He's got it all under control. We can remain calm, composed, and content. We can be known for our love, mercy, forgiveness, and blessing. Our names will be great. We can model our composure to our children and pass our reputations down through the generations. We don't retaliate. Instead, we are blessers (see Genesis 12:2–3).

Why are we able to apply the blessing of Abraham to our lives? It is because we are in Christ, so we are of the spiritual seed of Abraham. We share his spiritual lineage and inheritance. Galatians 3:29 says, *"And if ye be Christ's, then are ye Abraham's seed, and heirs according to the promise."*

Psalm 5:7 says, *"But as for me, I will come into thy house in the multitude of thy mercy: and in thy fear will I worship toward thy holy temple."* Mercy is so important and so fulfilling that the psalmist included it in his reasons for singing. Many of his songs focus on God's mercy, the effects of mercy, and the need for mercy. When we have something that good, we sing about it! Blessed are the merciful. Mercy is built up forever. God's faithfulness is surely established, and He will return mercy for mercy!

> *"I will sing of the mercies of the LORD forever: with my mouth will I make known thy faithfulness to all generations.*
>
> *For I have said, Mercy shall be built up for ever: thy faithfulness shalt thou establish in the very heavens."*
> (Psalm 89:1–2)

Beloved, it is our task and our mission to be a blessing. We cannot be a blessing to others and still operate through condemnation, criticism, or judgment. We can accomplish our mission of blessing only through people who love mercy and walk humbly with their God, in a spirit of love, mercy, and forgiveness. The church should be a place of mercy, not of condemnation. Yes, we must speak the Truth, and that may cause discomfort. However, we should operate from a place of love and mercy so others may be reconciled to God, just as we are.

Chapter 7

The Heart Is the Heart of All That Matters

Blessed Are the Pure in Heart

What do you consider the most important sentence in the Bible? We all have favorites and verses we've heard more than any others. But the most important one? Maybe Matthew 5:8 is it. If a verse reveals how to "see God," I believe that should be considered vital.

The entire purpose of Christ's mission on earth was to prepare the way for our ultimate destiny—to see Jesus and to see God for all eternity. Jesus was ready to reveal the critical truth—only the pure in heart will see God: "*Blessed are the pure in heart: for they shall see God*" (Matthew 5:8).

The Importance of the Heart: Seven Truths

Our hearts are our first and ultimate responsibility. Guarding our hearts is more important than keeping a job, the status of our bank account, and even our health. In fact, guarding, or keeping the heart, keeps our health. How much time do we spend each week keeping our hearts? Do we look after them with all diligence? *"Keep thy heart with all diligence; for out of it are the issues of life"* (Proverbs 4:23).

If we guard our hearts, we'll keep them trouble-free. If we accept trouble into them, we'll trouble other areas of our lives. It's an all-day task to stay free of trouble. Because we do not wish to have heart trouble in the physical sense, we must work to prevent it. Likewise, we must make the spiritual condition of our heart a top priority. This protects us physically, emotionally, mentally, and spiritually. Keep your heart with all diligence. John 14:1 instructs, *"Let not your heart be troubled...."*

Here are seven truths about the importance of the heart:

1. **From the heart come the issues of life.** Whatever we produce in our lives originated in the heart. The heart is the core of our being, the real you and me. When we say we wish to "get to the heart of a matter," we're talking about getting to the core, the root, or the real reason. Whatever develops in our hearts will come to the surface: *"But those things which proceed out of the mouth come forth from the heart; and they defile the man. For out of the heart proceed evil thoughts, murders, adulteries, fornications, thefts, false witness, blasphemies"* (Matthew 15:18–19).

   The heart controls our thinking, and our words and actions follow. Actions like theft, adultery, and murder are first formed in the heart. Jesus said if a man looks at a woman with lust, he has already committed adultery in his heart. He also said if we hate our brothers, we are murderers *in our hearts.*

   Our hearts control our imaginations, and that's where evil forms and works its way out: *"And God saw that the wickedness of man was great in the earth, and that every imagination of the thoughts of his heart was only evil continually"* (Genesis 6:5).

   However, Jesus explained that good also emanates from the heart. A man of good heart creates what is good, and a man of evil heart what is evil: "*A good man out of the good treasure of the heart bringeth forth good things: and an evil man out of the evil treasure bringeth forth evil things*" (Matthew 12:35).

2. **The unruly heart is treacherous.** Our hearts can trick us. They can be desperately wicked, deceiving us in the thoughts that eventually produce actions. David asked God to search him and know his heart. He asked God to test him and see if any wicked thing could be found: "*The heart is deceitful above all things, and desperately wicked: who can know it? I the LORD search the heart, I try the reins, even to give every man according to his ways, and according to the fruit of his doings*" (Jeremiah 17:9–10).

3. **God's primary concern is our hearts.** God looks past our outward condition to expose the root of our behavior. His focus is on our hearts, not what seems to be on the outside: "*For man looketh on the outward appearance, but the LORD looketh on the heart*" (1 Samuel 16:7).

4. **Civil law cannot change the heart.** Legalism is an attempt to apply laws to change behavior. Laws *can* change some behaviors, but they cannot change the heart. Psalm 119 says the undefiled are blessed as they walk in the laws of the Lord.

   Laws are good—without them, we would have total anarchy. However, civil laws break down in two ways. First, laws break down when culture redefines right and wrong, and things that were previously known as unlawful are no longer against the law. Second, civil law may not always be enforced so that even when good laws are retained, they lose their authority. Even good laws and proper enforcement address only outward behavior. Civil law is inadequate because it cannot change the heart.

5. **Our hearts can become defiled.** Outside influences can defile minds, but they cannot defile our hearts. It is our *response* to these outside influences that can defile our hearts, yet if we are aware and in control, our hearts remain preserved: *"And he saith unto them, Are ye so without understanding also? Do ye not perceive, that whatsoever thing from without entereth into the man, it cannot defile him"* (Mark 7:18).

   What happens when our response to evil is incorrect? What happens when we cultivate our own evil deep inside to inflict harm on others? We defile ourselves. What others may have attempted, we do to ourselves: *"And he said, That which cometh out of the man, that defileth the man. For from within, out of the heart of men, proceed evil thoughts, adulteries, fornications, murders, Thefts, covetousness, wickedness, deceit, lasciviousness, an evil eye, blasphemy, pride, foolishness: All these evil things come from within, and defile the man"* (Mark 7:20–23).

6. **The heart must be pure to produce Christian authenticity.** One of the greatest reasons people do not follow Jesus is the inconsistency in the lives of those who claim to follow Him. With the commercialization and industrialization of our churches, we've become a stumbling block to many. We look for ways to market our programs and services. Instead of having power over the world, we take on the ways of the world, and they enslave us.

   Also, our churches are full of hypocrites. Of course, the best place for hypocrites is to remain in our congregations, in hopes they'll one day become convicted; yet this hypocrisy keeps us from purity. Without purity, we cannot produce and reproduce authentic Christianity. We must clean up the inside as well as the outside:

"Woe unto you, scribes and Pharisees,
hypocrites! for ye make clean the outside of
the cup and of the platter, but within they are
full of extortion and excess.

Thou blind Pharisee, cleanse first that which
is within the cup and platter, that the outside of
them may be clean also.

Woe unto you, scribes and Pharisees,
hypocrites! for ye are like unto whited
sepulchres, which indeed appear beautiful
outward, but are within full of dead men's
bones, and of all uncleanness."

(Matthew 23:25–27)

7. **The condition of our hearts affects our vision.** How do we see the world? How do we see God? Without purity of heart, we cannot achieve purity of vision. The pure in heart will see God and the good in the world and in others. They will not develop a negative, critical, and condemning disposition toward everyone and everything around them. They will see their friends, spouses, children, parents, and everyone else in the best possible light. However, to the defiled of heart, nothing is pure. Their minds and even their consciences are defiled. Their consciences can break down and stop working.

The Bible says the conscience can become seared or completely ineffective. This happens to those who believe in God, yet deny Him with their actions:

"Unto the pure all things are pure: but
unto them that are defiled and unbelieving
is nothing pure; but even their mind and
conscience is defiled.

They profess that they know God; but in
works they deny him, being abominable,

85

and disobedient, and unto every good work reprobate." (Titus 1:15–16)

————————

Do we want to see God? We can recognize Him throughout His Word, in all of creation, and in the lives of others. We can see Him in our circumstances, our finances, our health, and our relationships. We can see Him when we seek peace and holiness: *"Follow peace with all men, and holiness, without which no man shall see the Lord"* (Hebrews 12:14).

Just as we want our physical hearts to be healthy, our spiritual hearts must stay pure. The condition of the heart is of prime importance. We must guard it. We must keep it according to the Word of God, or it can become ineffective, wicked, and defiled. From the heart springs the issue of life. How wonderful to know we can align our hearts with God's Word, and that one day we can see Him all around us and look into His face! Blessed are the pure in heart.

Chapter 8

Understanding the Functions of the Heart

Blessed Are the Pure in Heart

Our hearts are busy, aren't they? They sense needs. They notice wounds. They see tears. They observe scars. The stare at a world of worry, anxiety, pain, and uncertainty. One person might express those hurts from the heart. Another person might hold them in. However we respond, stress becomes deep. The thoughts and actions of our spiritual hearts reveal so much about us. And the results are huge.

We know of the blessed expectation of the pure in heart. We've come to an understanding that the heart is of prime importance to God and is at the core of who we are and what we do. The heart, the control center, is ever-ready to observe, analyze, decide, and guide. It's ready to instruct us.

What the Heart Does: Fifteen Key Functions

The heart is the foundation, the core, of our being. It is the center of our humanity, and we are to keep it pure. Here are fifteen key functions of the heart in our spiritual lives:

1. **The heart thinks.** Our thoughts come and go. In fact, we can quickly process dozens of things all at once. The heart, however, has thoughts that are settled. The heart thinks. It can think about good or evil at the deepest level:

   > *"For as he thinketh in his heart, so is he...."*
   >
   > (Proverbs 23:7)

   > *"For from within, out of the heart of men, proceed evil thoughts..."* (Mark 7:21)

   > *"Now Haman thought in his heart...."*
   >
   > (Esther 6:6)

   We must understand that the heart thinks, not just the mind. What it thinks pours out from us.

2. **The heart reasons.** The heart not only thinks; it also has a rational thinking process. It adds logic to information. When Jesus spoke to anyone, it was always about the heart. Luke 5:22 says, *"But when Jesus perceived their thoughts, he answering said unto them, What reason ye in your hearts?"*

   We all reason in our hearts. The scribes did this, and we do this. The heart adjudicates information and concludes the matters of life. *"But there was certain of the scribes sitting there, and reasoning in their hearts"* (Mark 2:6).

3. **The heart ponders.** The heart does this wonderful, private activity: it contemplates, giving adequate consideration to the information we hear. It considers

and reconsiders things that need private attention. Mary pondered what people said about Jesus. *"But Mary kept all these things, and pondered them in her heart"* (Luke 2:19). The men who heard the message of John also mused, or pondered, in their hearts. *"And as the people were in expectation, and all men mused in their hearts of John, whether he were the Christ, or not"* (Luke 3:15).

4. **The heart discerns.** Our minds generally jump to conclusions based on whatever information we feed them. Our hearts can discern beyond observation and scientific fact. Some may call it intuition because there are things the heart just knows. Blaise Pascal put it this way: "The heart has its reasons which reason knows nothing of. We know the truth not only by the reason, but by the heart."

   There are times when the heart knows we need to take an action but says, "Not now, not yet." This often applies to discipline in the home. We are not denying the problem; the heart is just slowing things down to produce the best result. Using our hearts will render a different outcome than using just our minds. When we make snap judgments, without using our hearts, we can become harsh and make decisions we regret. *"Whoso keepeth the commandment shall feel no evil thing: and a wise man's heart discerneth both time and judgment"* (Ecclesiastes 8:5).

5. **The heart talks.** Often, our hearts will speak to us when we are quiet. With the busyness of our lives, we don't give the heart time to speak. Conversely, our minds are always going and being filled with activities and noise. David instructs us on the importance of communing with and consulting our hearts: *"Stand in awe, and sin not: commune with your own heart upon your bed, and be still..."* (Psalm 4:4).

Learning to listen to our hearts knows no gender. Although it may be true that women are generally better at speaking from their hearts, this does not give men an excuse to consult only their minds. Thankfully the Bible gives us many examples of godly, heart-consulting men as examples. One is David. 1 Samuel 27:1 says, *"And David said in his heart...."* Many of the heroes of the faith routinely had conversations within their hearts. (Plus, men, we bless our wives when we speak from the heart.)

6. **The heart learns.** The heart will learn, so we cannot be left unadvised, undisciplined, or uncontrolled. It is up to us to instruct our hearts: *"Apply thine heart to instruction, and thine ears to words of knowledge"* (Proverbs 23:12).

7. **The heart memorizes and retains.** Our hearts remember our value systems. They are like reservoirs retaining our most valuable lessons. They will remind us and keep us in check when we start to go off track: *"My son, attend to my words; incline thine ear unto my sayings. Let them not depart from thine eyes; keep them in the midst of thine heart"* (Proverbs 4:20–21). *"Thy word have I hid in mine heart, that I might not sin against thee"* (Psalm 119:11).

8. **The heart meditates.** It's up to us to ensure our hearts meditate on the right things. Remember, it's the heart that processes data at the deepest level. Thoughts, words, and deeds come from the heart. We must not let our hearts meditate on evil. Our hearts should meditate on whatever is acceptable to God. *"Let the words of my mouth, and the meditation of my heart, be acceptable in thy sight, O LORD, my strength, and my redeemer"* (Psalm 19:14).

   While the mind processes quickly, the heart will meditate and slow things down. It sorts and accumulates, becoming the operational source out of which mental and physical activities take place. Psalm 49:3 says, *"My mouth shall speak of wisdom and the meditation of my heart shall be of understanding."*

9. **The heart understands.** The heart seeks understanding. Our minds can quickly discard and forget, but our hearts make sense of life. Look around at our society, and you will see people doing things that make no sense. They do not consult their hearts. *"So that thou incline thine ear unto wisdom, and apply thine heart to understanding..."* (Proverbs 2:2).

10. **The heart seeks knowledge.** People who have understanding desire knowledge. They are aware that they need more knowledge, and their hearts stretch after it. *"The heart of him that hath understanding seeketh knowledge: but the mouth of fools feedeth on foolishness"* (Proverbs 15:14).

11. **The heart can receive and believe the Word of God.** Our hearts are susceptible to the Word of God. When we talk about the Gospel, we want to reach the other person's heart because that's where the real comprehension occurs. We can present the Gospel and argue it out, mind to mind, debate with eloquent words, and disagree.

However, all it takes is one Spirit-inspired phrase to cause someone to walk away with a seed planted in the heart. His or her heart will ponder. It will hang onto those words and process them. The heart receives the Word and believes it, even after the mind forgets and discards it.

Once the heart has received and believed, then the head needs to be educated to line up with the heart. The mind is renewed, and then emotions begin to change until a new person emerges, full and complete. This is the process of discipleship. It starts first in the heart:

"But what saith it? The word is nigh thee,
even in thy mouth, and in thy heart: that is, the
word of faith, which we preach;

That if thou shalt confess with thy mouth the
Lord Jesus, and shalt believe in thine heart
that God hath raised him from the dead, thou
shalt be saved.

For with the heart man believeth unto
righteousness; and with the mouth confession
is made unto salvation." (Romans 10:8–10)

12. **The heart resolves.** Once the heart believes, it decides. It sets a holy and godly direction based on belief as God directs the steps.

13. **God speaks to the heart to reach our heads.** Satan speaks to our heads to get to our hearts. Often, our minds are too busy. When God speaks, His words just drop into our hearts. We need to slow down and listen. Be still, and know He is God.

14. **The heart controls generosity.** If people are generous or if they are stingy, they are that way because of their hearts. We reap what we sow, and we reap in kind what we sow. If we sow sparingly, we will reap sparingly. Generosity is voluntary, and it's decided in the heart. The Scriptures say one withholds and comes to poverty, but another spreads his generosity and has plenty (see Proverbs 11:24). When our hearts are in tune with God, we are generous. We delight to give—not out of necessity, but from a joyful heart:

"But this I say, He which soweth sparingly
shall reap also sparingly; and he which soweth
bountifully shall reap also bountifully.

Every man according as he purposeth in his
heart, so let him give; not grudgingly, or of

necessity: for God loveth a cheerful giver."
(2 Corinthians 9:6–7)

15. The heart loves. Jesus said to love God with all our hearts. This is the best purpose of the heart: *"And thou shalt love the Lord thy God with all thy heart, and with all thy soul, and with all thy mind, and with all thy strength: this is the first commandment"* (Mark 12:30).

A pure heart desires one thing above everything else: to love God. A heart with singleness of purpose is like pure gold, void of alloys. The heart that loves the Lord, as its all-consuming purpose, will be single and focused:

> *"The light of the body is the eye: if therefore thine eye be single, thy whole body shall be full of light.*
>
> *But if thine eye be evil, thy whole body shall be full of darkness. If therefore the light that is in thee be darkness, how great is that darkness!*
>
> *No man can serve two masters: for either he will hate the one, and love the other; or else he will hold to the one, and despise the other. Ye cannot serve God and mammon."*
>
> (Matthew 6:22–24)

We've looked at the ultimate importance of the heart and the wonderful things it can do. We know that to love God with all our hearts is right. What a privilege it is to love the God of all creation! How wonderful to know He desires our love. How awesome it is to know we can be pure in heart and see Him face to face! There is no greater reward.

Beloved, this is the real stuff of life. Realize that. Receive that. It is the reason we arise each new day with joy, hope, and gladness. Blessed are the pure in heart.

Chapter 9

How to Set Your Heart Right

Blessed Are the Pure in Heart

Our Lord does not give us an impossible task. Instead, He partners with us to accomplish His will, which is for our ultimate good, for our eternal blessedness. Can we hear these beautiful words enough? Blessed are the pure in heart, for they shall see God.

The following are eleven requirements we must meet before we can have purity of heart.

1. **Give up all previous heart ambitions.** In the book of Ezekiel, God said a day would come when the people would rid themselves of all detestable things, and He would give them a heart of flesh rather than a heart of stone. This points to a major difference between a heart that seeks God and one that does not.

   The heart seeking God is tender and gentle. It has the strength to do hard things, but with kindness. A stony, hard heart inspires crime, abuse, divorce, and all sorts of hardened acts in this world. God is not harsh, cruel, critical, or condemning with us. He is tender. He does not impose Himself on us, and we should not fear Him like we would a tyrant. We can even push Him away. We can grieve Him and quench the Holy Spirit, and He stills stays tender in His dealings with us.

2. **Call on the Lord.** Once we're ready to change our hard, artificial, stony hearts, we need to call on God, much like David: *"Create in me a clean heart, O God; and renew a right spirit in me"* (Psalm 51:10).

   One of the greatest Scriptures in Proverbs tells us it is possible to surrender our hearts to God. By conscious choice, we can offer our hearts to be taught, transformed, and purified. How does God do this? It remains a mystery, but we know the blood of Jesus and the workings of the Holy Spirit come together, and we become new. *"My son, give me thine heart, and let thine eyes observe my ways"* (Proverbs 23:26).

3. **Cooperate with God's work in your heart.** In other words, God will not force the purification of our hearts. He draws us to Himself tenderly. He will tell us what we should do, but He then waits for our response. Ezekiel 18:31 says, *"Cast away from you all transgressions, whereby ye have transgressed; and make you a new heart and a new spirit: for why will ye die, O house of Israel?"*

   There are two false ideas in Christianity. One is "mystical" in that God does everything, and we do nothing. The other school of thought is "humanistic" where we do everything, and God does nothing. The truth, I believe, is somewhere in the middle. We work *with* Him. Through His Word and the Holy Spirit, He instructs us. We then agree and call on Him to help us accomplish it.

4. **Love God wholeheartedly.** Remember, we want singularity of purpose, and we desire purity. There is no holier object for our affections than God. If something competes with Him, it will also compete for our time, money, talents, and behaviors. He should be our only obsession. *"Jesus said unto them, Thou shalt love the*

Lord thy God with all thy heart, and with all thy soul, and with all thy mind. This is the first and greatest commandment" (Matthew 22:37–38).

5. **Praise God wholeheartedly.** The Word tells us again and again we are to worship Him with joy and gladness. When you love Him with all your heart, you'll sing out with great rejoicing. *"I will praise thee, O Lord my God, with all my heart: and I will glorify thy name forevermore"* (Psalm 86:12).

6. **Trust God wholeheartedly.** God wants all of us, and He is trustworthy. There is nothing we cannot trust Him with, and nothing is too big or small for Him. Don't keep any area of your life separated from God's leadership. Let Him into your relationships, your vocation, your finances, and all your plans and pursuits. Proverbs 3:5–6 says, *"Trust in the Lord with all thine heart; and lean not unto thine own understanding. In all thy ways acknowledge him, and he shall direct thy paths."*

7. **Seek God wholeheartedly.** Like a man seeking a great treasure, we are to seek God with all our hearts. He is waiting and ready to meet us when we seek Him:

> *"And ye shall seek me, and find me, when ye shall search for me with all your heart.*
>
> *And I will be found of you, saith the Lord: and I will turn away your captivity, and I will gather you from all the nations, and from all the places whither I have driven you, saith the Lord; and I will bring you again into the place whence I caused you to be carried away captive."*
>
> (Jeremiah 29:13–14)

How much time do we spend looking for God? Where do we look? Do we search His Word? It's a beautiful thing to know that He wants to be found.

When find Him, He sets things in order. He takes away our captivity and sets us free.

8. **Serve God wholeheartedly.** When we serve God with a whole heart, everything we touch is blessed, and everything we do will prosper. I'm not speaking of prosperity teachings: you do this or that, and you'll get whatever you want. I'm speaking of a basic truth about our Lord: He wants us to be blessed. We serve, and He blesses, in all the ways He desires.

   Many men, upon their deathbeds, have expressed regret over not becoming a Christian. However, I don't know of any Christian on his deathbed who said he wished he had not served God. Serve Him with a full heart, from a heart of joy:

   > *"Because thou servedst not the LORD thy God with joyfulness, and with gladness of heart, for the abundance of all things;*
   > *Therefore shalt thou serve thine enemies which the LORD shall send against thee...."*
   > (Deuteronomy 28:47–48)

9. **Keep your heart happy.** God expects us to have happy hearts. He is not interested in pressing us down—that's what the enemy does. Religion loads us up with rules and regulations and discourages true peace and joy. God seeks relationship and has our best interests in mind. His joy is our strength.

10. **Commit your heart to what God shows you.** We must be careful to commit our hearts to Him, to follow and obey. We cannot become sidetracked, enticed, or tricked by others who offer alternatives to God. David followed God to do what was right. We read in 1 Kings 14:8, *"who followed me with all his heart, to do that only which was right in mine eyes."*

11. **Do regular heart maintenance.** This is essential if
   we are to have pure hearts. Jesus said we must not let
   trouble enter our hearts. We must consciously be aware
   when trouble tries to enter our hearts, so we can keep
   it out.

The Christian life is a glorious combination of two extremes
that seem incongruous. One is to be responsible, and the other is
to not give a care. We are responsible with our lives and the way
we live them, yet we are not to let the cares into our hearts. The
"cares" of this world belong to the Lord—1 Peter 5:7 instructs,
"Casting all your care upon him; for he careth for you."

Just as any other type of maintenance we perform, heart
maintenance is an ongoing activity. It is up to us. *"Keep thy heart
with all diligence; for out of it are the issues of life"* (Proverbs
4:23).

Chapter 10

The Ability to See as God Sees

Blessed Are the Pure in Heart

Many times, when astronauts entered space or walked on the moon, they became suddenly aware of this world's Creator. American astronaut James Erwin said after walking on the moon, "I felt the power of God as I've never felt it before."

Charles Duke, the tenth and youngest person to walk on the moon, said of his encounter in space, "I was able to look out the window to see this incredible sight of the whole circle of the Earth. Oceans were crystal blue, the land was brown, and the clouds and the snow were pure white. And that jewel of Earth was just hung up in the blackness of space." Six years after his walk on the moon, he met Jesus. "Now that I'm a believer, in my mind, I can see that sight and proclaim as the psalmist did," Duke explained. "The heavens declare the glory of God. The sky proclaims the work of his hands."

Buzz Aldrin was the pilot of the Apollo 11 mission and one of the first two humans to ever walk on the moon. On his historic trip into space, Aldrin took his Bible, a silver chalice, some bread, and sacramental wine. The first thing he did when he stepped out was to celebrate communion.

All these men saw or felt God in a new and mighty way. Thankfully for us, you do not need to be an astronaut to see God. He wants us to seek Him, and He's waiting to be found.

Ten Ways We Can See Him

Jesus taught the multitude that the pure in heart would see God. What does it mean to *see God*? How can we see Him?

1. **Simply realize it is possible!** It may seem beyond comprehension that our Lord *can* be seen. But Hebrews 12:14 says, *"Follow peace with all men, and holiness, without which no man shall see the Lord. ..."*

   Job struggled through a chain of disasters. When they ended, he declared, *"I have heard of thee by the hearing of the ear: but now mine eye seeth thee"* (Job 42:5).

2. **Know that we can see God, but not all of Him.** God allowed Moses to see part of His glory, but only from behind as God passed by. Moses was hidden in the cleft of a rock, and God covered him there with His hand. Moses saw Him only in passing.

   When I was young, I had a little contraption using magnets, wires, and a generator. I rigged it up and put it under a blanket in my wagon, waiting for the high-school boys to come by my house. I would ask if anyone had the courage to take the two wires in their hands while I cranked the generator. A few did and would shake from the electrical current. Of course, *I don't recommend doing this*, but here's how it relates to God: we can take a measured amount of Him, but not all.

   To be fully in His presence, we would be overcome, just as too much electricity can kill us. He is there, yet we cannot see Him in His totality. We learn in 1 Timothy 6:16, *"Who only hath immortality, dwelling in the light which no man can approach unto; whom no man hath seen, nor can see: to whom be honour and power everlasting. Amen."*

3. **Come out of hiding.** After eating of the tree of good and evil, Adam and Eve hid in the garden. They knew they had sinned and wanted to avoid their usual walk with God in the cool of the day. He called to them, and they stepped out, clothed. They were hiding. However, God wants us to step toward Him. Some can no longer hear Him. They cannot see Him or even sense His presence. They're hiding and perceive Him. However, we can see Him, if we so desire:

    > *"And in them is fulfilled the prophecy of Esaias, which saith, By hearing ye shall hear, and shall not understand; and seeing ye shall see, and shall not perceive:*
    >
    > *For this people's heart is waxed gross, and their ears are dull of hearing, and their eyes they have closed; lest at any time they should see with their eyes and hear with their ears, and should understand with their heart, and should be converted, and I should heal them.*
    >
    > *But blessed are your eyes, for they see: and your ears, for they hear."* (Matthew 13:14–16)

    God promised to seek and to save those who are lost. He does not drive us away. It's man who moves away from God. He says He will never reject us. We need to come out of hiding. He's ready to receive us.

4. **Celebrate God as He revealed Himself to us.** Many do not see God because they have a wrong concept of God's nature. They're looking for something that's not God, so they miss Him. Romans 1 speaks of those who knew God but did not glorify Him as God. They invented alternative ideas about God and worshiped

other things. They became fools, and God was forced to give them up:

> *"Because that, when they knew God, they glorified him not as God, neither were thankful; but became vain in their imaginations, and their foolish heart was darkened.*
>
> *Professing themselves to be wise, they became fools,*
>
> *And changed the glory of the uncorruptible God into an image made like to corruptible man, and to birds, and fourfooted beasts, and creeping things.*
>
> *Wherefore God also gave them up to uncleanness through the lusts of their own hearts, to dishonour their own bodies between themselves."* (Romans 1:21–24)

God is not corruptible; it is man who tries to change God's nature. He is the same yesterday, today, and forever. His Word works the same. When He must give someone up, it is because people chose, by their beliefs and actions, to separate from Him. We cannot exchange God for other things. We must see Him as He presents Himself.

5. **Look in the Scriptures.** God reveals Himself to us in many ways, but His primary source is in the Scriptures. We can understand Him by reading *His own words* about Himself. He revealed Himself to Samuel by His Word, such as in 1 Samuel 3:21: *"...for the LORD revealed himself to Samuel in Shiloh by the word of the LORD."*

6. **Look for Him in the cosmos.** Look for God in the heavens. He placed the sun, moon, stars, and entire galaxies to speak of His existence. Every day and every night, from every place on the planet, man can

look up and see the evidence of God: *"The heavens declare the glory of God; and the firmament sheweth his handywork. Day unto day uttereth speech, and night unto night sheweth knowledge. There is no speech nor language, where their voice is not heard"* (Psalm 19:1–3).

7. **Study His creation.** We can study His creative works all around us: the birds, fish, and animals. We can study how they live, grow, and interact. Also, every aspect of our planet—from the rocks on the ground to the clouds in the sky—speak of His magnificent handiwork. He holds the breath and soul of all mankind in His hands. Everything He created is an expression of His personality. Study what He has made, and study Him:

> *"But ask now the beasts, and they shall teach thee; and the fowls of the air, and they shall tell thee:*
>
> *Or speak to the earth, and it shall teach thee: and the fishes of the sea shall declare unto thee.*
>
> *Who knoweth not in all these that the hand of the* Lord *hath wrought this?*
>
> *In whose hand is the soul of every living thing, and the breath of all mankind."*   (Job 12:7–10)

8. **Act in the "drawing season" to see God.** There's a time when God can be found. We look for Him, we search for Him, and see Him all around us, but there is a time when we find Him. There's a time when He is near us. Isaiah 55:6 says, *"Seek ye the* Lord *while he may be found, call ye upon him while he is near."*

When we observe the sky, we see specific things at specific times. There are times when stars are more visible, the sun or moon is eclipsed, or a planet comes into better view. Maybe you've sensed Him while walking in the woods or along a beach. Or maybe you've felt His embrace as you've held a newborn.

Poetically speaking, He *gathers* us. If we don't pause in our busy lives, we may miss these points of time. The arrogant tell God to go away. The atheists pay Him no heed. His beloved people, however, seek these intimate times and seasons. His Word tells us about Him, and creation tells us about Him, but let's not ignore personal contact. Scripture tells us to be still and know He is God. He is found in stillness.

9. **Call, pray, seek, and search wholeheartedly.** Don't seek Him half-heartedly and expect to find Him in His entirety. He rewards people who diligently seek Him with more and more of Himself. He thinks of us, plans for us, answers our calls, and fights on our behalf. He wants us wholeheartedly. We will find Him when we desire the same:

> *"For I know the thoughts that I think toward you, saith the LORD, thoughts of peace, and not of evil, to give you an expected end.*
>
> *Then shall ye call upon me, and ye shall go and pray unto me, and I will hearken unto you.*
>
> *And ye shall seek me, and find me, when ye shall search for me with all your heart.*
>
> *And I will be found of you, saith the LORD: and I will turn away your captivity, and I will gather you from all the nations, and from all the places whither I have driven you, saith the LORD; and I will bring you again into the place whence I caused you to be carried away captive."*
>
> (Jeremiah 29:11–14)

10. **Have purity of heart.** The condition of our hearts affects our ability to see. Two people can look at the same creation, and one can see God, while the other sees something else. Two can witness the same event, hear the same words, or take part in the same action,

yet one sees God, and the other distorts it with evil. *"Unto the pure all things are pure: but unto them that are defiled and unbelieving is nothing pure; but even their mind and conscience is defiled"* (Titus 1:15).

Five Ways to Know We Are Seeing Him

We want to see Him. We know where to find Him, and He's always ready to receive us. However, what does it mean that the pure in heart will see Him? *Where* will we see Him? Here are five ways we will know we are casting our eyes on Him:

1. **We recognize Him in Scripture.** Sometimes when we read, the words seem to come alive—*there He is*. We feel Him consciously. He's speaking to us personally.

2. **We recognize Him in nature.** Anything that anyone has ever invented gives clues as to how those people think, what they desire, and what they have to offer. When we study God, how much more can we understand His creation?

3. **We see Him in others.** We are the body of Christ. When we look at our spouses, children, and other fellow heirs of God's grace, we should see Him. He should be visible in the people in whom He dwells, and they should see Him in us.

4. **We are amazed.** Our ultimate pursuit is to know God. To know Him, in His splendor, is overwhelming to contemplate. We could ponder Him for hours on end, and still, we would find no adequate words. How can anything compete with or compare to finding Him? Isaiah got a glimpse of Him and was amazed: *"In the year that King Uzziah died I saw also the LORD sitting upon a throne, high and lifted up, and his train filled the temple"* (Isaiah 6:1).

5. **We see need for change.** There is never a time in His presence that I don't come away realizing I need to change. I have no other hero. I have no other mentor.

There is no other perfect One. I want to be like Him. When I am in His presence, like Isaiah, I sense my need for change: "*Then said I, Woe is me! for I am undone; because I am a man of unclean lips, and I dwell in the midst of a people of unclean lips: for mine eyes have seen the King, the LORD of hosts*" (Isaiah 6:5).

Someday, We Will See Him Face to Face

Isaiah prophesied that the glory of God would be revealed, and all people would see Him at the same time. For now, we see Him only dimly, but someday, we will see Him face to face: "*For now we see through a glass darkly; but then face to face*" (1 Corinthians 13:12).

Beloved, right now we are the sons and daughters of God. What we will become, in the full beauty of His presence, is unknown. We will see Him and be like Him, however, and we will be changed forever:

> "*Beloved, now are we the sons of God, and it doth not yet appear what we shall be: but we know that, when he shall appear, we shall be like him; for we shall see him as he is.*
>
> *And every man that hath this hope in him purifieth himself, even as he is pure.*" (1 John 3:2–3)

To See Him, We Must Live in His Presence Now

There is something better than heaven and worse than hell. What's better than heaven? It is seeing His face when He says, "Well done, thou good and faithful servant, enter thou into the joy of the Lord." What's worse than hell? It is seeing His face when He says, "Depart from me. I never knew you." Seeing His face at that personal moment in time, when all has been decided, is something we will never forget.

God always has tears in His eyes when the rod is in His hand. Some say judgment happens in an instant—that the sinner stands just moments before God, and it's all over. Judgment day *is* coming.

The book of Revelation tells us that when Jesus returns, *everyone*—the pure and the impure—will see Him when He comes in the clouds: *"Behold, he cometh with clouds; and every eye shall see him, and they also which pierced him: and all kindreds of the earth shall wail because of him. Even so, Amen"* (Revelation 1:7).

When we die, there are no more chances. To see His blessed face, and to feel His open arms welcoming us to live with Him forever, we must live in His presence *now*. This should give us a sense of urgency as we tell others the glorious message of salvation. Which face of God do *we* wish to see? Which face do we wish for *others* to see? *"As for me, I will behold thy face in righteousness: I shall be satisfied, when I awake, with thy likeness"* (Psalm 17:15).

Beloved, please understand it is the pure in heart that will look upon His face forever. Blessed are the pure in heart.

Chapter 11

The Value of Living in Peace

Blessed Are the Peacemakers

Think of a recent time in your life when you felt peace. Maybe during a time with family or friends. Maybe when you were praying to God. Maybe by the ocean or on a mountain. Maybe after hearing good news about a deep concern.

Don't you cherish those moments? Don't you desire more of them?

The whole world speaks of peace. Nations want peace and, ironically, are willing to fight for it. Governments, on all levels, strive to legislate and enact laws they believe will bring peace. Every corporation, religious organization, hospital, school, family, and individual desires peace. Why, then, are we not all *at peace*? Apparently, true, biblical peace is hard to obtain and impossible for those who do not know God. Jesus says the peacemakers will be called the children of God: *"Blessed are the peacemakers: for they shall be called the children of God"* (Matthew 5:9).

Peace is the mental, emotional, physical, and spiritual condition in which there is freedom from disturbance, anxiety, turmoil, uncertainty, conflict, war, strife, fear, or violence. The list could go on and include freedom from self-condemnation, self-doubt, remorse, and regret. Peace is an invaluable possession.

The Infinite Value of Peace

Let's look at the infinite value God places on peace. Here are twenty-one key characteristics of God's—not the world's—peace.

1. **Peace is an essential, fundamental, foundational imperative of God's kingdom**. Three elements of His kingdom—being right, having peace, and having joy in the power of the Holy Spirit—set the course for all things: "*For the kingdom of God is not meat or drink; but righteousness, and peace, and joy in the Holy Ghost*" (Romans 14:17).

2. **Peace is an important part of God's identity.** The Scriptures refer to Him as the God of peace. He saw the need for man's peace and created a plan for everyone to experience it in this life and for eternity. Peace is at the core of God's heart and purpose: "*And the very God of peace sanctify you wholly...*" (1 Thess. 5:23).

3. **God is the initiator and author of peace.** The very concept of peace is His idea and His philosophy, which comes from His fundamental character of love. He wants peace for all He has created: "*For God is not the author of confusion, but of peace...*" (1 Corinthians 14:33).

4. **God's thoughts toward us are of peace.** God is not antagonistic or aggravating. He doesn't make trouble for us or wish us ill. He desires our peace: "*For I know the thoughts that I think toward you, saith the LORD, thoughts of peace, and not of evil...*" (Jeremiah 29:11).

   One of Satan's strategies is to convince us that he is good, and God is bad. Don't ever believe that God is your enemy or that He is the one who desires to steal, kill, and destroy. Instead, understand that God's thoughts and plans toward us are for loving, wonderful, and peaceful things.

5. **God wants peace for everyone.** When Jesus arrived, angels announced God's intentions for mankind.

Through Jesus, God sent us the way to peace, from a heart of love, with His goodwill toward us: "*And suddenly there was with the angel a multitude of the heavenly host praising God, and saying, Glory to God in the highest, and on earth peace, good will toward men*" (Luke 2:13–14).

6. **Peace is one of the main benefits of wisdom.** If wisdom does not produce peace, it is not wisdom. James said wisdom from above is peaceable: "*The wisdom from above is first pure, then peaceable...*" (James 3:17). Peace is the object and goal of wisdom: "*Happy is the man that findeth wisdom, and the man that getteth understanding. Her ways are ways of pleasantness, and all her paths are peace*" (Proverbs 3:13, 17).

7. **Peace is the work of righteousness.** Anyone doing the right thing is working toward peace and will gain quietness and assurance: "*And the work of righteousness shall be peace; and the effect of righteousness quietness and assurance forever*" (Isaiah 32:17).

8. **Peace will result when keeping the commandments.** God's commandments aren't intended to interfere with our happiness; they're intended to give us peace. They show the ways to produce peace in our lives: "*O that thou hadst hearkened to my commandments! then had thy peace been as a river, and thy righteousness as the waves of the sea*" (Isaiah 48:18).

9. **One of Christ's titles includes peace.** Jesus has many names or titles. In Isaiah, He is called the "Prince of Peace," and the peace He brings has no end. Isaiah 9:6–7 says, "*For unto us a child is born, unto us a son is given: and the government shall be upon his shoulder: and his name shall be called Wonderful, Counsellor, The mighty God, The everlasting Father, The Prince of Peace. Of the increase of his government and peace there shall be no end.*"

10. Peace is the primary purpose of Christ's coming. The purpose of God is to produce peace everywhere in the whole universe. Jesus came to bring God's peace, and without Him, peace would never come. He came to guide us into peace: *"Through the tender mercy of our God; whereby the dayspring from on high hath visited us, To give light to them that sit in darkness and in the shadow of death, to guide our feet into the way of peace"* (Luke 1:78–79).

Jesus said He came to teach us the path of peace. He wants us to rest, undisturbed by trouble. He wants us to remain in a peaceful condition: *"These things I have spoken unto you, that in me ye might have peace. In the world ye shall have tribulation: but be of good cheer; I have overcome the world"* (John 16:33).

11. Peace is one of the purposes of Calvary. Jesus came to trade His position and well-being to give us ours. That shows us that peace is of the utmost value. God wanted us to have it, and Jesus came to give it: *"But he was wounded for our transgressions, he was bruised for our iniquities: the chastisement of our peace was upon him; and with his stripes we are healed"* (Isaiah 53:5).

The blood of Jesus is all about peace. It's about reconciling all things to God. Our peace is so important that Christ gave up His life for it:

> *"And, having made peace through the blood of his cross, by him to reconcile all things unto himself; by him, I say, whether they be things in earth, or things in heaven.*
>
> *And you, that were sometime alienated and enemies in your mind by wicked works, yet now hath he reconciled."* (Colossians 1:20–21)

12. **Peace is the legacy Jesus left to us.** The world gives peace that is conditional and temporary. The peace that Jesus offered is a lasting peace that is not dependent on our circumstances: *"Peace I leave with you, my peace I give unto you: not as the world giveth, give I unto you. Let not your heart be troubled, neither let it be afraid"* (John 14:27).

13. **Peace is one of the nine by-products of the Holy Spirit.** One proof that the Holy Spirit is working in our lives is that we remain in a peaceful condition. This works together with the other outcomes of the Spirit's inner work, producing fruit that glorifies God and shows Him to others through us: *"But the fruit of the Spirit is love, joy, peace, longsuffering, gentleness, goodness, faith"* (Galatians 5:22).

14. **Peace is a proclamation when entering a home.** When we enter a home, we should greet those who live there with peace. Jesus instructs us to speak our desire for peace for our hosts. (Yes, we should say this aloud.) *"And into whatsoever house ye enter, first say, Peace be to this house"* (Luke 10:5).

15. **Peace is at the core of mental health.** When we have the peace of God, we will not turn to other, nonproductive or even destructive ways of obtaining it. We don't need to worry or drown our pain in drugs, alcohol, shopping, or anything else. Our condition is stable, peaceful, and untroubled. Only God can give us such peace: *"And the peace of God, which passeth all understanding, shall keep your hearts and minds through Christ Jesus"* (Philippians 4:7).

16. **Peace is the dominating force for victorious living.** We must allow the peace of God to rule our hearts. There are many other things that would like to take over our hearts, but with God in control, we'll be at peace: *"And let the peace of God rule in your hearts..."* (Colossians 3:15).

17. God speaks peace to whomever will listen. God speaks to us through the inner voice of the Holy Spirit. He always speaks in a consistent manner. He doesn't yell, scream, or condemn, and His message will always agree with His written Word. He speaks peace to His saints: *"I will hear what God the LORD will speak: for he will speak peace unto his people, and to his saints: but let them not turn again to folly"* (Psalm 85:8).

18. Peace inside us, and working out from us, is evidence that God is our Father. There is nothing better than knowing we belong to God. We can be happy to belong to our earthly parents and the others we hold dear, yet to be called a child of God is the grandest of them all. When we are full of His peace, and want to bring it to others, we are His! We are happy. We are blessed! *"Blessed are the peacemakers: for they shall be called the children of God"* (Matthew 5:9).

19. Peace is the true working of God's Word. God sends His Word to us for our encouragement and edification. His words are powerful and will accomplish exactly what He sent them to do. As we hear them, we are filled with joy and go in peace. Even creation applauds when the Word of God goes into our hearts:

> *"For as the rain cometh down, and the snow from heaven, and returneth not thither, but watereth the earth, and maketh it bring forth and bud, that it may give seed to the sower, and bread to the eater:*
>
> *So shall my word be that goeth forth out of my mouth: it shall not return unto me void, but it shall accomplish that which I please, and it shall prosper in the thing whereto I sent it.*
>
> *For ye shall go out with joy, and be led forth with peace: the mountains and the hills shall*

break forth before you into singing, and all the
trees of the field shall clap their hands. "

(Isaiah 55:10–12)

20. **Peace is mentioned more than four hundred times in the King James Version of the Bible.** When the same word is so often repeated, and in various contexts, we must conclude that it contains a vital message from God. He wants us to be well acquainted with, and living a life of, peace.

21. **Peace opens Genesis and closes Revelation.** The Bible opens with creation living in peace. This was God's plan from the beginning. When sin entered the world, that original peace was lost. The Prince of Peace came to restore lasting peace, and through His blood, peace will prevail! God puts infinite worth on peace. We all want it. He is the only way to get it.

Through Him, receive peace. And pass it on to a world so desperate for true peace.

Chapter 12

How to Have Inner Tranquility

Blessed Are the Peacemakers

Look back into your past. What hurts come to your mind? What disappointments do you remember?

Glance around the news cycles of today. The hurt abounds, doesn't it? Every story seems to provide more bad news, doesn't it?

Imagine the future. Will it become better? Are you afraid of where this world is going?

Events from our past, troubles of today, and worries about the future can destroy our peace—if we let them. For each conflict within us and around us, we can find a solution in God. He has provided peace through His Son.

Let's look at twenty-three ways our peace can be shaken, along with His responses that will lead us lead back to trust, calm, and a tranquil disposition:

1. **Unresolved guilt.** We cannot have guilt and peace at the same time. Guilt works against the conscience, shutting out peace and leaving us in turmoil. We can visit a psychologist and try all kinds of therapies and medications, but none of these can cleanse our conscience of guilt. Seeking the forgiveness of Jesus

and asking Him to wipe away our guilt is the only way we can receive total cleansing. With Him, all our guilt is gone: *"If we confess our sins, he is faithful and just to forgive us our sins, and to cleanse us from all unrighteousness"* (1 John 1:9).

2. **Unfulfilled selfishness.** We can lose our peace when we cannot obtain our selfish desires. The ego is a horrible taskmaster. The uncrucified, unsanctified ego can create almost limitless unattainable ambitions. The ego can drive us to exhaustion as we fail, time and again, to reach and grasp the impossible. A converted person no longer lives with selfish striving, but lives for the purposes of Jesus: *"And that he died for all, that they which live should not henceforth live unto themselves, but unto him which died for them, and rose again"* (2 Corinthians 5:15).

   We cannot allow our hearts to be ruled by ego rather than Jesus. He came to give us better reasons to live, better causes to support, and deeper pursuits to work toward, both for our peace and for greater fulfillment.

3. **Self-rejection.** Do you like yourself? You cannot have peace and be a self-rejecter. People who hate themselves try to escape their pain through diversions and amusements. They try to meet legitimate human needs through illegitimate methods. From a most tender age, people taught us to side with them against ourselves. God came to fix this. We are made in the image of God. He made no mistakes. We are uniquely formed, according to His purpose, and at the heart of His plans is pure love. We must remember, it is He who created us, and we have eternal value to the One who matters most: *"Of the Rock that begat thee thou art mindful, and hast forgotten God that formed thee"* (Deuteronomy 32:18).

   Psalm 100:3 says, *"Know ye that the Lord he is God: it is he that hath made us, and not we ourselves;*

we are his people, and the sheep of his pasture." He chose our gender, the day and time of our birth, and all our features. The things we may see as flaws are built-in reference points of identity and uniqueness, and a mark of ownership by God. We are His design!

Self-rejection doesn't just happen when we dislike a part of ourselves. It can also happen when we compare ourselves with others. The instinct and drive to compete happens in early childhood. We want to be first; we want to win. We want to be better than other people—we are taught to compete.

If we do not recognize God as our creator and designer and ourselves as valuable, unique, and indispensable, we will start comparing ourselves to others, and we will lose our peace. Parents, be careful not to compare your children to others, or they may compare themselves to others for the rest of their lives. This can have devastating consequences.

Once we believe we were created by design, and we value ourselves without comparing ourselves to others, then we can accept our title. We are kings and priests unto God! We are royalty. God is our Father, the King of Kings. He puts us in charge over His creation. We oversee and minister to others as trusted members of His kingdom:

> *"And from Jesus Christ, who is the faithful witness, and the first begotten of the dead, and the prince of the kings of the earth. Unto him that loved us, and washed us from our sins in his own blood,*
> *And hath made us kings and priests unto God and his Father; to him be glory and dominion for ever and ever. Amen."*   (Revelation 1:5–6)

4. **A sense of inadequacy.** God put the "real you" inside your body when He formed you and brought you

into being. Because we are formed and designed by the Almighty God, the all-knowing and all-powerful One, we can be sure that He can prepare us for this life. When we have His help, there is no circumstance, no trial, and no pain that we cannot overcome. He is greater than the stormy seas and wants us to also dwell in that place of peace: *"I can do all things through Christ which strengthens me"* (Philippians 4:13 NKJV).

5. **Self-condemnation.** Self-condemnation will steal our peace. It's similar to self-rejection, but instead of focusing on outward appearances or station in life, its criticism goes below the surface. Self-condemnation is a voice that speaks deep within our souls, telling us we're stupid, worthless, and can't do anything right. It throws the past into our faces and keeps us pressed into a corner of shame and ridicule. The voice that yells and screams of our failures is *not* the voice of God. Satan is the accuser, the enemy, who wants to keep us locked up and condemned.

  Who can condemn us? No one. Jesus died to take condemnation away: *"Who shall lay anything to the charge of God's elect? It is God that justifieth. Who is he that condemneth? It is Christ that died..."* (Romans 8:33–34). And Romans 8:1 says, *"There is therefore no condemnation to them which are in Christ Jesus, who walk not after the flesh, but after the Spirit."*

6. **Being wronged by others.** We have all been wronged by others. How do we respond? How do we let it affect us? God is more interested in our response than what was done to us. He will take care of the offender. In Matthew 18, Peter asks Jesus how many times he should forgive his brother. Jesus replied 490 times. It's not the number that's important, but what it represents: repeated forgiveness. Forgiveness neutralizes the power of the offender over us: *"Then came Peter to him, and said, Lord, how oft shall my brother sin*

against me, and I forgive him? till seven times? Jesus saith unto him, I say not unto thee, Until seven times: but, Until seventy times seven" (Matthew 18:21–22).

When someone sins against me, I'll give myself sixty seconds to complain about it, and then it's time to forgive. God wants us so trained to forgive that we do it quickly and consistently. It takes a big person to forgive and not hold a grudge. We can be that big person and continue our lives in peace.

7. **Anger and wrath.** We can't have anger and peace at the same time. When we're offended, we need to shake it off and let God avenge it in the way He sees fit. We are to forgive, to feed our hungry enemy, and, if he's thirsty, to give him a drink. If we are Christ-like, we will not render evil for evil; instead, we will keep our peace.

8. **Worry.** We cannot worry and have peace simultaneously. Jesus tells us not to worry in this life because God is already present in our tomorrow. Why worry when we can pray? We can prayerfully deal with life one day at a time: *"Take therefore no thought for the morrow: for the morrow shall take thought for the things of itself. Sufficient unto the day is the evil thereof"* (Matthew 6:34).

9. **Discouragement.** Sometimes, we don't see the progress we'd like to make and become discouraged. We may throw ourselves a pity party. Instead, we must put our hope in God, the one who never fails and never lets us down: *"Why art thou cast down, O my soul? and why art thou disquieted within me? hope thou in God..."* (Psalm 42:11).

10. **Stress.** When we're stressed, we need to find stillness. We must cast our cares upon God because He can handle them. As believers, we should maintain a care-free attitude; this will keep our peace: *"Be still, and know that I am God..."* (Psalm 46:10). *"Casting all*

your care upon him; for he careth for you" (1 Peter 5:7).

11. **Trials, tests, and temptation.** Our peace can certainly be destroyed by trials, tests, and temptation. However, if we handle them as God's Word instructs, we can maintain our peace and add to our maturity. These trials come to test our faith. We should be joyful as we face difficulties, knowing God cares for us and will help us through them. Our times of trials, tests, and temptation can be some of our closest times with God. We can watch Him work on our behalf. What a joy that is! *"My brethren, count it all joy when ye fall into divers temptations; Knowing this, that the trying of your faith worketh patience"* (James 1:2–3).

God takes us through various trials in life to produce the personal qualities that can help others. When we have experienced God's comfort through trials, we can better assist others as they go through their own trials. The process is like high school algebra. We didn't start with the hardest problems first. Instead, the teacher started at the beginning, and once we mastered each set, we got harder ones. So it goes with the trials and tests of life—they become harder as we gain maturity.

12. **Doubts.** We need to believe our beliefs and doubt our doubts. What God says is true. We must focus on His Word and leave doubting behind. Doubts can dissolve peace: *"And Jesus answering saith unto them, Have faith in God"* (Mark 11:22).

13. **Mental and emotional disturbances.** What should we do with mental and emotional disturbances? They come at us from every direction, attempting to carry away our peace. We must keep our minds on God. We must not let our thoughts move away from Him but stay fixed: *"Thou wilt keep him in perfect peace, whose mind is stayed on thee: because he trusteth in thee.*

Trust ye in the LORD for ever: for in the LORD JEHOVAH is everlasting strength" (Isaiah 26:3–4).

14. **Noise.** Noise can take our peace, and music can drain us. Even ambient noise can become a deterrent to a mind desiring peace and tranquility. We must wisely choose what goes into our ears.

15. **The choices of others.** The poor choices of others may cause us to become critical and judgmental. We can become cynical with everything we judge is wrong in the world or in other people. However, we *can* make a decision about a matter without sitting in judgment or condemnation. Judging is beyond our jurisdiction. God is the only qualified judge.

16. **Non-acceptance of others.** From whom do we seek acceptance? Jesus said not to be surprised if the world hates us because it hated Him first. He also said it is not good to be spoken well of by everyone. If everyone likes us, including the ungodly, we may be compromising ourselves to win the affections of men: "*Woe unto you, when all men shall speak well of you...*" (Luke 6:26).

    As Christians, we should always seek the honor that comes from God, not from men. Love those who don't accept you, but seek acceptance only from God.

17. **National and international distress.** Jesus said we would hear of wars and rumors of war. He knew this and said to not be troubled. We are not at peace because the world is at peace; we are at peace because we have the peace of God in our hearts and thoughts of His promises in our minds: "*And ye shall hear of wars and rumours of wars: see that ye be not troubled: for all these things must come to pass, but the end is not yet*" (Matthew 24:6).

    We cannot allow ourselves to become riled up, disturbed, or distressed about world events. We are only human-sized. We must move forward with our own business and maintain our own peace. We can take our place on our knees in prayer, but not overly concern ourselves with God-sized matters: *"Lord, my heart is not haughty, nor mine eyes lofty: neither do I exercise myself in great matters, or in things too high for me"* (Psalm 131:1).

18. **Reports of bad news.** How much good news do you hear? These days it doesn't seem the media is concerned with good news. Most of the news we hear is bad, and there's plenty of it. From every side, we hear the worst of humanity, and it can take our peace in an instant! *"But his word was in mine heart as a burning fire shut up in my bones, and I was weary with forbearing, and I could not stay. For I heard the defaming of many, fear on every side. Report, say they, and we will report it..."* (Jeremiah 20:9–10).

   We need to study the Word of God rather than all the negative reports. We need to meditate on His Word rather than what's on the TV, radio, or in the newspapers. If we start to obsess about what goes on in this world, we will have no peace. More than guided missiles, we need guided men, women, and children!

19. **Loneliness.** God said it was not good for man to be alone and that a wife is his companion. Some people have no peace because they want a companion. God will bring someone to us to share our lives. When that happens, we marry and stay married. We need strong marriages. These relationships bring peace, not only to us, but also to our families and our society: *"And the* LORD GOD *said, It is not good that the man should be alone; I will make him an help meet for him"* (Genesis 2:18). *"...Yet is she thy companion, and the wife of thy covenant"* (Malachi 2:14).

20. **Being abandoned by parents.** There are many ways parents can abandon their children. Parents may still be in the home yet are emotionally unavailable. If something is missing from your family or your

childhood, stay close to the Lord, and watch for His alternate provision. He promised to be a Father to the fatherless. The Church can get on board with this and learn to father the fatherless: *"When my father and my mother forsake me, then the LORD will take me up"* (Psalm 27:10).

21. **Having wayward children.** Is there anything more devastating than wayward children? The ache, the trouble, the loss of peace, the worry, and the concern can be overwhelming. Carefully watch your children's companions. Peers can lead our children away into all sorts of trouble: *"But thus saith the LORD, Even the captives of the mighty shall be taken away, and the prey of the terrible shall be delivered: for I will contend with him that contendeth with thee, and I will save thy children"* (Isaiah 49:25).

    We must pray and never give up on our children because God wants to deliver them from captivity. He wants to bring them to Himself. We must trust Him. When we pray, we can ask Him to send someone who can bring our wayward child back to Him as we continue to stand in hope. If the Lord encourages you to pray for someone—even if they seem unknown or a puzzle to you—obey and pray. You may be the one who prays another person's child home to safety.

22. **Past sorrows.** How do we handle past sorrows? One way is to realize that sorrow is better than laughter. People who have experienced sorrow have a deeper sensitivity to those around them. They will also have more wisdom to share if they responded properly to their own sorrow. In this sorrowful, fallen world, they are uniquely gifted to build and strengthen others. A fool is out for folly, a good time, and entertainment. Sorrow can mature us, sensitize us, and make us useful: *"Sorrow is better than laughter: for by the sadness of the countenance the heart is made better. The heart of*

the wise is in the house of mourning; but the heart of fools is in the house of mirth" (Ecclesiastes 7:3–4).

23. **Weariness.** Many things can make us weary— even the study of good things. There's an amazing connection between our physical condition and our spiritual, mental, and emotional condition. Jesus, our Good Shepherd, says to come away, to lie down, to be still, and be restored: *"He maketh me to lie down in green pastures: he leadeth me beside the still waters. He restoreth my soul…"* (Psalm 23:2–3).

The Singular Way to God's Way of Peace

The way to peace is not hard, yet the way without it is impassable. God has made it simple for us to find peace. If we dwell on what He wants us to dwell on, we will be at peace. We must meditate upon Him and His promises. We automatically know how to meditate on our worries and doubts. We are naturally prone to focus our thinking on what's wrong. However, we can *train ourselves* to meditate on what's right—the Word of God: *"Meditate upon these things; give thyself wholly to them; that thy profiting may appear to all"* (1 Timothy 4:15).

Personal peace is at the heart of God's commands. They are meant to keep us steady, stable, and calm. They keep us from worry, stress, striving, and doubt. A mind that meditates on Him is a mind at peace. When we have peace with God, and with ourselves, we are ready to make peace with others: *"Blessed are the peacemakers: for they shall be called the children of God"* (Matthew 5:9).

Chapter 13

How to Get Along with Others

Peace with Others—The Clash of Kingdoms

Can you control the weather? If you are a fan, can you control if your team wins a ball game? Can you be in charge of all decisions made throughout the world? Of course, we cannot control all things. But we must choose to pursue that which matters most.

There is so much we cannot control. But peace—that which we crave and desire, that which sometimes seems impossible—is something we must pursue.

Peace inside our hearts and peace with God are personal and internal. We have control of these areas based on our beliefs and choices. We know God is for our peace and values it greatly in His relationship with each one of us. However, being a peacemaker can present unique challenges because it partially relies on the willingness of others. Jesus did not present us with an impossible goal when He talked about peacemaking. As the Prince of Peace, He was acutely aware of things that whisk peace away. He was acquainted with the opposing forces we face each day. I call this "the clash of kingdoms."

There are two kingdoms. First is God's kingdom, which seeks peace. The second, the world's kingdom, seeks dominance (to destroy peace). When these kingdoms are in opposition, we are caught in the clash zone. These two kingdoms have differing standards and ideologies. They have different kings and different ways of functioning. Just as in Jesus's day, the world's kingdom will ridicule, hate, and persecute the people of God's kingdom. However, the One who overcame left us with hope. He says we can retain our peace, and even be cheerful, while the clash of kingdoms rages on: *"These things I have spoken unto you, that in me ye might have peace. In the world ye shall have tribulation: but be of good cheer; I have overcome the world"* (John 16:33).

How can we be successful in overcoming, as Jesus was? If we align ourselves with God's Word, we can face each battle and walk out victorious.

Jesus's Rules of Engagement

In Matthew 10, Jesus shows how we can retain our peace, even when we are challenged by another kingdom. Here are seventeen practical life management strategies for retaining our peace:

1. **Avoid being the offender.** In other words, don't go looking for trouble—do not be on the offense. Jesus describes it as going about our business as if we are sheep among wolves. We don't go out in ignorance or stupidity. We know what's out there, but still we go out. Jesus said to be wise yet harmless as we journey through this world: *"Behold, I send you forth as sheep in the midst of wolves: be ye therefore wise as serpents and harmless as doves"* (Matthew 10:16).

2. **Shake it off.** We need to shake off the offenses that cross our path. Jesus said whoever does not receive us does not receive Him. We don't stick around wounded and crushed; instead, we leave and shake the dust from our feet. We also don't bite back as wolves would do. We are kind, exchanging good for evil. We feed our hungry enemy and give a drink to our thirsty foe. We are harmless. Then we leave. We don't take everything personally. We go in peace: *"And whosoever shall not*

receive you, nor hear your words, when ye depart out of that house or city, shake of the dust of your feet" (Matthew 10:14).

3. **Realize people who are in the world are in deep trouble.** Trouble and judgment are *already* coming to people whose kingdom clashes with God's. Matthew 10:15 says, *"Verily I say unto you, It shall be more tolerable for the land of Sodom and Gomorrah in the day of judgment, than for that city."* Knowing the fate of the lost world should move us to compassion instead of conflict.

4. **Stay alert!** Although we have compassion, we must also stay alert. People will mock us, show their disdain for us, demonstrate against us, and persecute us. Daily, Christians are on trial and face death for their beliefs. This has been happening across the globe for centuries. This may come to America as well: *"But be aware of men: for they will deliver you up to councils, and they will scourge you in their synagogues"* (Matthew 10:17).

5. **Realize that some issues may become legal problems.** We may face governments, councils, or other ruling authorities in this clash of kingdoms. The world may come against us in the form of lawsuits. Just like the synagogues in Jesus's day, our own places of worship may come under attack. Denominations may accuse other denominations of bigotry or religious fanaticism: *"And ye shall be brought before governors and kings for my sake, for a testimony against them and the Gentiles"* (Matthew 10:18).

6. **Stay calm as God gives us wisdom.** We don't have to worry about what we'll say when we are asked to explain ourselves. The Holy Spirit will give us the right words at the right time. It doesn't mean the outcome will go in our favor, but the words we have spoken will accomplish the will of God. He will give us a wise

response that keeps with His point of view. Even if we have little education or experience, God does not want us to worry about it. He will give us His words: *"But when they deliver you up, take no thought how or what ye shall speak: for it will be given you in that same hour what ye shall speak"* (Matthew 10:19).

7. **Realize the Holy Spirit is the real speaker.** People in the world's kingdom don't know who they're dealing with. They may think they can freely mock, attack, tease, or ridicule God's standards. They may believe they can defeat us, yet the truth is that the Holy Spirit will be the speaker, not us. We can count on Him to give the perfect reply: *"For it is not ye that speak, but the Spirit of your Father which speaketh in you"* (Matthew 10:20).

8. **Realize the clash may happen in our families.** Some of the relationships we hold most dear may be caught up in the clash of kingdoms. From young and tender ages, our children are exposed to this world more and are exposed to less and less of God. Public schools have banned prayer and adopted evolution as fact. Peers often influence kids more than their parents—and 43 percent of the children in America live with only their mother in the home.

As a result, communication within the home suffers. The battle of kingdoms may be fought within our own families. Jesus warned that such divisions may even come to physical harm and the literal killing of one another: *"And the brother shall deliver up the brother to death, and the father the child: and the children shall rise up against their parents, and cause them to be put to death"* (Matthew 10:21).

9. **Expect to be hated for Christ's sake.** If we hide our identity as Christians, we won't have to worry about the clash of the two kingdoms. If we don't stand for biblical values or speak out for Christ's sake, we'll be

accepted by the world. However, if we *do* represent Jesus in the world, then we must expect to be as hated as He was: *"Woe unto you, when all men shall speak well of you! for so did their fathers to the false prophets"* (Luke 6:26). *"If the world hate you, ye know that it hated me before it hated you"* (John 15:18).

If we give up our lives, personal ambitions, and well-being on this earth, we will keep them for heaven. Conversely, if we attempt to keep our earthly lives from trouble and conflict, we will lose our lives in eternity.

10. **Realize there is refuge from the clash.** When we experience persecution, we can leave the battle to regain our peace. We can find people who are like-minded and be encouraged as we share our struggles and victories. We do not have to stay within the clash zone forever: *"But when they persecute you in this city, flee ye into another..."* (Matthew 10:23).

11. **Invest in others.** When we encounter someone in the world's kingdom who will not listen, we can take our message to others. Because there are others waiting to hear from us, there is no need to be bogged down by the unresponsive. We move on, taking with us the words of life: *"For verily I say unto you, Ye shall not have gone over the cities of Israel, till the Son of man be come"* (Matthew 10:23).

12. **Be satisfied and at peace with rejection.** When we represent Jesus, we will be treated as He was. Our Master was hated and mistreated, and we are to be like Him. We should not invite mistreatment—due to obnoxious behavior or a know-it-all attitude—but rather we receive rejection because of our Christ-like nature. What they did to Him they will do to us, and we gladly join in His suffering: *"It is enough for the disciple that he be as his master, and the servant as his lord"* (Matthew 10:25).

13. **Expect to be called evil or a messenger of the devil.** Some may call us religious nuts, while others may accuse us of having demons. We may be called "the devil" or simply out of our minds. People made the same accusations against Jesus, and we may be treated as our Master was. There is no better way to live, and what a privilege to be counted among His! *"But when the Pharisees heard it, they said, This fellow doth not cast out devils, but by Beelzebub the prince of the devils"* (Matthew 12:24).

14. **Do not fear because the truth will prevail.** In the end, when God restores all things as they should be, the Truth will come out. The Spirit will speak to us, in the quiet place, uncovering things we must deal with personally. He will also bring out truths that the kingdom of this world would rather hide. What was once done in secret will be revealed, and the fate of those who oppose our message will be uncovered: *"Fear them not therefore: for there is nothing covered, that shall not be revealed; and hid, that shall not be known"* (Matthew 10:26).

   We must not fear the people who persecute us—not even unto our death. They can destroy our bodies but cannot touch our souls. Laying aside our fear of man, we must continue to speak as God directs us: *"And fear not them which kill the body, but are not able to kill the soul: but rather fear him which is able to destroy both soul and body in hell"* (Matthew 10:28).

15. **Let the fear of God overcome the fear of man.** Fear of man is a trap. As if we're paralyzed, fear of man trips us up and stops us. It takes us out of the arena and makes us ineffective. Fear of the Lord, however, brings wisdom and keeps us safe. It sustains us, provides direction, and ensures our relationship with God for today and tomorrow. Our trust is in God alone; all others will fail us and trap us: *"The fear of man*

bringeth a snare: but whoso putteth his trust in the LORD shall be safe" (Proverbs 29:25).

16. **Remember your personal worth to God.** God tracks every detail of our lives. He even sees every sparrow that falls to the ground. If He keeps track of the birds, how much more must He be interested in us! He knows the difficulties we encounter in this world, and He promises to never forget us. Because He is fully aware of the sparrow's fate, we can be sure He is fully aware of us. He cares for us and places great value on our lives: *"Are not two sparrows sold for a farthing? and one of them shall not fall on the ground without your Father"* (Matthew 10:29).

17. **Realize that God accepts you.** In the clash zone, we should confess Jesus before men. If we do, Jesus will also confess us before His Father in heaven. We will not be denied in heaven when we zealously stand for Him: *"But whosoever shall deny me before men, him will I also deny before my Father which is in heaven"* (Matthew 10:33).

———

The clash of kingdoms is inevitable. Jesus tells us that this conflict exists, and He did not come to keep us from it, but to keep us *through* it. He also came to *bring* it. The clash zone is necessary. It separates those who will believe and receive the kingdom of God, through Jesus, and those who will not. It is an eternal issue, and that's where the conflict lies. He did not come to give peace to all, but only to those who receive Him:

> *"Think not that I am come to send peace on earth: I came not to send peace, but a sword.*
>
> *For I am come to set a man at variance against his father, and the daughter against her mother, and the daughter in law against her mother in law."*
>
> (Matthew 10:34–35)

These two kingdoms have irreconcilable differences. They are on a necessary, daily collision course. We do our best to keep the peace within the guidelines of Scripture. We do not seek to provoke others because of our own pride, although our Christ-like standards will indeed provoke them. We are humble and gentle; we are kind to those who use us, hate us, and persecute us. We continue forward, with inner peace, relying on our God of peace in a world that knows none.

Chapter 14

The Why and How to Make Peace

Peace with Others—
Our Responsibility to Make Things Right

W ho are peacemakers? What do they do? In this world of division, war, stress, and uncertainty, how can peacemakers change things?

Peacemakers *actively* pursue peace. They are not complacent, lazy, or negligent about making things right between themselves and others when necessary. Sometimes, we need great courage to step toward another person with a desired outcome of restoration and reconciliation. We may be tempted to hang back in a cold war, quietly avoid the other person, or justify our feelings of ambivalence. We may be fearful of confrontation or lack experience in making peace.

Our Biblical Responsibility toward Peace

The following are five elements of our biblical responsibility toward peace:

1. **Peace is a non-optional mandate from God.** Paul, in writing to the Corinthians, urged God's people to be like-minded and undivided. He wanted them

to be joined together. This was no suggestion, but a mandate. He called for the proper functioning of the whole Church and to the individuals within it:

> *"Now I beseech you, brethren, by the name of our Lord Jesus Christ, that ye all speak the same thing, and that there be no divisions among you; but that ye be perfectly joined together in the same mind and in the same judgment."* (1 Corinthians 1:10)

2. **Peace should be important to us because it's important to God.** If it is possible (and there will be times when it isn't), we must live at peace with all men. We aren't allowed to select with whom we will be peaceable. When no resolution has been reached, we also can't allow time and distance to smooth things into a pseudo form of peace. The Holy Spirit will remind us of people with whom we must pursue peace: "If it be possible, as much as lieth in you, live peaceably with all men" (Romans 12:18).

3. **Peace is the normal and consistent path of wisdom.** James says that wisdom from above is pure and peaceful. Wisdom that does not seek peace is not wisdom. Ideas that create conflict among spouses, families, workplaces, and congregations are not wise. God's wisdom pursues peace. In the book of Proverbs, wisdom is personified as a woman. Sorry, men! What's important is what wisdom is like: *"Her ways are ways of pleasantness, and all her paths are peace"* (Proverbs 3:17).

4. **Peace is more important than our offerings.** Before we give our offerings to the Lord, we must be at peace with each other. If we know someone has said or done something against us, we must first reconcile with him or her. After clearing up the relationship, we are then to go back to complete our offering. We should act with

speed and urgency. Our gift waits at the altar for us to return with a peaceful and obedient heart in right standing before God:

> *"Therefore if thou bring thy gift to the altar,*
> *and there rememberest that thy brother hath*
> *ought against thee;*
> *Leave there thy gift before the altar, and go thy*
> *way; first be reconciled to thy brother, and then*
> *come and offer thy gift."*   (Matthew 5:23–24)

5. **Peace is attainable.** God does not command that we reach the unreachable. Therefore, peaceful resolution is something we can attain. Many Scriptures illustrate how God helped His people, who were in difficult circumstances, conquer evil-doing with forgiveness or coldness with kindness. For example, Joseph, who had been sold into slavery by his jealous brothers, was able to forgive them. Once reunited, he embraced them with kisses and weeping. Joseph was human, yet he remained at peace within himself and made peace with his brothers.

Peace is not the only benefit of walking in obedience. When our actions please the Lord, he gives us much more. He will even make our enemies at peace with us. Proverbs 16:7 says, *"When a man's ways please the LORD, he maketh even his enemies to be at peace with him."*

Peace (the mental, emotional, physical, and spiritual condition in which there is freedom from disturbance, anxiety, and conflict) is a hallmark of people who follow God's commands and live in His love. It is His will that we diligently work toward peace.

Think about how the world will change as we pursue that peace. Think about how relationships, families, businesses, churches, and individuals will begin living differently by including the pursuit of peace as a key part of their life management system.

Twelve Principles of Reconciliation

The condition of our hearts will improve our ability to find peace. Therefore, reconciliation is a key aspect to finding peace. The following are twelve principles of reconciliation:

1. **Be reconciled with God.** We cannot begin to make peace with others until we have a peaceful relationship with God. The reconciliation process must start with our relationship with Him. Once we are at peace with Him, we can proceed to seek peace in our other relationships. Jesus reconciled us with the Father. Through His work of reconciliation, we can see many parallels to how we reconcile with others: "*And all things are of God, who hath reconciled us to himself by Jesus Christ...*" (2 Corinthians 5:18).

2. **Ensure that your goal is peace through reconciliation.** Unfortunately, we can't just run away. We also can't condemn, abuse, point the finger, argue, or debate. We are called to reconciliation. We must make it the goal of our energies, focus, time, talent, money, and treasure. We must aim to be peacemakers. God reconciled us to Himself through Jesus and has given us the ministry of reconciliation among ourselves. 2 Corinthians 5:18 says that God "*hath given to us the ministry of reconciliation.*"

3. **See yourself as a person who blesses others.** We can bless others through our role as peacemaker. Even when we are persecuted, we must maintain our role to bless. We keep our eyes fixed on the goal of reconciliation. Even when someone persecutes us, they should still be the targets of our blessing. If we treat them as they have treated us, then we are no longer at peace. A peacemaker, instead, returns good for evil. "*Bless them which persecute you: bless and curse not*" (Romans 12:14).

4. **Genuinely care for others.** We must genuinely care about the people with whom we seek reconciliation. We are not out to manipulate them for our own good. Instead, we are to show them real love. We know our caring is genuine when we can rejoice with others in the good and weep with others in times of trouble: *"Rejoice with them that do rejoice, and weep with them that weep"* (Romans 12:15).

5. **Take interest in how others think.** The Scripture says that understanding is a wellspring of life. As we try to understand how others process information, we can better reach them with a peaceful resolution.

6. **Avoid coming across to others as a know-it-all.** We cannot approach other people with pride, conceit, or in any other way that belittles them. The goal is not to stir up negative emotions but rather to reach a peaceful conclusion.

7. **Lower yourself (be humble).** We are not to speak to others in a condescending way. We, instead, should condescend our own standing on their behalf. That means we come from our high position to a lower one. God, who laid aside His crown, power, and garments of kingship, came down to Earth to be born of a woman. He *lowered himself* to our level so He could reconcile us to Him. This is the greatest example of our ministry of reconciliation with others. We don't stand in an elevated position. Instead, with a pure heart, we sincerely condescend before others in the hope we can win them over. Romans 12:16 says, *"Mind not the high things, but condescend to men of low estate. Be not wise in your own conceits."*

8. **Return good for the evil done to you.** This point cannot be overemphasized. When we strike back, we get into arguments, debates, and try to outwit each other. We can prolong the strife and disharmony and refuse to forgive. This is not the way of reconciliation:

"*Recompense to no man evil for evil...*" (Romans 12:17).

9. **Be honest.** When we engage with others, we must be completely honest. If they think we're conning them, manipulating them, or being deceitful, our efforts will not work. We must not use excuses or massage the truth. We must be dead honest: "*Provide things honest in the sight of all men*" (Romans 12:17).

10. **Know that reconciliation is the opposite of revenge.** We should always remain peaceful blessers who seek a peaceful resolution. God will handle any consequences that are due to the people who committed the offense: "*Dearly beloved, avenge not yourselves, but rather give place unto wrath: for it is written, Vengeance is mine; I will repay, saith the Lord*" (Romans 12:18).

11. **Proactively do good things for the other person.** It is not enough to keep our peace when others rail against us. We must actively do them good. As Christians, God empowers us to do good for others. We do not fall in line with our culture that tells us to walk away in disgust, to get them back, or simmer forever in our anger. We seek only the best for our offender. We provide whatever he is lacking: "*Therefore if thine enemy hunger, feed him; if he thirst, give him drink: for in so doing thou shalt heap coals of fire on his head*" (Romans 12:20).

What does it mean to heap coals of fire on our enemy's head? Doesn't that sound like the way of the world? In New Testament times, travel was done by foot, which means travelers were out in the elements. During cold weather, the traveler would start on his journey with hot coals, or heated rocks, wrapped in a blanket that he carried on his head. When it was time to rest, he covered himself with his heated blanket and drew the rocks close to his side. Through this practice, his life was sustained. When we proactively do good things for others through our ministry of reconciliation, we sustain their lives. This genuine concern for other's well-being is true reconciliation.

Also consider giving your enemy a gift, in secret. Don't gather attention or create fanfare. Quietly give, and the Holy Spirit will do the rest. We pray in secret, fast in secret, and give in secret. Then God, who sees what happens in secret, rewards openly. His reward of peace goes to both the giver and receiver of the quiet gift: "*A gift in secret pacifieth anger: and a reward in the bosom strong wrath*" (Proverbs 21:14).

That is how to truly make a difference. That is how to change the world.

12. **Never give up in your hope to reconcile.** Sometimes, a situation can appear impossible. We must never give up hope, no matter how bleak the situation may seem. Things can change in an instant. We are to stand in our peaceful place of prayer—blessing, giving, and waiting—to be the vessel of reconciliation. As we are diligent to do our part to overcome evil with good, we also wait upon the Holy Spirit to do His work for the good: "*Be not overcome of evil, but overcome evil with good*" (Romans 12:21).

We can actively pursue reconciliation with others once we understand our biblical responsibility to work toward peace and have made sure we're in a good condition before God. With Jesus's example, we can move toward our brother or sister.

Examine Yourself First

Be warned! Reconciliation doesn't begin by examining the other person's wrongs. Instead, Scripture instructs us to examine our own hearts first. Ask yourself, "Is there something I need to correct from my side of the problem?" Reconciliation should always start with self-evaluation. We straighten out ourselves before attempting to straighten out our brother:

"And why beholdest thou the mote that is in thy brother's eye, but considerest not the beam that is in thine own eye?

Or how wilt thou say to thy brother, Let me pull out the mote out of thine eye; and, behold, a beam is in thine own eye?

Thou hypocrite, first cast out the beam out of thine own eye; and then shalt thou see clearly to cast out the mote out of thy brother's eye.

Give not that which is holy unto the dogs, neither cast ye your pearls before swine, lest they trample them under their feet, and turn again and rend you."

(Matthew 7:3–6)

To clearly see (and avoid being a hypocrite), we first need to take care of the sin in our own lives. Reconciling with others requires that we have clear vision. Think of the precision, care, and sensitivity it would take to remove even a speck of dust from another person's eye. We do so cautiously, slowly, and gently. It is the same when we approach an errant brother or sister. Regardless of the amount of wrongdoing on their part, we must own 100 percent of our own wrongdoing. It's not enough to say that the other guy is 90 percent wrong and we are just 10 percent wrong. We must accept the full responsibility of *our* part and step toward the other person with the goal of reconciliation.

How to Approach an Offended Brother or Sister

Approaching our offended brother or sister in an appropriate way sets the stage for a successful reconciliation. Here are three techniques for accomplishing that:

1. **Repent and confess.** If we cover up our side of the problem, reconciliation will not happen. There will be no success, and we will not prosper. However, we receive mercy when we confess before God. God

will intervene, and we will receive the answer to our problem. Proverbs 28:13 says, *"He that covereth his sins shall not prosper: but whoso confesseth and forsaketh them shall have mercy."*

The apostle Paul said he *exercised himself* at being right with God and man. Clearly, Paul valued a clear conscience and believed it was worth the ongoing effort. Acts 24:16 says, *"And herein do I exercise myself, to have always a conscious void of offense toward God, and toward men."*

Likewise, Timothy went into ministry with nothing but faith and a clear conscience. These two things were pivotal to his success. Without them, he could not have preached to the masses without shipwrecking his faith: *"Holding faith, and a good conscience; which some having put away concerning faith have made shipwreck"* (1 Timothy 1:19).

2. **Be the one to make restitution, if possible.** Restitution is part of clearing our conscience. Whenever it applies and is possible, we must repay the person we've offended. If we've stolen, we must make up for the loss. Sometimes we do this by returning the object, and at other times, it's a cash payment. Repentance doesn't end with the mind, thoughts, or words—it is also exercised through deeds: *"Bring forth therefore fruits meet for repentance"* (Matthew 3:8).

    The Bible tells the story of a tax collector named Zacchaeus. After his encounter with Jesus, Zacchaeus acknowledged his thievery and repaid each person four times what he had taken. Salvation came to the entire household of Zacchaeus. Repentance works from the inside out. Our children and families are watching. When our actions meet our profession of faith, our families will be positively impacted: *"If I have taken anything from any man by false accusation, I restore him fourfold. And Jesus said unto him, This day is salvation come to this house"* (Luke 19:8–9).

It may be more comfortable for you just to apologize, but *humbly asking for forgiveness* is the real mission of peace. We need to put ourselves in a vulnerable position by asking a question of the other person. It's humbling to do this and to wait for their answer. Stating that we're sorry and walking away does not give the other person the chance to give a heartfelt reply. Asking for forgiveness allows both parties to clear their conscience of bitterness. We can rehearse our lines, so to speak, before going to the other person, but as we humble ourselves, we must ask for forgiveness.

3. **Give the other person your promise of future intentions.** The conclusion of repentance is to promise not to repeat the offending action. We don't confess our wrongdoing to God and ask the offended person for forgiveness, only to carelessly continue with the same offense. We stop doing the hurtful action. Our behavior must keep step with our words. We assure the other person of our intention to discontinue the hurt, and then we carry it out.

In reconciliation, another goal is to *win the other person over*. This doesn't mean winning *against* them, but rather working to win them back. We must build a new relationship and establish peace in an enduring way.

Jesus is the perfect example of reconciliation. His words concerning the reconciliation of nations reflect our individual need for reconciliation. We were once without Christ and were alienated and disconnected from God. We were estranged, hopeless from His covenants and promises. This was the condition of the whole world. This was the reason Jesus came— to produce reconciliation: *"That at that time ye were without Christ, being aliens from the commonwealth of Israel, and strangers from the covenants of promise, having no hope, and without God in the world"* (Ephesians 2:12).

There was a time when we were far away from God. We needed to be brought near Him. This is what Jesus did when He reconciled us to the Father through His shed blood on the cross. He made the way for unity between God and humanity. Jesus is our peace, and He made us one with God. Jesus broke down the wall that was between God and us and eternally removed the hostility, animosity, bitterness, and resentment. He united two into one and established peace:

"But now in Christ Jesus ye who sometimes were far off are made nigh by the blood of Christ.

For he is our peace, who hath made both one, and hath broken down the middle wall of partition between us;

Having abolished in his flesh the enmity, even the law of commandments contained in ordinances; for to make in himself of twain one new man, so making peace." (Ephesians 2:13–15)

In 2 Corinthians 5:19, we are told, *"To wit, that God was in Christ, reconciling the world unto himself, not imputing their trespasses unto them; and hath committed unto us the word of reconciliation."* This is our goal when reconciling with others: to draw them near, to break down the walls that divide us, to get rid of bitterness and resentment, and to unite us. This is true peace.

Reconciliation removes the barriers. They may be emotional barriers, and the two parties no longer speak to each other. They may be geographical barriers, and they have moved apart physically. In our ministry of reconciliation, we help bring down any barriers and all hostility through sincere acts of love. When we, as imitators of Christ, cancel the debts of others, we set anew the course for a new relationship. We are ministers of reconciliation in a world of brokenness, unforgiving spirit, and strife. This is a blessed function of every believer. Peace is indeed possible! Blessed are the peacemakers.

147

Chapter 15

How to Destroy Animosity

Peace with Others—Tearing Down the Wall

Years ago, I walked the Berlin Wall. It was built to separate two groups of people. Some people had loved ones on the other side of the wall. They wanted to embrace each other and live near each other again, but it was illegal. In 1987, President Ronald Reagan said to Mikhail Gorbachev, "Tear down this wall!" Two years later, it crumbled to the ground, reuniting loved ones and giving greater freedoms to the countries on either side.

Walls are meant to be sturdy and strong. Walk into one, and you will be quickly reminded that they don't move. Sometimes, this describes how we feel about a broken relationship. The wall of hurt separating us seems too thick to penetrate and too high to climb. Yet, at the same time, we are given the ministry of reconciliation. We should unite ourselves with others and help others do the same. We can't teach what we do not know, and we can't lead where we do not go. So we must start with ourselves.

We've learned about confession and forgiveness. We first go to God and confess, and then we go to our brother or sister to seek forgiveness. We "face the wall," so to speak. It is important to remember the wall didn't go up in a day, so taking it down will also take time. As we work toward the wall's destruction, we should take an honest look at the animosity that helped establish it. Examine the hostility, friction, antagonism, and bitterness that strengthened it. It takes hard work and wisdom to win back what was lost between our brothers and sisters. The good news is that God will repay us for our efforts in the ministry of reconciliation. Proverbs 11:30–31 says, "*The fruit of the righteous is a tree of life; and he that winneth souls is wise. Behold, the righteous shall be recompensed in the earth. ...*"

Because God gives us very clear directions, our task is simple. However, it is *not* easy because deconstructing the wall involves the will of another person. They could be a fellow Christian, a spouse, a parent, a child, another family member, a friend, an acquaintance, or a business partner. The walls that divide are well fortified—like the iron bars of a castle. Proverbs 18:19 says, "*A brother offended is harder to be won than a strong city; and their contentions are like the bars of a castle.*"

The New Living Translation says it this way: "*An offended friend is harder to win back than a fortified city. Arguments separate friends like a gate locked with bars*" (Proverbs 18:19).

So how do we win a person back? We start with our words. They carry the power to build or destroy and to hurt or to heal. Words can satisfy the mind as food does the stomach; they can be as gratifying as a plentiful harvest: "*Death and life are in the power of the tongue: and they that love it shall eat the fruit thereof*" (Proverbs 18:21).

We need to practice tearing down the walls with those closest to us. Once we learn to do this with our spouse, children, and other family members, we can expand outward and teach others how to do the same. Be cautioned: some may say there's nothing wrong and deny the conflict exists. Others may want to discuss the problem, only to become defiant, defensive, and opinionated. They may want to dwell *only* on the injustice done to them and stubbornly refuse to move past it. Some may use the silent treatment, while others will show outright fury. Each of these scenarios represents a formidable wall.

Another way people "keep the walls up" during conflict is to refuse to ask a wise mediator for help. Some are discouraged not to go to an elder or the pastor for help. Others do not seek counsel because of an unteachable spirit and the assumption they know it all. This is dangerous because their lives become a secret, dark world.

Tips for Breaking Down the Walls

Here are eleven life management strategies for breaking down the walls to foster peace with others:

1. **Start with pure motives.** We want the walls to crumble because we love the other person. Any other motive will not work: *"This is my commandment, That ye love one another, as I have loved you"* (John 15:12).

2. **Change your thoughts toward the other person.** That means we cannot dwell on the offense or speak poorly of the other person to others. Our negative thoughts build a stronger wall. If our thoughts do not change, our behavior will be hypocritical, shallow, empty, and ineffective. Then our attempts to reconcile are manipulative. God loves the other person, and we show obedience to Him through our actions of love to them. Love others with the love of God. We have the power of the Almighty God behind us when we do things His way:

   > *"For the weapons of our warfare are not carnal, but mighty through God to the pulling down of strong holds;*
   > *Casting down imaginations, and every high thing that exalteth itself against the knowledge of God, and bringing into captivity every thought to the obedience of Christ."*
   > (2 Corinthians 10:4–5)

   Pure motives and loving thoughts will result in outward actions.

3. **Express love by doing good things.** Good deeds are a clear sign that we are pursuing peace. Psalm 34:14 says, *"Depart from evil, and do good; seek peace, and pursue it."*

   When we are doing genuine deeds of kindness and peace on the offended person's behalf, he or she will find it harder to lash back, ridicule us, or maintain their animosity. In our ministry of reconciliation, we do the opposite of what the world does. Often, this is the opposite of what the other party may expect. We are to love them, bless them, do good for them, and pray for them. We put them in a position of receiving goodness. This is the way the children of God conduct themselves. We love:

   > *"Ye have heard that it hath been said, Thou shalt love thy neighbor, and hate thine enemy.*
   >
   > *But I say unto you, Love your enemies, bless them that curse you, do good to them that hate you, and pray for them which despitefully use you, and persecute you;*
   >
   > *That ye may be the children of your Father which is in heaven...."* (Matthew 5:43–45)

4. **Listen without interruption.** Too often, we interrupt to get *our* opinion across. Love doesn't do that. Instead, it is patient, kind, and yielding. When we listen without interruption, a great dynamic happens—mentally, emotionally, and spiritually—in us and the other person. It tells them they are important enough to be heard, and it lowers their anger as they talk it out. They become pacified. Some cracks appear in the dividing wall, and animosity lessens as we remain calm: *"If the spirit of the ruler rise up against thee, leave not thy place; for yielding pacifieth great offenses"* (Ecclesiastes 10:4).

   When we interrupt to point out the errors in the other person's thinking, we do this to our shame. We must humbly approach others with ears ready to listen and a heart ready to hear; a haughty attitude will only reinforce the wall: *"Before destruction the heart of a man is haughty, and before honor comes humility. He that answereth a matter before he heareth it, it is folly and shame unto him"* (Proverbs 18:12–13).

5. **Avoid discussing the conflict with others.** As soon as we start telling others, we strengthen the wall. Third parties have no right to know unless that third party is a qualified counselor or trusted godly advisor. Usually when we seek others out, it is for pity and self-justification. Our words can spread in all directions and can even reach the person with whom we have a conflict. We should speak only to the person who is directly involved. Sometimes it helps to tell them we've kept quiet on the matter. This shows our intention to respect and honor them and resolve the conflict: *"Debate thy cause with thy neighbour himself; and discover not a secret to another: Lest he that heareth it put thee to shame, and thine infamy turn not away"* (Proverbs 25:9–10).

6. **Speak godly words.** After we have listened, we will have our turn to speak. We must exercise self-control and remember the goal is to tear down the wall. We go to the other person with the right motives and from a heart of love. He or she may have said things to stir us up, but we have pure motives and continue to pursue peace. We keep ourselves from saying negative things. We speak godly words: *"Keep thy tongue from evil, and thy lips from speaking guile. Depart from evil, and do good; seek peace, and pursue it"* (Psalm 34:13–14).

When we speak with another person, we want to be ready with godly speech that wins our brother. We're not in a contest of who's right and who's wrong. The goal is not to win a contest but to win the heart. We don't just go to talk. We've preplanned what we'll say

153

with wisdom and words that speak healing. We speak fitting and timely words, words that go to the heart, to produce the best result. Proverbs 15:23 says, *"A man hath joy by the answer of his mouth: and a word spoken is due season, how good is it!"*

Godly words are:

> **Spoken softly:** *"A soft answer turneth away wrath: but grievous words stir up anger"* (Proverbs 15:1).

> **Spoken in love:** *"But speaking the truth in love, may grow up into him in all things, which is the head, even Christ..."* (Ephesians 4:15).

> **Spoken graciously:** *"Let your speech be always with grace, seasoned with salt, that ye may know how ye ought to answer every man"* (Colossians 4:6).

Godly words are:

> **Not spoken loftily (haughtily):** *"They are corrupt, and speak wickedly concerning oppression: they speak loftily"* (Psalm 73:8).

> **Not spoken with a stiff neck (stubbornly):** *"Lift not up your horn on high: speak not with a stiff neck"* (Psalm 75:5).

> **Not spoken hastily:** *"Go not forth hastily to strive, lest thou know not what to do in the end thereof, when thy neighbour hath put thee to shame"* (Proverbs 25:8).

> **Not spoken with evil motives:** *"Speak not evil one of another, brethren. He that speaketh evil of his brother, and judgeth his brother, speaketh evil of the law, and judgeth the law: but if thou judge the law, thou art not a doer of the law, but a judge"* (James 4:11).

7. **Consider giving a private gift.** Sometimes, in addition to the gift of our words, it will be appropriate to give a thoughtful gift before we start reconciliation and again as the wall is falling. Gifts should be tasteful and meaningful, but not expensive. This is one of those times when the adage "It's the thought that counts" applies. Just as the argument is kept between the two parties, so is the gift: *"A gift in secret pacifieth anger: and a reward in the bosom strong wrath"* (Proverbs 21:14).

8. **Seek God in private prayer.** Jesus said to speak to the mountain, and it would be removed. Likewise, we are to speak to the wall—to seek God in private prayer. When our motives are right, we can tell that wall to come down:

   > *"And Jesus answering saith unto them, Have faith in God.*
   >
   > *For verily I say unto you, That whosoever shall say unto this mountain, Be thou removed, and be thou cast into the sea; and shall not doubt in his heart, but shall believe that those things which he saith shall come to pass; he shall have whatsoever he saith."*   (Mark 11:22–23)

   Through our words and deeds, we speak life to the person and death to the dividing wall. We are proactive and determined to win the soul of our brother or sister. Our words are powerful tools in our ministry of reconciliation. They will produce the fruit that works toward peace. Proverbs 18:21 says, *"Death and life are in the power of the tongue; and they that love it shall eat the fruit thereof."*

9. **Remove animosity.** Jesus said, *"Blessed are the peacemakers: for they shall be called the children of God"* (Matthew 5:9). We know peace is of the utmost importance to God and should be to us as well. This

process of peace making is a ministry. It's a job that takes concentration, effort, and time. We want to see it through to completion.

Animosity is a strong feeling of dislike or hatred—ill will or resentment tending toward active hostility.

It produces ill feelings of hatred, loathing, malice, spite, and contempt. Even when these feelings are kept silent, they can build and deepen over time. We want to give others the opportunity to be at peace with us by dissolving any resentment and lingering hard feelings.

One of the first and best ways to remove animosity is to *forgive the other person*. It's not enough to just receive their forgiveness; we need to forgive them as well.

It is important that we not only forgive, but that we also *restrain from any form of retaliation*. While the wall is falling, we are to remain patient, kind, gentle, and loving. This helps to restore the bond of peace. We wait. We keep the right attitude. We allow peace to rule in our hearts. True peace is worth the time:

> *"Put on therefore, as the elect of God, holy*
> *and beloved, bowels of mercies, kindness,*
> *humbleness of mind, meekness, longsuffering;*
>
> *Forbearing one another, and forgiving one*
> *another, if any man have a quarrel against any:*
> *even as Christ forgave you, so also do ye.*
>
> *And above all these things put on charity,*
> *which is the bond of perfectness."*
>
> (Colossians 3:12–14)

There is a lot at stake here. Forgiveness is an extreme act that takes place between two human beings. Our forgiveness from the Father depends on our forgiveness of others. God will not give us what we withhold from another. His love forgives, so our task is

to treat others the way God treats us. He's watching to
see if we follow His lead:

> *"And when ye stand praying, forgive, if ye*
> *have ought against any: that your Father*
> *also which is in heaven may forgive you your*
> *trespasses. But if ye do not forgive, neither will*
> *your Father which is in heaven forgive you*
> *your trespasses."*   (Mark 11:25)

If we are to stop animosity, we must also *stop
imputing other people's wrongdoing.* If we are full of
hostility, we become fault-finders. If we are focused on
the negative, we will see every negative thing about the
other person, and we will always be in accusation mode.
This just increases animosity. We must stop adding
every wrong to their account. If we can't get over our
bitterness and resentment, we have not forgiven them.
We must balance the intellectual knowledge of their
wrong, while not holding it against them. Keeping
records is not our job; instead, we are to release the
wrongs. This is what Christ did for us. He no longer
keeps track of our transgressions but reconciles us to
God: *"And all things are of God, who hath reconciled
us to himself by Jesus Christ, and hath given to us the
ministry of reconciliation"* (2 Corinthians 5:18).

To remove animosity from our relationships, we
must also *stop carrying grudges.* When we share the
details of an argument, we can cause others to become
the bearer of a grudge on our behalf. (This is a good
reason to keep our offenses quiet.) Likewise, we may
also hold grudges on behalf of others. Each affected
person must forgive for the work to be completed.
In 2 Corinthians 2:10, we are instructed, *"To whom
ye forgive anything, I forgive also: for if I forgave
anything, to whom I forgave it, for your sakes forgave
I it in the person of Christ...."*

We can count on the law of *reciprocity*, which we trust that if we sow love, love will return to us. This law works in the positive and the negative. If we're critical, we will reap criticism. When we remove our animosity, we can sow good seed and look forward to a future harvest. This is exciting. We can transform a person's life through the law of reciprocity. Galatians 6:7 says, *"Be not deceived; God is not mocked: for whatsoever a man soweth, that shall he also reap."*

Don't give up after a few days of chipping away at the animosity. Do not become weary in doing good. It's not enough to stay spiritually minded for a month or two. We should continue sowing good things toward the other person if we desire full reconciliation. We continue to do the right thing toward them as we wait for the season when they will respond: *"And let us not be weary in well doing: for in due season we shall reap, if we faint not"* (Galatians 6:9).

There may be times when we need to call in a third party to assist. We need to make sure this person is a known peacemaker. Unwise counselors are troublemakers and do not reunite! We must be sure the one coming to our aid desires peace and reconciliation for everyone involved:

> *"Moreover if thy brother shall trespass against thee, go and tell him his fault between thee and him alone: if he shall hear thee, thou hast gained thy brother.*
> *But if he will not hear thee, then take with thee one or two more, that in the mouth of two or three witnesses every word may be established."* (Matthew 18:15–16)

10. Use the "Second-Mile Principle" with narcissists.
Sometimes, the person we wish to reconcile with is extremely self-loving, self-admiring, and egotistical.

This is sometimes referred to as a narcissistic personality. Narcissists can only relate to others in a manner that contributes to their own self-centeredness. They require an excessive amount of admiration and praise from others. They lack empathy and don't care for others unless doing so contributes to their own self-crafted image. Narcissists have an overinflated sense of entitlement. They simply *react* (instead of *interacting*) with everything in the world outside their own self-exaltation.

Although this is usually called a personality disorder, it is the fundamental condition of anyone who has not given himself or herself up to God (salvation). Narcissism complicates the process of tearing down the wall because the narcissist may not respond to our attempts at peacemaking. They may enjoy the good things we do for them and expect more without returning good to us. God has given us instructions concerning this situation. I call it the Second Mile Principle: *"And whosoever shall compel thee to go a mile, go with him twain"* (Matthew 5:41).

In New Testament times, a Roman soldier had the legal right to command a Jewish person to carry his gear for one mile. This was not an honorable task. Romans and Jews were enemies. It might have seemed that Jesus made it worse when He instructed them to go an extra mile by choice. But He wanted this service to Rome to be done with joy, not begrudgingly. What happens when two people walk together? We can imagine a conversation. Perhaps it took reaching mile number two to get into deeper things, to dispel prejudices, and create a temporary bond. Maybe going the second mile allowed the sharing of ideas and the breaking down of walls.

When dealing with a narcissist, we may need to go the second mile. The first one may not yield the desired result, so we go farther. However, we do not keep going.

We don't wish to reinforce his sense of entitlement. If we do that, we will continue to enable him and will not achieve the intention of the Lord's instruction. Jesus did not tell us to pursue a person forever—serving, walking, and attempting to stay joyful—to the point of abuse.

Going the second mile can take people by surprise, often softening their disposition. Jesus said when someone compels us to go one mile, we should go two. However, He never said five, ten, twenty, or more were necessary. We must follow this as precisely as He meant it. Scriptures address the problem of overdoing it. One wise man or woman may not be enough to win the soul of the narcissist. Do not try this to the point of self-abuse and destruction. Ecclesiastes 7:16 says, "*Be not righteous over much; neither make thyself over wise: why shouldest thou destroy thyself?*"

We can do what is required, but we cannot change the hearts of all men. We confess to God and ask for forgiveness from the offended person. However, some will not relent. In the case of narcissists, we must walk away. They do not value God's ways or the health and well-being of the relationship. Our mental health is of paramount importance to God. So, beloved, let us be diligent in following His words with precision and then be satisfied. Having done everything we can to obey Him, we stop pursuing the narcissist.

11. **Understand the role of suffering in making peace.** Many of us do not know how to suffer properly. If we do the right thing and suffer for it, we are honorable in His sight. But if we suffer with a good attitude after committing a wrongdoing, there is no glory in that. In that case, we deserved the trouble. When we have gone the extra mile, walked in God's ways, and set a course for reconciliation, we may suffer for doing right.

In learning to suffer, we do not sin in retaliation at the other person. We don't continually confront them, hold grudges, get others in on it, sulk, stew, or sit in self-pity. We are joyful because we were obedient and did what was required. Then we go forward:

> *"For this is thankworthy, if a man for conscience toward God endure grief, suffering wrongfully.*
>
> *For what glory is it, if, when ye be buffeted for your faults, ye shall take it patiently? but if, when ye do well, and suffer for it, ye take it patiently, this is acceptable with God.*
>
> *For even hereunto were ye called: because Christ also suffered for us, leaving us an example, that ye should follow his steps:*
>
> *Who did no sin, neither was guile found in his mouth:*
>
> *Who, when he was reviled, reviled not again; when he suffered, he threatened not; but committed himself to him that judgeth righteously:*
>
> *Who his own self bare our sins in his own body on the tree, that we, being dead to sins, should live unto righteousness: by whose stripes ye were healed."*   (1 Peter 2:19–24)

Our ministry of reconciliation can be a tough one. Not everyone wants to follow the same principles we do, but many will. Happy are the peacemakers. It is always worth the try—a good, honest, and Christ-like try. God will reward!

Chapter 16

Recognizing Your Divine Connection

The Children of God

How far have you traveled in your life? How many continents and countries have you visited? During each adventure, you needed identification. Traveling without your driver's license, your passport, or your visa could get you in trouble. You needed to provide proof of who you truly are.

It is a tragic thing to travel across the stage of time and not know who you are, what you possess, and if you accomplished your purpose. No one wants to stand facing an eternal question mark. God wants us to know who we are as His children.

Jesus said the peacemakers *shall be called the children of God.* That is an identity we surely want.

What It Means to Be a Child of God

The Bible shows us what it means to be a child of God. The following are three key explanations of what this means.

1. To be a child of God means that **God is our Father.** God Himself, the Creator of the universe, is our Father. That's why Jesus taught us in Matthew 6:9 to pray: *"After this manner therefore pray ye: Our Father which*

art in heaven, Hallowed be thy name." Our response to His name is to *hallow* it, or hold it in high esteem.

God personally created us. We are the product of our Father, the offspring of God. *He* made us; we did not make ourselves. We are His people. He put us here, and He makes no mistakes. He didn't put us here to lose or to wander aimlessly. He put us here to *win*, and the best way to achieve that is to realize that He created us and we are His: "*Know ye that the* LORD *he is God: It is he that hath made us, and not we ourselves; we are his people, and the sheep of his pasture*" (Psalm 100:3).

2. **God designed our personal characteristics.** God shaped us, contoured us, gifted us, and deposited His image within each one of us. He gave each of us exactly what He wanted us to have, down to the smallest detail. There's no need to compare ourselves with others. He made us just right!

   It's hard to discover our true selves if we're trying to be like others. At a very young age, we enter competitions. We compete with others and compare our grades, sports, appearance, strength, and just about anything else we can. As children of God, we dare not compare because we are each God's specific workmanship: "*For we are his workmanship, created in Christ Jesus unto good works, which God hath before ordained that we should walk in them*" (Ephesians 2:10).

3. As children of God, **we are loved.** God loves us so much that we are called His sons and daughters in Christ. This is amazing! Our big God loves us little people. When we fully accept this, we see that we are not so little. He has big plans and big purposes for each of us that last throughout eternity: "*Behold, what manner of love the Father hath bestowed upon us, that we should be called the sons of God: therefore*

the world knoweth us not, because it knew him not"
(1 John 3:1).

God Is the Father of Spirits

We could take any one of those truths—that He is our Father, that He designed our personal details, and that He loves us—and meditate on it for hours. This should bring us great emotional energy, mental well-being, wholeness, and a sense of celebration. But there's more—God is the Father of spirits. Hebrews 12:9 says, *"Furthermore we have had fathers of our flesh which corrected us, and we gave them reverence: shall we not much rather be in subjection unto the Father of spirits, and live?"*

He puts a spirit inside each baby's body. The spirit inside us is the real, true us. He created our bodies, but He didn't stop there. He put the real *us* inside. We are fashioned and formed and given a spirit. We are set apart from the rest of His creation, and we are dearly loved. We can take that blessed verse, John 3:16, and put our names right in the middle of it: *"For God so loved...[put your name here]...that He gave His only begotten Son, that whosoever believeth in him should not perish, but have everlasting life"* (John 3:16, insertion mine).

God Knows Us

As children of God, *we are under His watchful eye.* God sees us. He's not casual or random about it. He searches us. We are different than all other works of His creation. Unlike the animals, which are ruled by instinct, we are made in His creative likeness. When he created us, He made creators. People are in the same category as Him. He didn't just set us in motion and walk away. He looks at us. He searches, and He knows us. There is no detail about our lives—past or present—He doesn't know. He knows when we sit down and stand up (see Psalm 139:1–4). (In a poetic sense, sitting down and standing up could refer to Him knowing our weaknesses and our strengths.)

He understands our thoughts—not from far off, but up close. To be a child of God means we have a Father who keeps an eye on us continuously. He knows every word before we speak it. He knows us to the very depths of our hearts and the heights of our thoughts. He even keeps track of the number of hairs on our heads. We are of great importance to Him. We are loved: "*But the very hairs of your head are all numbered*" (Matthew 10:30).

> "*O LORD, thou hast searched me, and known me.*
>
> *Thou knowest my downsitting and mine uprising, thou understandest my thought afar off.*
>
> *Thou compassest my path and my lying down, and art acquainted with all my ways.*
>
> *For there is not a word in my tongue, but, lo, O LORD, thou knowest it altogether.*"   (Psalm 139:1–4)

We Are All Brothers and Sisters

Being children of God makes us *all brothers and sisters*. We all have one Father, one Master—Christ. In fact, the New Testament refers to as "brothers" 294 times. (This terminology includes our "sisters" as well.) We are all brethren. When we look at our spouses, our children, and others in the body of Christ. we are looking at our brothers and sisters. This should cause us to look at them differently. We have brothers and sisters in our homes every day. We are eating, sleeping, and conversing with them on a regular basis. We are all siblings of one Father: "*But be not ye called Rabbi: for one is your Master, even Christ; and all ye are brethren*" (Matthew 23:8).

If we are all God's children, that makes Jesus like an elder brother. Jesus is the Son of God. He came in the flesh, died, rose, and ascended to the Father. He is the firstborn among us. He is our Brother because we share the Father. Romans 8:29 says, "*For whom he did foreknow, he did also predestinate to be conformed to the image of his Son, that he might be the firstborn among many brethren.*"

We are a family and live out family values. This is about family—the family of God. The whole family in heaven and on the earth bears the name of Jesus Christ. God's plan revolves around parents and families. Likewise, we—in microcosm with our fathers, mothers, and children—represent a small snapshot of the bigger family of God. Just think: as Christians, we have family we haven't met yet: *"For this cause I bow my knees unto the Father of our Lord Jesus Christ, Of whom the whole family in heaven and earth is named"* (Ephesians 3:14–15).

Family values are not optional. Obedience is the duty of a good and proper child. Likewise, we are to follow our Heavenly Father. This is what we do. We are His dear children, and we follow Him. Ephesians 5:1 says, *"Be ye therefore followers of God, as dear children."*

We Have the Gift of the Holy Spirit

Because we are the children of God, His Spirit reveals itself to our spirit. We know we belong to Him. The real us inside *knows* we are His. How we value ourselves determines how we care for ourselves, so we must never forget who we are in Christ. Romans 8:16 says, *"The Spirit itself beareth witness with our spirit, that we are the children of God."*

As His children, we love like our Father. We do what He does and show love, even when people do not love us in return. Also, we do good to those who have not earned it. A child behaves like his or her father. It's the evidence that we belong to the same family. God is the head of our eternal family, so we do what He does.

God doesn't ask us to do something He won't do. He sends His blessings to everyone. We too, should bless everyone. He doesn't hold back the light from the evil because they're evil. Instead, He sends them rain, which is a sign of blessing. We live "love" like our Father:

> *"But I say unto you, Love your enemies, bless them*
> *that curse you, do good to them that hate you, and*
> *pray for them which despitefully use you,*
> *and persecute you;*
>
> *That ye may be the children of your Father which is*
> *in heaven: for he maketh his sun to rise on the evil*

*and on the good, and sendeth rain on the just and
on the unjust."* (Matthew 5:44–45)

We have put our faith in Jesus Christ to become children of God. Galatians 3:26 says, *"For ye are all children of God by faith in Jesus Christ...."* When we put our faith in Jesus, our sins are forgiven. We should be full of joy about this! He forgives and cleanses His children. We are condemnation-free. We belong to God. 1 John 2:12, says, *"I write to you, little children, because your sins are forgiven you for his name's sake."*

Through the forgiveness of our sins, we have been given an amazing amount of freedom and glorious liberty. When God delivers us from corruption, we are no longer enslaved and no longer in bondage. We belong to God, and Satan no longer has a hold on us: *"Because the creature itself also shall be delivered from the bondage of corruption into the glorious liberty of the children of God"* (Romans 8:21).

We Will Live Eternally

For children of God, death on earth is merely a transition from one life to the other. As children of God, we will never die. Much like the angels in heaven, our lives never end. He designed us from the beginning to live forever: *"Neither can they die any more: for they are equal unto the angels; and are the children of God..."* (Luke 20:36).

We don't have to worry about tomorrow. For ages to come, He is going to show the exceeding riches of His grace. Because we are His children, our future is bright:

> *"And hath raised us up together, and made us sit together in heavenly places in Christ Jesus:*
>
> *That in the ages to come he might shew the exceeding riches of his grace in his kindness toward us through Christ Jesus."* (Ephesians 2:6–7)

As His children, we are the heirs of everything He is and has and are joint heirs with Christ. This is a blessed, eternal belonging:

"The Spirit itself beareth witness with our spirit, that we are the children of God: And if children, then heirs; heirs of God, and joint-heirs with Christ..." (Romans 8:16–17).

Right now, on this earth, we are the sons and daughters of God. We don't have all the details yet, but we know when He appears that we will be like Him: *"Beloved, now are we the sons of God, and it doth not yet appear what we shall be: but we know that, when he shall appear, we shall be like him; for we shall see him as he is"* (1 John 3:2).

As children of God, we are His jewels. We belong to Him. Malachi 3:17 says, *"And they shall be mine, saith the LORD of hosts, in that day when I make up my jewels; and I will spare them, as a man spareth his own son that serveth him."*

He saves up His children's tears. Imagine that! He saves every tear we shed. The Message Bible says, *"You've kept track of my every toss and turn through the sleepless nights, Each tear entered into your ledger, each ache written in your book"* (Psalm 56:8).

He cares for us. He sees our every need and hears our every call. A real Father knows when His child isn't sleeping, when the child is tossing and turning, hurting, or weeping. God also calls us the apple of His eye (see Zechariah 2:8). That means we are in the very center of His vision. The pupil is the most sensitive part of the whole body. The prophet said whoever touches God's children sticks their finger in His eye. He is sensitive about us.

There is no greater position in the universe than to belong to Him. When the world comes in, disruptions try to control us, and conflicts arise, we must remember whom we belong to as we cling to our Father. When we do things His way, we dwell in peace and make peace. Blessed are the peacemakers, for they shall be called the children of God.

Chapter 17

The Joy of Being Persecuted for Being Right

Blessed Are They Who Are Persecuted and Reviled

Most of us would not consider it a great day if people treated us hatefully. Most of us do not wake in the morning hoping to be attacked verbally by others. Be honest. Do you feel blessed when you're persecuted? How about when people hate you? Do you feel blessed when people gossip about you? Who can react positively to such things?

Jesus stated that people who experience these types of persecutions are blessed! Also, He says a reward awaits them in heaven. What a very different life management system. What a different perspective needed in His times and in our times: *"Blessed are ye, when men shall revile you, and persecute you, and shall say all manner of evil against you falsely, for my sake"* (Matthew 5:10–11).

We Will Be Persecuted
for Believing His Truth

Truth is designed to modify our emotional responses to life's situations. We ponder a certain thought pattern until it produces a corresponding emotion. These thoughts come from our value systems, and our value systems come from our beliefs.

What is the Truth? God is our Father. We are His children. We were created to be somebody. When we grasp that Jesus died for us, we should feel even more of our personal value. When we ponder and believe who we truly are, we can better combat the outer forms of persecution. What would happen to our emotional responses if we accepted the truth that all things work together for our good? What if we believed that each thing in our lives would work out for our best? Romans 8:28 says, *"And we know that all things work together for good to them that love God, to them who are the called according to his purpose."*

God designed Truth to work in our lives and change our emotional response from negative to positive and from hopelessness to sufficiency. God reveals additional truths concerning us.

He will never leave us! He will never forsake us or turn us away (see Matthew 28:20, Hebrews 13:5). He will be with us until the very end of the earth. These truths should cause great rejoicing. They should produce change in how we think and in how we feel. They should cause us to respond to outside negativity in a new way and with confidence in Him. We need more of His truths to go deep inside us. The truth is, we can no longer be condemned. If we believe in Him, then our sins are gone. Completely *gone*. We can face the world, and those in it, on a higher level when we know who we are and can hang on to the Truth of God's Word. Romans 8:1 says, *"There is therefore now no condemnation to them which are in Christ Jesus...."* *"I have swept away your offenses like a cloud, your sins like the morning mist..."* (Isaiah 44:22 NIV).

Truth is the antidote for sinfulness. It is the passport to mental health, emotional strength, and social stability. Jesus says we're going to be persecuted for doing the right thing. We'll be persecuted for believing the Truth. Jesus wants us to know we'll *also* be blessed for it. Our society does not want to hear or speak the Truth. Satan doesn't want others to hear the Truth, either. Our world is far from God and doesn't know Him: "*And they bend their tongues like their bow for lies: but they are not valiant for the truth upon the earth; for they proceed from evil to evil, and they know not me, saith the LORD*" (Jeremiah 9:3).

Even in our closest relationships, a time is coming when Truth will be hard to find. It will be hard to trust the words and actions of the people around us because they would rather substitute truth with lies and slander. Jeremiah 9:4–5 says, "*Take ye heed every one of his neighbor, and trust ye not in any brother: for every brother will utterly supplant, and every neighbor will walk with slanders. And they will deceive everyone his neighbor, and will not speak the truth: they have taught their tongue to speak lies, and weary themselves to commit iniquity.*"

The Truth Will Set Us Free

The children of God believe the Truth. We know it. The truth is incarnated into our lives, and that's what sets our freedom into motion. When we have Truth in our hearts, we have freedom in our minds. We must choose the Truth and maintain it: "*Then said Jesus to those Jews which believed on him, If ye continue in my word, then are ye my disciples indeed: And ye shall know the truth, and the truth shall make you free*" (John 8:31–32).

David said that God desires truth in our "inward parts"—that is, in our hearts. If we have the Truth in our hearts, it doesn't matter what others say: "*Behold, thou desirest truth in the inward parts: and in the hidden part thou shalt make me to know wisdom*" (Psalm 51:6).

Truth is powerful and lasts forever. However, sometimes, we speak incorrect ideas, philosophies, and concepts that we've learned from others: "*The lip of truth shall be established for ever: but a lying tongue is but for a moment*" (Proverbs 12:19).

John said Jesus had no greater joy than to know His children walked in Truth. We have no idea how He expressed that joy, but we know it was real. He rejoiced when He knew His disciples grasped and maintained the Truth as their daily walk and belief. Our walks with the Lord will bring great rejoicing to others. Likewise, others walking in Truth will bring joy to us: "*I have no greater joy than to hear that my children walk in truth*" (3 John 1:4).

The Truth also has the power to protect us, change us, and alter our emotional responses when we're persecuted or falsely accused. It keeps us steady when everything around us crumbles. The Truth stands, and we stand in it.

It *is* a blessing to be persecuted and criticized. It's also a blessing when others speak against us for Jesus's sake. We rejoice and are exceedingly glad because we know our reward is in heaven. We should understand Jesus's message so well that persecution means nothing. In fact, it becomes a joy. This is not a religious version of masochism. We are not to suffer as murderers, adulterers, or fornicators do. If we suffer for doing the right thing, then our suffering is acceptable to the Lord.

Three Categories of Persecution

There are three categories of persecution listed in Jesus's life management system:

1. **Being reviled—that is, being made fun of or mocked.** This could happen on the job, at school, in our neighborhoods, and even in our families. When we're the ones doing the right things right, others will notice. Those who disagree most likely will mock us.

2. **Experiencing persistent disagreement.** Those who disagree with the Truth will be persistent—they won't let up. They may taunt us, gossip about us, and get others to join in the abuse. In various parts of the world, this can even end in death. When we refuse to follow the lies of false religions and peoples, they will hate us.

3. **Being falsely accused.** Persecution can come in the form of false accusation. People will make things up, misinterpret us, or use our good words and deeds against us. When we are mocked, lied about, nagged, and persecuted, how do we maintain our composure?

Do we remain calm, even to the point of rejoicing? We remember God's Truth in our hearts and meditate on it in our minds.

Five Aspects of God's Truth to Remember During Persecution

The following are four aspects of God's Truth that we should remember when we are being persecuted because we follow Him. These facts should encourage us.

1. **We will inherit the kingdom of heaven.** This is the greatest outcome of all. Yes, we may see and hear many horrible things. We may suffer and even die at the hands of our enemies. However, *we will* inherit heaven. We will be with our Lord. This Truth, this promise, makes a firm foundation for our faith and is a real and vital reason to rejoice: *"Blessed are they which are persecuted for righteousness' sake: for theirs is the kingdom of heaven"* (Matthew 5:10).

2. **We will be rewarded in heaven.** It's certainly a wonderful thing to inherit a place in God's heaven, but it doesn't stop there. We are rewarded when we arrive: *"Rejoice, and be exceeding glad: for great is your reward in heaven: for so persecuted they the prophets which were before you"* (Matthew 5:12).

3. **We're in the same category as the prophets.** The prophets represented "God on earth," and they were persecuted for telling the truth. This is the same position we stand in as we stand up for God's Truth. We're in good company to be among the prophets. We receive the same persecution and the same reward: *"For so persecuted they the prophets which were before you"* (Matthew 5:12).

4. **We bring the sting to the world, but also flavor and preservation.** Jesus described believers as "the salt of the earth." Salt brings flavor to food and preserves it.

Salt can also sting. Just ask anyone who has ever gotten salt into a wound! We are here to make a difference and to heighten God's effect on the world. We are to show the way to eternal life and to preserve life. Our godly lives will always stand against ungodliness. Be warned: if we stop taking a stand for what is right, or lose our saltiness, we are useless: "*Ye are the salt of the earth: but if the salt have lost his savour, wherewith shall it be salted? it is thenceforth good for nothing, but to be cast out, and to be trodden under foot of men*" (Matthew 5:13).

5. **We are the light of the world.** Jesus describes His followers as the light of the world and a city set on a hill that cannot be hidden. We don't light a candle and put it under a basket. We put it where everyone can see it. It illuminates our path and keeps us from stumbling about. A single candle can light an entire house: "*Ye are the light of the world. A city that is set on a hill cannot be hid. Neither do men light a candle, and put it under a bushel, but on a candlestick; and it giveth light unto all that are in the house*" (Matthew 5:14–15).

So, why are we persecuted as we spread light? Sinful men love the darkness because it conceals their wrongs. Light, on the other hand, exposes the sins they want to keep hidden in darkness. Everyone who does evil hates the light of Truth. That means they will hate us: "*For everyone that doeth evil hateth the light, neither cometh to the light, lest his deeds should be reproved*" (John 3:20).

Jesus says we can count on persecution, but He also tells us we will be rewarded. His promises are true. They make it all worth it. The real blessing comes in knowing that this world, with its trouble, including its persecutions, is not the end. We will be welcomed in heaven.

Chapter 18

What It Means to Be Salt

You Are the Salt of the Earth

S alt is a fascinating substance and an interesting metaphor for the believer. Most salt is mined below the earth, but in Bolivia, you can find salt stacks above ground. The Dead Sea holds a great amount of salt. Its salinity is about 34 percent, in contrast to the ocean, which is approximately 3 percent.

The Many Virtues of Salt

Salt is valuable; for one thing, it's an exfoliant. That's why so many bathe in the Dead Sea—the salt softens the skin by sloughing away dead skin cells. Salt prevents things from decaying and cures food for storage. It can take away the itch of an insect bite. When it's gargled, salt can soothe a sore throat. It can extinguish a grease fire. Salt can remove stains, water marks, and even eliminate odors. It de-ices roads to make them safer for driving. Salt is said to have more than 14,000 uses. So, when Jesus compares us to the salt of the earth, He is comparing us to an item of great value. We are an essential element to have on this planet.

Up until now, Jesus had been speaking to the crowd about spiritual virtues and their resulting rewards, in a general sense. He had spoken about the poor in spirit, those who mourn, the meek, those who hunger and thirst after righteousness, the merciful, the pure in heart, the peacemakers, and those who are persecuted. He then became more direct:

> *"Blessed are ye, when men shall revile you, and*
> *persecute you, and say all manner of evil against*
> *you falsely, for my name sake.*
> *Rejoice, and be exceeding glad: for great is your*
> *reward in heaven...."* (Matthew 5:11–12)

He continues to address them more personally as He describes believers as the salt of the earth. Unlike many of the other godly characteristics Jesus had mentioned to this point, "saltiness" was not something they were to pursue. Instead, He explains who the believer, in Him, already *is* (salt) and what would happen if the believer discontinued their pursuit:

> *"Ye are the salt of the earth: but if the salt have*
> *lost his savor, wherewith shall it be salted? it is*
> *thenceforth good for nothing, but to be cast out,*
> *and to be trodden under foot of men."*
> (Matthew 5:13)

One of the most common uses for salt is that of a preserver. For salt to effectively preserve, however, there must be *enough* of it. You cannot preserve meat with only two grains of salt.

For example, when God was about to destroy Sodom and Gomorrah, Abraham stepped in to plead for the righteous who may be found there. He negotiated with God on their behalf. He pleaded their case, even down to just ten righteous people. Would God destroy the ten along with the wicked? No. The real tragedy, however, was not the destruction of the cities, but that Lot, Abraham's nephew, was not influential there. He was not salty. He could not sway people to God's cause, not even ten people.

I believe there is plenty of salt in our country to preserve it—many more than ten souls! Imagine, however, if our country was without the preservation of Christians. Imagine if the world was without the influence of Christ. Righteousness preserves nations. It raises them above the nations that fall:

"Righteousness exalteth a nation: but sin is a reproach to any people." (Proverbs 14:34)

A society without Christ is absolute chaos. Without the Holy Spirit working in and through believers, our societies will find death. We will find large-scale killing due to religion, ethnicity, or any other reason that can enter the heart of evil people. One day, the Church will be taken out of the earth, and the Holy Spirit will leave. The anti-Christ will be revealed, and there will be cataclysmic destruction of the entire planet, saved only by the return of Jesus Christ.

In the meantime, let's remember His words. We are the salt of the earth. We hinder national decay. As Christians lose their influence on Congress, the Supreme Court, and the president, we tumble toward chaos and destruction. First it happens spiritually and socially, and then militarily. We need to remain salty and keep our godly influence. Each one of us is valuable to the preservation of our families, our workplaces, our communities, our local governments, and the nation.

In addition to preserving, salt penetrates. Think of the impact Christian Americans have on countries throughout the world. The Gospel message is preached as believers provide humanitarian aid in the name of Jesus and stand up for Christ-like principles toward others.

Salt also cleanses. If we put salt in a wound, it stings, but it also cleanses and kills bacteria. In the times of the prophet Elisha, they had a water problem. In 2 Kings, we read how the prophet healed and purified the water by using salt. We, too, should have a cleansing effect on those around us. Every day, we rub shoulders with all kinds of people. Does our presence make any difference in their lives over the next guy? Everybody is contagious to some degree, so what are we spreading?

We cannot compromise biblical principles on any subject. We keep ourselves cleansed by continually going before God in prayer. We are the difference in this world:

> *"If my people, which are called by my name, shall*
> *humble themselves, and pray, and seek my face,*
> *and turn from their wicked ways; then will I hear*
> *from heaven, and will forgive their sin, and will*
> *heal their land."* (2 Chronicles 7:14)

Salt also enhances flavor. We want food to taste its best, and salt can enhance flavor and perk up an otherwise tasteless dish. We, as believers, should do the same to the world around us. We should make it more pleasant, joyful, and improved. Others should be drawn to us because our lives make their lives better.

We should be the gentlest and most kind, loving, giving, and humble people others know. If we are not, we may have lost our saltiness. For salt to lose its saltiness, it must lose its physical composition. The most common way this happens is when it is diluted. Likewise, believers lose their "saltiness" when they allow God's truth to be diluted in their lives:

> *"Can that which is unsavory be eaten without salt?*
> *or is there any taste in the white of an egg?"*
>
> (Job 6:6)

Jesus came to give us an abundant, genuine life. He wants us to live connected to Him—the Living God. He came to bless us and not to curse us. We should do the same for those around us. We should bring the flavor to life.

One of the ways we can bring flavor to others is in how we speak to them. It's so important for us to know how to answer them. We don't speak in anger, and we don't want to come across as self-righteous or condescending. The words from our lips should be gracious. We should be known as the ones who answer with kindness. There is no room in our conversation for rolling our eyes, sarcastic remarks, or harsh tones. We should never be judgmental or annoyed. We should speak with flavor—seasoned with salt—so that our words have the potential to be well received:

> *"Let your speech be always with grace, seasoned*
> *with salt, that ye may know how ye ought to answer*
> *every man. "* (Colossians 4:6)

Salt can eliminate problems. Salt is toxic to slugs, for example. If you have a yard full of slugs, salt will rid you of the problem. In our spiritual lives, we need to remove the things that rob us of the life God intended for His children. Drug addition, alcohol abuse, and other immoral behavior should be poisoned. To God, we are like the sweet savor of Christ.

Likewise, we are a sweet savor to fellow Christians. However, to those who perish, we are the savor of death. We enhance the flavor of the good. Conversely, we aren't just resistant to evil but cause it great damage:

> *"For we are unto God a sweet savor of Christ, in*
> *them that are saved, and in them that perish:*
>
> *To the one we are the savor of death unto death;*
> *and to the other the savor of life unto life...."*
> (2 Corinthians 2:15–16)

Salt creates thirst. Think back to when Jesus was at the well in Samaria. When He spoke salty words to the woman at the well, she recognized her need for a drink of the living water only He could provide. The woman then asked Him for water, so she would never thirst again. He created the *real* thirst in her, inside her soul. Our lives should provide the salt that causes others to thirst.

However, these wonderful aspects of salt can disappear. If we lose our Christian virtues, we lose our usefulness. If we, the salt of the world, lose our savor, the earth *won't* be salted. In New Testament times, they tossed garbage out into the streets where it was trampled. If we lose our usefulness as salt, what good are we? We've lost our influence. In fact, we could be trampled by this world since we no longer stand for the Christian principles we once followed.

We Cannot Let the World Dilute Our Impact

Salt can lose its usefulness due to contamination with other products or chemicals. We cannot allow the world to come in and contaminate our salt. It's extremely important that we never compromise because compromise leads to contamination. We should be who we want others to be:

> *"And there shall ye remember your ways, and all your doings, wherein ye have been defiled; and ye shall lothe yourselves in your own sight for all your evils that ye have committed."* (Ezekiel 20:43)

Another way that salt loses its effectiveness is when it stays in the salt shaker. If it doesn't come in contact with the food, it does no good. Sometimes we are like that. Sometimes the Church is like that. We are not called to isolate ourselves; rather, we must find a way to live in this culture without allowing it to affect us. We can have contact with the world but not love it.

What is Jesus telling us? He came to tell us that we are of great value. We are needed in God's love plan for the world. We bring flavor, cleansing, and preservation to the things that should be enhanced, healed, and kept safe. We are the salt of the earth. Let's keep our distinctive zest for the kingdom of God.

Chapter 19

What It Means to Be Light

You Are the Light of the World

When describing yourself to someone, you could mention your name, your address, your phone number, and your job title. You could reveal your family history and your doctrinal beliefs. You could mention your height, weight, talents, gifts, and areas of interest. You could state your testimony and your favorite experiences. But do you say of yourself, "I am the light of the world"?

Jesus describes believers as the salt of the earth, and now He also says we are the light of the world. While salt works in secret and can be added inconspicuously, light is open and visible. Our role is to be the light that shines through the darkness, illuminating the right path for those around us. This job is exclusive to Christians—no one else can do it: "*Ye are the light of the world. A city that is set on an hill cannot be hid*" (Matthew 5:14).

We are to be like a city on a hill. God is interested not only in our "salt" that preserves behind the scenes; He's also interested in how we are publicly perceived. He wants us in plain sight, not hidden, silent, or dim: "*Neither do men light a candle, and put it under a bushel, but on a candlestick; and it giveth light unto all that are in the house*" (Matthew 5:15).

Many people hide their light due to fear or a feeling of inadequacy. Others are apathetic to others' needs and isolate themselves. God wants the glow of His children to influence others. He wants our lives to produce beams of life that lead to Him: "*Let your light so shine before men, that they may see your good works, and glorify your Father which is in heaven*" (Matthew 5:16).

How We Become the Light in a Dark World

For each of us to become a person that is a light to the world, we must first understand *how* we become a light. Here are six ways we can become a light that shines and illuminates the way for others to trust Him:

1. **First, we must come to *the Light*.** Jesus is the Light of the world, and we have no light to share with others until we partake of His. We must receive Him, and His light then shines through us. John 8:12 says, "*Then spake Jesus again unto them, saying, I am the light of the world: he that followeth me shall not walk in darkness, but shall have the light of life.*"

   Many do not choose to receive the Light because they hate what the light exposes. They choose to cling to their evil deeds performed in darkness. The reasons are not intellectual or scientific—they are moral. We cannot come to Jesus, the Light, and insist on keeping immoral ways. They are incompatible with light: "*And this is the condemnation, that light is come into the world, and men loved darkness rather than light, because their deeds were evil*" (John 3:19).

   Sadly, many of the bestselling or critically acclaimed movies in "Hellywood" are the ones with the most darkness. It seems that the more immoral, violent, and perverted a movie is, the better it's received. The "news" is much the same. Bad news sells and draws in more viewers than uplifting stories.

   To be light, we first come to the Light. We seek Truth and expose our deeds. We want to obey, to grow, and to mature. We align our actions with God's desires as we grow spiritually and seek His approval. Then we take that light into the dark world: "*But he that doeth truth cometh to the light, that his deeds may be made manifest, that they are wrought in God*" (John 3:21).

2. **We must leave every form of darkness behind.** We cannot mix light with darkness. They cannot coexist. While darkness cannot put out light, the smallest amount of light can extinguish the dark. With the light of God's Word, we will know how to handle life's tests, trials, disappointments, and hurts. We will also know how to deal with life's consequences.

    We are not to attempt to mix light and darkness. Instead, we are to have no part of our lives left in darkness:

    > "*Take heed therefore that the light which is in thee be not darkness.*
    > *If thy whole body therefore be full of light, having no part dark, the whole shall be full of light, as when the bright shining of a candle doth give thee light.*"   (Luke 11:35–36)

    If we allow darkness in any area in our lives, we can guarantee failure in that area. We can create disaster if we are in the dark about how to conduct our marriages, discipline our children, earn and manage money, or grow in the workplace. John 12:46 says, "*I am come a light into the world, that whosoever believeth on me should not abide in darkness.*"

    Jesus has called us a chosen generation, a royal priesthood, a holy nation, and a peculiar people. We are called to be unique, different. Our responses should also reflect that difference. His marvelous light shines through in the way we conduct business, raise our families, interact with our brothers and sisters, and view the world. 1 Peter 2:9 says it this way: "*But ye are a chosen generation, a royal priesthood, an holy nation, a peculiar people; that ye should shew forth the praises of him who hath called you out of darkness into his marvelous light."*

Our futures are not determined by what others do or say to us, but by our responses. It's almost as if God cares more about how well we respond to situations than what those situations entail. We have the advantage of marvelous light. We were not meant to stumble about, as if in darkness. He wants us to keep the light before us so we can respond to others with His light and maintain our peace. When we respond in the light, we cannot be damaged.

3. **We must follow Jesus.** We don't follow a church, a denomination, or a religion. We follow Jesus. Darkness will try to influence our decisions, our emotions, or our reactions. If we're truly following Him, however, we will not walk in darkness. We belong to Him and walk in His light, and we have life at its best: *"Then spake Jesus again unto them, saying, I am the light of the world: he that followeth me shall not walk in darkness, but shall have the light of life"* (John 8:12).

4. **We must walk consistently in the light.** As Christians, we always walk in the light. This is not an occasional blast or beam from a laser or flashlight. It's perpetual. For the past twenty years in America, the Church has been lazy and undisciplined. In its efforts to "win the world," it has become more like the world. This strategy isn't working. If there is no difference between the ways of the world and the Christian's ways, then we are not fulfilling our role as the light. There is no room in the life of a light-bearer to bicker, gossip, complain, lie, cheat, steal, or practice immorality.

We walk in light by walking in the Word. In the psalms, David describes the Word of God as a lamp to his feet and light to his path. With everything properly illuminated, or understood through biblical principles, we walk with precision and wisdom.

5. **We must walk in love.** Jesus's listeners had heard many commandments, but He wanted them to hear a new one. The old commandment instructed followers to love God with all their hearts, souls, minds, and strength, and to love their neighbors as themselves. The new commandment was to love one another as *He* loved them! We would no longer love others as we love ourselves. Instead, we were called to an even higher standard: to love others *His* way with *His* love: "*A new commandment I give unto you, That ye love one another; as I have loved you, that ye also love one another*" (John 13:34).

This new commandment means I should treat my wife the way God treats me. I should treat my children the way God treats me. I should treat people in my business the way God treats me. This is a new focus. The true Light gave further instructions. He did not give us the right to hate anyone. We may hate their words or actions or the consequences of an interaction with them, but we are not allowed to hate *them*. Jesus said it took nothing extra to love those who love us.

Even those of the world can do that. However, if we love those who do unloving things to us, then we are loving them as God loves us:

> "*Again, a new commandment I write unto you, which thing is true in him and in you: because the darkness is past, and the true light now shineth.*
>
> *He that saith he is in the light, and hateth his brother, is in darkness even until now.*
>
> *He that loveth his brother abideth in the light, and there is none occasion of stumbling in him.*" (1 John 2:8–10)

Much like the conversation between Jesus and a certain lawyer in Luke 10, we may ask, "Who is my brother?" Is it a sibling—someone of our flesh and blood? Is it a brother or sister in the Lord? Much like the term "neighbor" in Luke 10, the use of "brother" also indicates that Jesus means for us to love *everyone*.

If you have ever wandered around in darkness, you know how frightening it is to walk "blind." Many people live with their hatred, anxiety, bitterness, resentment, and unforgiveness year after year. The darkness and sense of hopelessness get deeper and deeper. To stumble, fall, and hurt themselves seems inevitable.

6. **We must believe in the Light.** Do we believe? This is not about being religious. It's not about church attendance or going through some ritual. This is about *really believing* in Jesus. We cannot depend on our own skills or understanding. He and He alone gives us life and light. 1 John 1:1–5 says, "*In the beginning was the Word, and the Word was with God, and the Word was God. The same was in the beginning with God. All things were made by him; and without him was not anything made that was made. In him was life; and the life was the light of men.*"

Practical Ways to Let Our Light Shine

The ultimate life management system gives us practical ways to be bright, shining examples of His goodness in the world. Here are three.

1. **Do good works.** Jesus wants us to let our light shine through good works that glorify God. However, when we do good works, people tend to give us personal credit. We need to give their praise to Jesus. We can accept their thanks while also sharing our motivation to follow His instructions. Or we can let them know

we're doing what He would do. Once we are saved, good works will naturally follow.

We are created to do good works as His representatives on this earth. As His people, we bring glory to Him when we walk in the light and do good works: "*For we are his workmanship, created in Christ Jesus unto good works, which God hath before ordained that we should walk in them*" (Ephesians 2:10).

2. **Talk to others about the glories of Jesus.** We let our light shine by the words we speak. We don't need to "preach." Instead, we just talk about Jesus. God, who commanded the light to shine out of the darkness, has shined light into our hearts to give off light. We take in His light, and we reflect it back out into the world. It is easy to talk about our passions, so Jesus's glory should be the center of our conversation.

3. **Seize the opportunity to share Him every day.** It is time, right now, to let our light shine. The day is coming when we can spread no more light. In Revelation 18, we read about the fall of Babylon the Great. This foreshadows the destruction of all the nations of the world. When that day of reckoning happens, the light will no longer shine in this world. The voice of the bridegroom, Jesus, and of His bride, the Church, will no longer be heard. We must make the most of every opportunity because eternity is at stake. We seize each day and use it to shine the light of the Gospel.

Some of the questions we face today are "Have we come out of darkness? Are we walking in the light as He is in the light? Are all our actions and deeds brought to the light so we can know if they are of God?" Ask yourself if you are applying the light of Jesus into every area of your life—from your personal life to your marriage, family, and beyond.

God has called us out of the darkness into His marvelous light. Let's put our candles on candlesticks and set His light in us as a city on a hill, shining for Him!

Chapter 20

How to Season and Shine

The Christian's Mandate

A strange notion has crept into American theology. It's called *practical theology*—if it works in practice, we make it part of our theology; if it does not work in practice, we strike it from our theology. So we will do good to our enemies only if it changes them. If it doesn't change them, we can quit doing it. That is what practical theology would say.

Jesus teaches differently. If we are kind to our enemies and they don't change, that is irrelevant. We aren't to be kind because we *may* receive a blessing. Instead, we are to rejoice even if everything that we have done is rejected and we are still hated.

You are the light, and you are the salt. What you do can never be contingent on the reaction or response of another. Beloved, I want this to be an encouragement to you. I want this to set you free from the bondage of needing the praise of others. You don't *need* their kudos. You don't *need* their strokes. You don't *need* anything from anyone but God.

Who is in charge if your behavior can be controlled by another's response or lack thereof? They are. God doesn't want to share His Lordship of your life with anyone else. That is what makes you indomitable. Nobody can conquer you because it doesn't matter what anyone says or does. It only matters that the Lord approves.

Jesus Clarifies the Law of Moses

So far in His inaugural address, Jesus has spoken of Christian virtues and their rewards. He has informed His followers that they are the salt of the earth and the light of the world. At this point, He brings up the law of Moses. His audience was well aware of the rules and regulations of the day.

The law of Moses, with the addition of rabbinical interpretation and add-on commands, was the standard. Jesus started with what they knew and clarified the terms. Then He gave divine instructions about the Christian walk that seasons like salt and shines like light.

The believer's light originates in God's glory and then rises upon us:

> *"Arise, shine; for thy light is come, and the glory of the* LORD *is risen upon thee.*
>
> *For behold, the darkness shall cover the earth, and gross darkness the people: but the* LORD *shall arise upon thee, and his glory shall be seen upon thee."*
>
> (Isaiah 60:1–2)

Daniel tells us that the wise shine as brightly as the firmament and that those who bring others to God shine as stars: *"And they that be wise shall shine as the brightness of the firmament; and they that turn many to righteousness as the stars for ever and ever"* (Daniel 12:3).

God, who commands light, shines in our hearts so we may emit the light of knowledge of His glory: *"For God, who commanded the light to shine out of darkness, hath shined in our hearts, to give the light of the knowledge of the glory of God in the face of Jesus Christ"* (2 Corinthians 4:6).

Paul, writing to the Philippians, says, *"That he may be blameless and harmless, the sons of God, without rebuke, in the midst of a crooked and perverse nation, among whom ye shine as lights in the world; Holding forth the word of life...*" (Philippians 2:15–16).

We know that our light comes from God and directs back to Him. However, non-Christians may also seem to shine a light of goodness from a higher power other than God. What makes believers in the one true God of Israel different from the rest? What do they look like, and how do they function? Jesus went to the Law of Moses to illustrate who is of God and who is not.

It's important to note that Jesus did not come to destroy the law (the rules and regulations of the day). He came to add divine emphasis to the law and to accurately explain and instruct His people about their requirements under the law. Matthew 5:17 says, "*Think not that I have come to destroy the law, or the prophets: I am not come to destroy, but to fulfill.*" His explanation of the law set rabbinical interpretations aside. This divided followers into two categories: those who truly follow the heart of the law and those who merely follow its words only, without an obedient heart.

The law was, and still is, active and necessary. (It was and is still wrong to steal, to kill, and to commit adultery. It was and is still right to give to the poor, to be impartial in judgment, and be kind to strangers.) Jesus came to fulfill the law. In other words, He came to model and explain how to correctly live it out—to deliver our ultimate life management system.

While the Jews focused on the outward demonstration of the law, Jesus placed a greater emphasis on its inner workings: "*For verily I say unto you, Til heaven and earth pass, one jot or one tittle shall in no wise pass from the law, until all be fulfilled*" (Matthew 5:18).

What is a *jot* or *tittle*? It is the smallest stroke of a pen in the Hebrew language. This could be the letter *yud* or perhaps the tiny flourishes added to some of its letters. Jesus said not one tiny bit of the law was insignificant, not even a jot or a tittle.

Jesus came to set things straight concerning adherence to the law. He was clear that it was not to be ignored or disobeyed. This should help us realize the importance of obeying and teaching the corrected law. In fact, those who accurately follow and teach the law through the lens of Christ Jesus will receive esteem in heaven:

> *"Whosoever therefore shall break one of these least commandments, and teach men so, he shall be called the least in the kingdom of heaven: but whosoever shall do and teach them, the same shall be called great in the kingdom of heaven."*
>
> (Matthew 5:19)

The scribes and Pharisees, known as the most religious among the Jews, followed the exact letter of the law while harboring opposition to it in their hearts. They tended to be cruel and judgmental to those they taught. The Pharisees added manmade stipulations and commentary and taught others that they must abide by their additions. Some of their laws may have preserved a society, but they would not get them into the kingdom of heaven: *"For I say unto you, That except your righteousness shall exceed the righteousness of the scribes and Pharisees, ye shall in no case enter into the kingdom of heaven"* (Matthew 5:20).

"Do Not Murder" Becomes "Do Not Be Angry"

So, how did Jesus interpret and apply the law to believers? Jesus intensifies the commands by expanding the focus from just outward rules to include inward heart attitudes.

The law that God gave to Moses said we should not kill. Matthew 5:21 says, *"Ye have heard that it was said by them of old time, Thou shalt not kill; and whosoever shall kill shall be in danger of the judgment."* Jesus agreed with the law that we should not kill. However, He takes it a step further. The command "do not murder" becomes "do not be angry."

Jesus exposes the heart behind the action. Although every person with an angry heart doesn't murder, they still possess the same heart of vengeance and hatred that a murderer would have. The malice is equal, even if the action will not be taken:

> *"But I say unto you, That whosoever is angry with his brother without a cause shall be in danger*

*of the judgment: and whosoever shall say to his
brother, Raca, shall be in danger of the council: but
whosoever shall say, Thou fool, shall be in danger
of hell fire."*   (Matthew 5:22)

Anger can cause people to be temporarily insane. At that moment, they aren't thinking or believing straight. Unfortunately, some people stay angry for an extended time. As their anger lingers, they aren't thinking correctly. Jesus expects us not to kill others, but He also says we are not to even have the same heart condition as a killer.

Likewise, He tells us not to call people names. We refrain from "killing" with our words. In New Testament times, the Sanhedrin, or council, was the ruling body of Judaism. If a person said to his brother, *Raca,* or "empty head," he was in danger of facing the Sanhedrin. Jesus told us not to call our brother a fool, or we may be in danger of hell fire. He intensified the law.

In our walk of seasoning and light, we are not allowed to call someone an idiot or a jerk or to tell them they're crazy. We will not be a light to the world if we speak like others do. Calling people names robs their lives, a little at a time, which is the opposite of bringing light to them. Jesus was teaching us not to murder in the flesh and also not to commit murder in the spirit or with the tongue.

We Are to Clear Up Wrongs

Another difference in the kingdom of Jesus is that we are to stop what we're doing and clear up wrongs. This is *not* how other kingdoms work. The world just keeps going about its business. People don't stop to right wrongs and resolve differences, especially with other people.

Jesus tells us to *make wrongs right* with people around us before offering our gifts to God. He did not want us moving forward with unresolved conflict. If we push ahead, we will not have the ability to affect others. Our light will be damaged:

> *"Therefore if thou bring thy gift to the altar, and there rememberest that thy brother hath ought against thee;*
>
> *Leave there thy gift before the altar, and go thy way; first be reconciled to thy brother, and then come and offer thy gift."* (Matthew 5:23–24)

Jesus said he wanted us to learn to *resolve issues without litigation*. In the Old Testament, people were continuously going to the council to have their differences resolved. In His new kingdom, we should make agreements and clear any issues between us and the other person without resorting to the courts. We need to get clarity and seek resolution while the person is still in a relationship with us. When they walk away, our opportunity and connection is lost. It is better to have a lean loss than a fat lawsuit:

> *"Agree with thine adversary quickly, whiles thou art in the way with him; lest at any time the adversary deliver thee to the judge, and the judge deliver thee to the officer, and thou be cast into prison."* (Matthew 5:25)

"Do Not Commit Adultery" Becomes "Do Not Lust"

Jesus also clarified the subject of adultery. He knew His audience had a definition for it, yet He made a new one. He did not do away with the law concerning adultery; instead, He broadened its scope. "Do not commit adultery" becomes "do not lust."

In His kingdom, to look upon a woman with lust was to commit adultery in the heart. A man who doesn't sleep with his neighbor's wife, but would if he could, has the same heart as the man who commits the act. Jesus desires moral purity, not just in our actions, but also in our hearts, minds, and emotions:

> *"Ye have heard that it was said by them of old time, Thou shalt not commit adultery:*

*But I say unto you, that whosoever looketh on a
woman to lust after her hath committed adultery
with her already in his heart."* (Matthew 5:27–28)

Jesus says to fight sin with purpose, not casually. *We are to be
strict, not casual, with ourselves regarding sin.* If we cannot learn
how to control our eyes, for example, Jesus says it's better to pluck
out our eye and throw it away, so we lose just an eye and not our
soul. We are not to be casual in our avoidance of pornography. I
know one preacher who sat in front of his computer screen with
a piece of bread and cup of grape juice. He did his communion
right there. He was reminded of the shed blood and broken body
of Christ for his salvation. He stayed away from every page
unacceptable to our Lord.

Matthew 5:29–30 instructs us on how seriously we should
view our sin: *"And if thy right eye offend thee, pluck it out, and cast
it from thee: for it is profitable for thee that one of thy members
should perish, and not that thy whole body should be cast into hell.
And if thy right hand offend thee, cut it off, and cast it from thee:
for it is profitable for thee that one of thy members should perish,
and not that thy whole body should be cast into hell."*

"Divorce" Becomes
"No Divorce, Except for Fornication"

The law said divorce was acceptable. Jesus did not do away
with divorce but explained that it should be done only in the case
of fornication.

In Deuteronomy 24, it says that a man may divorce his wife
if he finds some uncleanness in her. This referred to her lack of
virginity. However, through the mishandling of Scripture, people
believed it to mean that a man can divorce his wife for anything he
did not like about her. Jesus said a man can divorce his wife only
in the case of adultery. Otherwise, if she were to remarry, she and
her new husband would be considered adulterers.

In the new kingdom, divorce is not as acceptable as it used to
be:

> *"It hath been said, Whosoever shall put away his wife, let him give her a writing of divorcement:*
>
> *But I say unto you, That whosoever shall put away his wife, saving for the cause of fornication, causeth her to commit adultery: and whosoever shall marry her that is divorced committeth adultery."* (Matthew 5:31–32)

The word "fornication" is actually the Greek word *porneia,* the word from which we get "pornography." Adultery is only one form of *porneia.* "Fornication" is a broader word that includes many and all forms of sexual perversion.

"Keeping Oaths" Becomes "Keeping Your Word"

Jesus talked a lot about our actions toward others, but He did not forget about our words. In the new kingdom, keeping oaths becomes keeping your word. In other words, we don't have to swear an oath to demonstrate our commitment or seriousness. Instead, we just keep our word.

Jesus takes this idea one step further and says believers are not to make sworn declarations because it is evil. It is a common practice in court for witnesses to "swear an oath" on the Bible to tell the truth. I don't ever do that when I go to court because of this verse. (You shouldn't, either.) The law allows people who follow the Scriptures to simply say, "I will tell the truth." No swearing is necessary:

> *"Again, ye have heard that it hath been said by them of old time, Thou shalt not forswear thyself, but shalt perform unto the Lord thine oaths:*
>
> *But I say unto you, Swear not at all; neither by heaven; for it is God's throne:*
>
> *Nor by the earth; for it is his footstool: neither by Jerusalem; for it is the city of the great King.*

Neither shalt thou swear by thy head, because thou
canst not make one hair white or black.

But let your communication be, Yea, yea; Nay, nay:
for whatsoever is more than these cometh of evil."

(Matthew 5:33–37)

"Retaliation" Becomes "Nonresistance"

The Old Testament law said if someone knocks out your tooth, you are justified to knock out his or her tooth. Likewise, if someone wounds you, you could wound him or her back. Jesus changed how His people were to handle retaliation.

In Jesus's kingdom, *retaliation becomes nonresistance*. Jesus said that for us to be salt and light, we need to do things differently. We need to stand out from secular culture, and that means we cannot seek retaliation or vengeance. In this new kingdom, God participates with us, and He'll take care of those who do us wrong:

"Ye have heard that it hath been said, An eye for an
eye, and a tooth for a tooth:

But I say unto you, That ye resist not evil: but
whosoever shall smite thee on thy right cheek, turn
to him the other also.

And if any man will sue thee at the law, and take
away thy coat, let him have thy cloak also.

And whosoever shall compel you to go a mile, go
with him twain.

Give to him that asketh thee, and from him that
would borrow of thee turn not thou away."

(Matthew 5:38–42)

"Hate Your Enemy" Becomes "Love Your Enemy"

Moreover, Jesus not only changed how we acted toward our enemies; He also wants us to think differently about them. "Hate your enemy" becomes "love your enemy." God loves His enemies. Christ died for us. He loved us even while we were His enemies. Even those of the world love those who love them and do good to those who do good to them. We, the salt and light of the world, are called to an even higher standard of love. This sets us apart.

When we are cursed, we bless. When we are hated, we do good for the hater. When we are used, we pray for the user. (Prayer brings us—our situation and our responses—to the throne room of God.) Communicating with Him and going in the same direction as His Word brings us into contact with God. Is there anything greater?

If we do not turn to prayer, we will turn to self-pity. Self-pity turns to bitterness. Bitterness will cause us to treat the other person the way they have treated us (or worse). It's a downward spiral. Instead, we are to be proactive with our good attitude and good deeds. This concept is revolutionary and unexpected. And it's of God.

Anyone can love their friends, but if that's all we do, we are no different from everyone else. Instead, we greet those who snub us. We speak kindly to those who'd rather not see us. It's OK if they turn the other way or remain silent. We're pleasing God. We're being light. We're being salt.

Matthew 5:43–48 says it this way: "*Ye have heard that it hath been said, Thou shalt love thy neighbour, and hate thine enemy. But I say unto you, Love your enemies, bless them that curse you, do good to them that hate you, and pray for them which despitefully use you, and persecute you; That ye may be the children of your Father which is in heaven: for he maketh his sun to rise on the evil and on the good, and sendeth rain on the just and on the unjust. For if ye love them which love you, what reward have ye? do not even the publicans the same? And if ye salute your brethren only, what do ye more than others? do not even the publicans so? Be ye therefore perfect, even as your Father which is in heaven is perfect."*

In Jesus's new kingdom, we must change our thinking. As we seek Jesus, we will get better and better at exercising His updated and corrected commands. They will become habit, and we will perfect them just as we perfect ourselves. These new and different godly approaches are proof of our relationship with Him. We listen to Jesus's voice and hear something new and defining.

Chapter 21

What to Do in Secret

The Hidden Life of Giving and Praying

We are often alerted when there is an emergency. We are warned about possible severe weather or an accident on the road or when traffic is backed up. Public information is important for safety.

But not everything is to be made public. Not everything is to be placed on display.

As Jesus progresses in His inaugural message, He goes deeper and deeper into the private lives of His followers. Jewish society was based on an outward show of works. Jesus, however, addressed the *hidden* areas of their hearts. If His teachings were received in their hearts, He knew their corresponding actions would be pure, true, and consistently fluid.

He targeted two specific areas that had become a public spectacle: giving and prayer. In His kingdom, these two acts would no longer be put on display. He wanted personal, godly attitudes and actions cultivated in private. These personal acts would not only be rewarded openly by God; they would prove to be the source that draws others into His kingdom.

Why We Need to Give in Secret

It was common practice during Jesus's day for followers to sound a trumpet to call attention to themselves. They wanted the approval of men for their good deeds, and that's exactly what they got. That was it. It was all over. There was nothing left to receive from God.

We don't need a trumpet to call attention to our giving. In fact, we shouldn't let anyone know. Do not do your charitable giving in front of other people so you can impress them. If you do, your Father will not reward you. When you do your giving in secret, then your Father, who sees in secret, will reward you openly:

> *"Take heed that ye do not your alms before men, to be seen of them: otherwise ye have no reward of your Father which is in heaven.*
>
> *Therefore when thou doest thine alms, do not sound a trumpet before thee, as the hypocrites do in the synagogues and in the streets, that they may have glory of men. Verily I say unto you, They have their reward.*
>
> *But when thou doest alms, let not thy left hand know what thy right hand doeth:*
>
> *That thine alms may be in secret: and thy Father which seeth in secret himself shall reward thee openly."*
> (Matthew 6:1–4)

The following are five reasons why it is wise to give in secret:

1. **To confirm our real loyalty is to God.** Jesus taught a phenomenal concept in Matthew 25:35–40, which, in the English Standard Version, says, "*'For I was hungry and you gave me food, I was thirsty and you gave me drink, I was a stranger and you welcomed me, I was naked and you clothed me, I was sick and you visited me, I was in prison and you came to me.' Then the righteous will answer him, saying, 'Lord, when did we see you hungry and feed you, or thirsty and give*

you drink? And when did we see you a stranger and welcome you, or naked and clothe you? And when did we see you sick or in prison and visit you?' And the King will answer them, 'Truly, I say to you, as you did it to one of the least of these my brothers, you did it to me.'"

This is one of the most vital kingdom principles: whenever we serve in the kingdom, we are really serving the King. We live in His name and do to others in His name. Because of who He is and what He has done for us, we do also for Him.

2. **To assure any reward will come from God.** We don't need the accolades of men. We are off track the moment we require the approval and applause of men. If we are working for the accolades of others and they do not reciprocate, we will often become sullen and no longer wish to do them good. This petty reaction indicates we did the deed to get praise and thanks from people. The reward from God is so much more. He knows the reward that best fits each one of us, and His intimate knowledge of what encourages us is so much sweeter than what any person can do.

3. **To connect with God.** God *loves* to reward His children, and what a joy it is to receive from Him! Receiving from God shows us the evidence of His work in our lives, and we can enjoy our connection with Him. This alone is reward enough! In God's kingdom, we don't look to men to gain self-worth or appreciation. We are to look to the real source—our Heavenly Father. This keeps our motives pure even when men do not respond. With our eyes on the Lord, we remain the difference in this world. Hebrews 11:6 says, *"But without faith it is impossible to please him: for he that cometh to God must believe that he is, and that he is a rewarder of them that diligently seek him."*

4. **To avoid the loss of benefits.** Jesus said if we give "to be seen," then we will get a reward from men. The problem is that the world's reward is temporary. It's over about as quickly as our giving. When God honors, He gives both temporal as well as eternal rewards. In fact, He is the best giver of all. How good to hear the words, *"Well done, thou good and faithful servant: thou hast been faithful over a few things, I will make thee ruler over many..."* (Matthew 25:21).

5. **To avoid the glory of men.** One of the biggest blessings in our lives is that of a good and encouraging human father. Some of us didn't get that, so that is why God had a back-up plan. He is our Father. If He says we are doing well, then we are doing well. We don't need anyone else's approval. Our sense of well-being—mentally, emotionally, and spiritually—is best obtained from God.

   If we rely on the praise of men, we will be dependent on the praise and approval of the created rather than the Creator. No one but God should rule our lives. We can honor and respect others, but they should never replace God in our lives. They don't have the qualifications. They don't possess the love, wisdom, power, or inclination to choose our highest good.

Why We Need to Pray in Secret

Next, Jesus says we should pray in secret. Just as with giving, we want to avoid hypocrisy. We don't pray to be seen, whether that's in a church, a synagogue, or on the street. It's not about monologues that will impress people. It's not about the length, repetition, tone of voice, or time of day. Prayer is communion with God. It's sacred, precious, and intimate. When we pray, it's just Him and us. He alone sees, hears, and decides the outcome. He rewards:

> *"And when thou prayest, thou shalt not be as the hypocrites are: for they love to pray standing in*

the synagogues and in the corners of the streets,
that they may be seen of men. Verily I say unto you,
They have their reward.

But thou, when thou prayest, enter into thy closet,
and when thou hast shut thy door, pray to thy
Father which is in secret; and thy Father which
seeth in secret shall reward thee openly.

But when ye pray, use not vain repetitions, as the
heathen do: for they think that they shall be heard
for their much speaking.

Be not ye therefore like unto them: for your Father
knoweth what things ye have need of, before ye ask
him."   (Matthew 6:5–8)

The following are five reasons why it is wise to pray in secret:

1. **Because prayer is between God and us.** Prayer is vertical, not horizontal. It is a spiritual event, not a social one. Even when we pray corporately, our focus is on God, not each other.

2. **Because any response will come from God.** Prayer is a conversation between God and you, and the only response should be from God. The Father Who sees you pray in secret will reward you openly. We leave all outcomes to Him.

3. **Because we have no audience but God.** Prayer should not have a human audience. It is the time when God has our attention. He may want to say something very personal to speak to our hearts. He also may need to convict our hearts of a sinful attitude or response, and His rebuke is private. (Much like we wouldn't correct a child publicly, we want to give our Father an opportunity to speak privately to us.) He may need to speak with the special comfort or assurance that only He can give. There are times for others to join us in

prayer, but that should not be the *only* time we spend talking to God.

4. **To avoid loss of benefit.** If we pray to be seen, that's all we get—the eyes of men. They might think we're a person of great piety. They may even tell others they saw us praying, but usually that's as far as the "reward" goes. When we settle for man's praise, attention, or reward, we can stop God's reward for prayer.

5. **To follow Jesus's example.** How did Jesus pray? Jesus sought private time with His Father. He sent the multitudes away and withdrew to quiet places to pray. When He was troubled, he stepped away for prayer. When He was weary from taking care of others, He went away to recuperate through prayer. He knew there were times to turn aside, even from those closest to Him, for prayer:

    > *"And when he had sent the multitudes away,*
    > *he went up into a mountain apart to pray:*
    > *and when the evening was come, he was there*
    > *alone."*   (Matthew 14:23)

    > *"And in the morning, rising up a great while*
    > *before day, he went out, and departed into a*
    > *solitary place, and there prayed.*
    > *And Simon and they that were with him*
    > *followed after him.*
    > *And when they had found him, they said unto*
    > *him, All men seek for thee."*   (Mark 1:35–37)

    > *"And He withdrew himself into the wilderness,*
    > *and prayed."*   (Luke 5:16)

"And it came to pass in those days, that he went out into a mountain to pray, and continued all night in prayer to God.

And when it was day, he called unto him his disciples: and of them he chose twelve, whom also he named apostles."　　　(Luke 6:12–13)

How to Pray in Secret

If you are not sure how to pray in secret, privately, here are some suggestions:

1. **Change your geography.** Find a place that is quiet and out of the way. Your quiet place may be a room in your house, outside while on a walk, or in your car. Find out what works best for you. Also, try to incorporate opportunities to get away from your normal daily life for the day just to pray.

2. **Get alone with God.** We go away to be with God. Yes, there are times to pray with our spouses, families, and fellow believers. However, there are also times we must turn aside to pray alone. It takes wisdom to know when to pray together and when to be alone with God.

3. **Close the door.** When I was a kid, I couldn't imagine praying in my closet. There was no room in there for me! But when He talked about the "prayer closet," Jesus was telling us to go someplace where we can keep everyone out. With the "door" closed, we can focus on Him and us. This doesn't have to be a literal door. If your quiet spot is a special chair, for example, be sure to let others know you want privacy while you're there. Even small children can learn to respect Mom or Dad's quiet spot!

4. **Get real with God.** Authenticity happens behind a closed door. It's where the "God and us stuff" happens.

When we are in that private place with God, no one else's opinion matters. It's a safe place to be real.

5. **Expect intimate communication.** We can talk to God about anything. He's not going to interrupt, tell us off, "one-up" our story, or tune us out. We get to enjoy a real and vital relationship with Him. We are not like the religious people of Jesus's day, with their fake connection to the Father. He will listen and use the inner voice of the Holy Spirit to communicate with our hearts and minds. When He gives advice, comfort, or direction in that quiet place, we know it is not from anyone else. We can expect Him to speak in the quiet place.

6. **Fast in secret.** Prayer accompanied by fasting can often deepen our connection with God. When we fast, we must not tell everyone. Otherwise, our motives are wrong, and we will miss the point. We fast in secret because it is another opportunity for us to commune with God.

> *"Moreover when ye fast, be not, as the hypocrites, of a sad countenance: for they disfigure their faces, that they may appear unto men to fast. Verily I say unto you, They have their reward.*
>
> *But thou, when thou fastest, anoint thine head, and wash thy face;*
>
> *That thou appear not unto men to fast, but unto thy Father which is in secret: and thy Father, which seeth in secret, shall reward thee openly."* (Matthew 6:16–18)

How to Pray

Jesus taught us how to pray. We know it as the Lord's Prayer. He didn't mean for us to just repeat each word of the prayer, over and over, as our normal mode of prayer. Yes, we do pray the exact prayer at times, but He meant for us to pray in a similar manner. The style of the prayer, or how to approach prayer in general, is the important lesson. It addresses certain topics in a certain order. That's what we can learn from it:

> *"After this manner therefore pray ye: Our Father which art in heaven, Hallowed be thy name.*
>
> *Thy kingdom come, Thy will be done in earth, as it is in heaven.*
>
> *Give us this day our daily bread.*
>
> *And forgive us our debts, as we forgive our debtors.*
>
> *And lead us not into temptation, but deliver us from evil: For thine is the kingdom, and the power, and the glory, for ever. Amen."* (Matthew 6:9–13)

The Seven Key Elements of Prayer

The Lord's Prayer includes the following seven key elements of communication that we need to aim to include in our prayers to Him:

1. **We pray to our heavenly Father.** First, Jesus teaches us to address the Father as "Our Father in heaven." When we start any conversation, we need to know with whom we're speaking: *"After this manner pray ye: Our Father which art in heaven..."* (Matthew 6:9).

2. **We talk and listen reverently and respectfully.** Next, we approach Him with *hallowedness*—that is, with honor toward His holiness. We speak to Him with respect and yield to Him as our Father, not like some distant god to whom we are unrelated. He is our *Father*. Matthew 6:9 continues, saying, *"Our Father which art in heaven, Hallowed be thy name..."*

3. **We pray with the big picture in mind.** Our Father is all about His kingdom. Jesus taught that this new

kingdom, built on new principles, had a new leader. We align ourselves with Him for the bigger picture and the greatest good: *"Thy kingdom come, Thy will be done in earth, as it is in heaven..."* (Matthew 6:10).

4. **We pray for the will of God.** The will of God is exactly what we would choose if we knew all the facts. Most people stop praying at this point because they want *their* will, not God's. In fact, we have this false notion that if we get enough people praying the same thing, we'll get God to do what He otherwise wouldn't do. Wrong.

God is smarter than us. He loves us more than anyone else can, and He has more power to carry out the wonderful things we associate with His love. When we know the Scripture, we can pray in agreement with *His words*. What if we are still unsure of His will? We have the help of the Holy Spirit, who prays on our behalf, and He *does* know the will of God.

We can be confident that the Holy Spirit will intercede for us: *"Likewise the Spirit also helpeth our infirmities: for we know not what we should pray for as we ought: but the Spirit itself maketh intercession for us with groanings which cannot be uttered. And he that searcheth the hearts knoweth what is the mind of the Spirit, because he maketh intercession for the saints according to the will of God"* (Romans 8:26–27).

5. **We request our daily needs.** "Our daily bread" is a phrase that refers to the things we need each day. Bread is a necessary staple and a centerpiece in nearly every culture. It stands for the basic building block or requirement for daily provision. We take our requests to God for everything we need: *"Give us this day our daily bread"* (Matthew 6:11).

God knows what we need before we ask, but He still wants us to ask. This keeps us in communication. We should always be aware of where our help comes from; we are utterly dependent on our heavenly Father, and He loves to show His fatherhood to His children: "*For your Father knoweth what things ye have need of, before ye ask him*" (Matthew 6:8).

"Without God, I cannot, and without me, He will not." My earthly father drilled that thought into my memory, and it's true and applicable in bringing our requests to God. We do our part, and God does His. This keeps us in relationship with Him and holds us accountable to Him.

6. **We confidently ask for forgiveness.** We forgive others, and God forgives us. In the same way we forgive, we are forgiven. This is a critical and fundamental concept we all must grasp: "*And forgive us our debts as we forgive our debtors*" (Matthew 6:12).

7. **We ask for wise leadership.** The Holy Spirit leads us in what is true, which helps us avoid temptation. If we stay in an attitude of prayer throughout the day, God is free to warn and instruct us. His wise counsel can keep us out of trouble, and He can tell us what to say in any situation. He can save us money and prompt us to give to those in need. He can tell us where and when to go or why to stay away. We need our wise and loving heavenly Father to direct us, moment by moment, and then temptations will fade: "*And lead us not into temptation...*" (Matthew 6:13).

God is watching. He will let temptation go only so far, and then He'll provide the way of escape. He does not allow us to be tempted beyond our ability to turn away from it. He is there every moment:

"*There hath no temptation taken you but such as is common to man: but God is faithful, who will not suffer you to be tempted above that ye are able; but will with the temptation also make a way to escape, that ye may be able to bear it*" (1 Corinthians 10:13).

Resisting Temptation

God is not the tempter. The Holy Spirit led Jesus away into the wilderness to be tempted by the devil. The devil is the tempter, and we get ourselves into trouble when we cooperate with him. If we do not deal with temptation properly, it will lead to sin, and when we keep going, sin will bring death:

> *"Let no man say when he is tempted, I am tempted of God: for God cannot be tempted with evil, neither tempteth he any man."*   (James 1:13)

> *"Then was Jesus led up of the Spirit into the wilderness to be tempted of the devil."* (Matthew 4:1)

> *"But every man is tempted, when he is drawn away of his own lust, and enticed.*
> *Then when lust hath conceived, it bringeth forth sin: and sin, when it is finished, bringeth forth death."*   (James 1:14–15)

We cannot allow ourselves to dwell on, or meditate about, a temptation. We must hold ourselves back from fleshly lusts because they war against our very souls, minds, and emotions. They will suck us into a blizzard of emotion and trap us. We shun these lusts. We cannot be casual about this; we must be alert and ready to remove the temptation: *"Dearly beloved, I beseech you as strangers and pilgrims, abstain from fleshly lusts, which war against the soul..."* (1 Peter 2:11).

One way to abstain from lusts is to kill, or crucify, them. We have nothing to do with them whatsoever. We don't go where they are, and we don't read their words. We give them no opportunity. They are dead to us: *"And they that are Christ's have crucified the flesh with the affections and lusts"* (Galatians 5:24).

In our battle against temptation, we must learn the principles of fleeing and following. We should never fight if God says flee, and we should never flee if God says fight. Some people think they are so strong they don't need to flee. That's a fool's argument. It's smart to flee many situations. If you're in an enclosed room and someone lets in a lion, you're going to find out how to get out of that room as soon as possible. That's not weak or stupid—it's smart. You want to save yourself.

It is the same with temptation; sometimes, we must flee or physically run away. There are other times we resist the devil, and we hold our ground, as Jesus did in the wilderness. We follow His example and resist with the Word of God. We resist, and *Satan* flees. However, the Bible is clear when it comes to lust—we flee: *"Flee fornication. Every sin that a man doeth is without the body; but he that committeth fornication sinneth against his own body"* (1 Corinthians 6:18).

Job said he made a covenant with his eyes that he would not look at a woman with lust. It's good to have strategies in place before the occasion presents itself. A promise to God and oneself, combined with practical ways to avoid the temptation, are powerful tools. Job 31:1 says, *"I made a covenant with mine eyes; why then should I think upon a maid?"*

Paul encouraged young Pastor Timothy to flee from youthful lusts and to follow the right things. We run away from sin and pursue those things that God approves: *"Flee also youthful lusts: but follow righteousness, faith, charity, peace, with them that call on the Lord out of a pure heart"* (2 Timothy 2:22).

How to Resist Temptation

As part of your ultimate life management system, the following are five practical ways to resist temptation:

1. **Request deliverance from evil.** When we pray, we should ask to be safe from the effect and influence of a sinful society. From the government all the way down to the individual citizen, America is in a state of wickedness. We pray to be delivered from it.

2. **Focus on the kingdom.** Our prayers need to be bigger than "me, mine, and ours." They should be about the

whole of God's kingdom and each person in it. We remember that the kingdom belongs to Him, and we want to support His will and His ways.

3. **Remember that He is the power.** We can count on this: God is the power, has the power, and exercises His power. It's about His might, not ours or anyone else's.

4. **Let your motivation be for His glory.** As Matthew 6:13 says, *"For thine is the kingdom and the power and the glory...."* Everything that is not sin we do for the glory of God. Blinking glorifies God. Sneezing glorifies God. Even when we nourish ourselves, it's for His glory. He is the one who feeds us. He wants our good. He is a loving, watchful, and fully involved God, and to glorify Him is fitting: *"Whether therefore ye eat, or drink, or whatsoever ye do, do all to the glory of God"* (1 Corinthians 10:31).

5. **Realize that forever is at stake.** We conclude our prayers with the acknowledgment that God's way, His plan, and His kingdom, are all forever. We acknowledge Him in His rightful place, and we remain humble. This world is not our home. His kingdom is not of this world. What a blessing it is to be counted among the children of the King!

We give, fast, and pray in secret. We keep ourselves to God. We do not need the praise of people, who are imperfect as we are. We look higher. We want the reward that is reserved for those who diligently seek God. Nothing is sweeter!

Chapter 22

The Power of Forgiveness

Forgive, and Be Forgiven

After Jesus presented His model prayer, He elaborated on a single, sobering line. In Matthew 6:14–15, Jesus says, *"For if ye forgive men their trespasses, your heavenly Father will also forgive you: But if ye forgive not men their trespasses, neither will your Father forgive your trespasses."*

Jesus added the big little word—"if." God repeats this word throughout the Bible. It carries the weight of one outcome versus another: if you have faith, if you believe, if you hold to my teaching, if you love me, and in His prayer—if you forgive. If you forgive men their trespasses, your heavenly Father will also forgive you. However, if you don't forgive, your heavenly Father will not forgive you. The question is, to forgive or not to forgive? Those are the only two options, and each comes with its own result.

Jesus says if we forgive others, our heavenly Father will forgive us. If we don't forgive others, He will not forgive us. This is a wonderful and miserable concept all at once. It may seem simple to forgive others because we know we want the forgiveness. However, once we are in a situation in which we must forgive, the task doesn't seem as simple. Our own forgiveness is based on our obedience. That is sobering.

The Consequences and Benefits of Forgiveness

We can evaluate the importance of this matter by evaluating the severity of its consequences and the magnitude of its benefits. For example, there are three levels of thievery, each with different consequences: petty theft, theft, and grand theft. All three are wrong, but their penalties are different. If we steal something under the value of forty dollars, the consequences are different than if we steal something that is worth more than ten thousand dollars. Different laws apply, and the penalties change accordingly. We know the importance of a matter by the severity of its consequences.

The Scriptures tell us to compare the severity and the goodness of God. Without understanding His severity, we cannot overfeed ourselves with the goodness of God. We need a balance, or we will become too soft or too hard in our perceptions of Him. God granted you and me forgiveness through the blood of Jesus. For Him to cut off His forgiveness because we do not forgive others is the most severe consequence of all: "*Behold therefore the goodness and the severity of God: on them which fell, severity; but toward thee, goodness, if thou continue in his goodness: otherwise thou also shalt be cut off*" (Romans 11:22).

Next, we can determine how important a thing is by examining the magnitude of its benefits. The more important a thing is, the bigger the benefit. God's full intention is to fill us with goodness. He wants us to be blessed in this life and the next. Jesus said He came to give us a life that is abundant. He wants to give *more*. When we forgive, we get the *more* God desires for us. We get the goodness, not the severity.

You have probably heard the phrase, "I owe you an apology." When an offense occurs, it naturally creates a debt–debtor relationship. Forgiveness is the act of setting someone free from an obligation—a debt—they "owe" us due to some wrong committed against us. (That is the basis of civil law.) Forgiveness sets that person free from compensating us what we lost. If our loss was monetary, they owe us money. If we forgive them, we cancel their debt.

What Forgiveness Involves

There are three elements of forgiveness. First, an injury or offense must have occurred. Someone hurt us somehow. Second, there is a debt to be paid due to the injury. We know when we've been injured, and we know they owe us something. This is true even if we can't name what they owe us or put a value to it. And third, the debt canceled. We don't try to collect it. It is as if it never happened. That's how forgiveness works.

Here are seven facts about forgiveness:

1. **Forgiveness has nothing to do with the other person.** Forgiveness is not dependent on other people. It would be nice if those who wronged us came back to us on their knees, humbly apologizing, and begging for our forgiveness, but usually they don't. More likely, they will go happily through life thinking they haven't done anything wrong. Perhaps they even believe we deserved the damage they did to us. Forgiving has nothing to do with the other person, and it has nothing to do with their attitude. It is not about them; it's about us.

2. **Forgiveness takes place in our hearts and minds.** Forgiveness is an internal exercise that has both inward and outward results. It takes place within our hearts.

3. **Forgiveness is giving up our right to get even**. We willingly give up our right to retaliate or to even the score. We do not repay *in kind* but with *kindness*.

4. **Forgiveness is a promise not to use people's past sins or offenses against them.** Forgiveness doesn't keep a record of offenses. This is exactly what the Lord did for us—He canceled our debt. In fact, in Corinthians, it says He does not count our trespasses against us. Through the cross, Jesus canceled our debts and cast them out of the way. Forgiveness is a promise not to use people's past sins or offenses against them ever again.

5. **Forgiveness releases God to deal with offenders.** Forgiveness allows God to deal with the offenders. Because forgiveness and pardon are two different things, in some cases, this means He releases the laws of the land to deal with the offender. We may not have the legal right and authority to pardon someone, but we do have to forgive them. By taking our hands off the situation, we release God to do what should be done in their case.

6. **Forgiveness cannot be occasional.** Forgiveness cannot be on again, off again. It's not something we do just occasionally. It's not something we'll do for one person and not for another. It must be a long-term, general policy that we are forgivers.

7. **Forgiveness is a great spiritual act.** Forgiveness is a God-like activity and one of the greatest spiritual acts a human can do. It surrenders our right to tip the scales back to our favor. (That is His business.) Instead, we must always focus on the forgiveness *we* have received. Through Jesus Christ, we are provided forgiveness and cleansing for our past wrongs. He wipes our sins out as if they had never happened. It says in Scripture that our sins are never to be remembered against us anymore—never. When He forgives, the offense is put out of existence, and the debt has been canceled. As He cancels the debt of our sins, so must we forgive the debt of others. It is the most God-like activity.

Writer, theologian, and Christian apologist C. S. Lewis put it this way: "To be a Christian means to forgive the inexcusable in others because God has forgiven the inexcusable in you."

There is no justification for what they did—it's inexcusable. So are the wrongs we commit. This is a key emphasis of Jesus's inaugural address. He's introducing, for the first time, a new kingdom and a new concept. He is calling His people to let their lights shine and to be the salt that seasons. He says these people are *also* forgivers of every transgression. His kingdom is for forgivers.

We don't want God to remember *our* sins. However, we may remember the sins others have done against us. I've talked to people who were damaged forty years ago. Today they know the details as clearly as the day the offense happened. They meditate on it, and they cannot forget it. Why is it that we want God to forget our sins, but we remember everyone else's?

We must remember that the greatness of the matter depends on two basics: the severity of the consequences and the magnitude of the blessing.

The Consequences of Unforgiveness

In the book of Luke, Peter went to Jesus and asked how often he should forgive his brother who had sinned against him. He asked if seven times was enough. Jesus said seven times was not enough. Instead, we are to forgive seventy times seven, or 490 times. This was the forgiveness required in a *single day*.

Jesus's response to Peter's question was not to give him a specific numerical limit; rather, it signified to him (and us) that forgiveness is an ongoing process. Jesus wants His kingdom made up of people who know how to continually forgive.

To illustrate His point, Jesus told Peter a story was about a certain king who was checking on the debts of his servants. One owed him ten thousand talents. This equaled about twenty years' worth of a day-laborer's wages. The servant didn't have the money to pay his debt. His lord, the king, commanded that the man, his wife, and their children be sold into slavery and that all their possessions be sold to make the payment. The money would go toward the repayment of the debt.

Upon hearing this, the servant fell to his knees and pleaded with his lord, saying, "Give me some time. Have patience with me, and I will pay you everything." The king was moved with compassion, freed his servant, and forgave the huge debt.

Afterward, the same servant went out and searched for a fellow servant who owed him money—a hundred pence, or about one day's wages. He laid his hands on him, took him by the throat, and demanded repayment. His fellow servant fell and begged for patience as he paid his debt, but his cries went unheeded. The servant, who owed the king so much, had this fellow thrown into debtor's prison.

Other servants watched what was happening. They were saddened by what they saw, and they went to their lord and told him what had happened. The lord summoned his unforgiving servant and called him wicked. He recounted how he had forgiven the servant's huge debt. The lord rebuked his servant because he did not show the same compassion to his fellow servant. The wicked servant had been forgiven a great fortune, yet he refused to pardon the small amount owed to him. The lord was angry and delivered him to the tormentors, until he could pay all that was due the king. The king rescinded his previous forgiveness! To *rescind* means to revoke, cancel, remove, repeal, to take away.

At the end of the story, the Scripture says, *"So likewise shall my heavenly Father do also unto you, if ye from your hearts forgive not everyone his brother their trespasses"* (Matthew 18:35).

Key Concepts about Forgiveness

In the parable of the unforgiving servant, Jesus illustrates several key concepts for believers:

- When we don't forgive, we are termed "wicked" by the Lord. That's a frightening status.

- When we don't forgive, we anger the Lord. He has given us everything freely, including forgiveness through Jesus Christ. When we withhold what He has given to us, we anger Him.

- When we don't forgive, our forgiveness is taken back from us. This may be a shock to us, but in the story of the king, he took back the forgiveness he had originally extended. His wicked servant did not forgive; therefore, he lost his forgiveness.

- When we don't forgive, we become prisoners of our own doing. The king turned his unforgiving servant over to the tormentors. When we don't forgive, we prolong our own torment. Because of our unwillingness to give others what God had given us, our torment is self-inflicted.

- When we don't forgive, we are tortured by endless cycles of retaliation. Our minds go through ongoing periods of bitterness and resentment. Dwelling on things will weaken and destroy us.

- When we don't forget the transgression against us, we have not truly forgiven them. The whole thing is still alive within us.

- When we don't forgive, we contaminate others. If a father or mother is unforgiving, their children will also be unforgiving. Children first learn these concepts at home. Bitter parents will raise bitter children. When a root of bitterness springs up, it troubles us. Hebrews 12:15 says, "*Looking diligently lest any man fail of the grace of God; lest any root of bitterness springing up trouble you, and thereby many be defiled.*"

The Benefits of Forgiving

Forgiving others benefits us in many ways. Here are twelve powerful benefits:

1. **We maintain our forgiven status with God.** What do we think of our redemption? Do we think enough of it to keep it? If we value the forgiveness we have received from our heavenly Father, then we must forgive others.

2. **The healing forgiveness brings is therapeutic.** Forgiveness is the greatest healing therapy on the planet. We won't need a psychiatrist, alcohol, or any synthetic thing to bring us peace. Conversely, to not forgive is mental poisoning.

3. **We are no longer victims.** We stay a victim if we can't forgive the transgressor and the transgressions. If the transgression is still active, it is still damaging us.

4. **We change our future for the better.** Forgiveness can't change the past, but it does change the future. Forgiveness means tomorrow will be a much better

day because the past will no longer affect it. We are free from the cheating, lying, betrayal, or abuse of the past. Our past will not touch our future.

5. **We unlock the handcuffs of hatred.** Hatred exists in the non-forgiver. It may not be directed at someone currently in our lives, but as we look back, we still remember. Although the anger is focused on the past, hate becomes the condition of our hearts and our minds today. Hatred spills over like venom in our bloodstream. It goes to all parts of the body and will affect every part of our lives. We were never designed to live with hatred.

   Dutch-born Christian Corrie Ten Boom and her family took great risks to help Jews during World War II. These risks eventually led Corrie and many in her immediate family to be captured. Her father and sister both died in concentration camps, and Corrie endured horrific treatment at the hands of the Nazis. Yet she knew the power of forgiveness. In her book *The Hiding Place*, she said, "Forgiveness is the key that unlocks the door of resentment and the handcuffs of hatred. It is a power that breaks the chains of bitterness and the shackles of selfishness."

   Forgiveness unlocks the handcuffs of hatred—wow, what power! We don't consciously stop hating; it just happens as we forgive. Jesus says His kingdom is for forgivers because it's the forgivers who know how to extinguish the horrors of the past and put an end to hatred.

6. **We get closure for past wrongs.** Forgiveness ends past hurts. When we forgive, we terminate the things that sought to stay alive. We move on in peace.

7. **Forgiveness creates a new way to remember.** When we look back with the filter of forgiveness, we don't just see the damage. The pain fades. Many things that once brought a sting may, instead, bring a chuckle.

Be warned: Satan is the accuser. He will remind us of that person who did us wrong. Although their actions were a reality, he will only remind us of half the truth. He will not remind us that we forgave the person, for example. So we must remind ourselves that we have forgiven and see that memory as a cause for rejoicing. We were victorious. We forgave.

8. **We release God to deal with the offender.** If God isn't dealing with our offenders, it is because we are unforgiving. Unforgiveness is just an attempt to get even. It's a way of retaliating—even if only in our minds. It is our vengeance—God is not involved. God says vengeance is His to repay. God knows how and when to avenge us, but He does it only for people who forgive. Even then, we are warned not to rejoice when our enemy falls, or God may stop punishing them. Vengeance is a serious matter; we must leave it to God.

9. **We manifest love.** Forgiveness is evidence of love. In the Phillips translation, 1 Corinthians 13:6 says, *"Love...does not keep an account of evil or gloat over the wickedness of other people...."* The grace of God produces several character qualities that empower us to forgive. One of them is mercy. Obviously, an unforgiving person is not a merciful person. Jesus said the merciful are blessed because they have obtained mercy.

   Another character quality is love. This form of love suffers long and is kind to the one who causes suffering. Jesus, in His inaugural address, told us to love our enemies and bless those who curse us. Unless I am a forgiver, I cannot do these things. However, when I have canceled others' debt, I am free. Love shows mercy and offers freedom. It is one of the greatest benefits of being a forgiver.

10. **We improve our health.** Anger is expensive—it damages our blood, cells, and bones. The book of

Proverbs says bitterness dries the bones. Anger affects our bodily systems and our mental capacity. It strains our emotions and causes all kinds of breakdowns of body and soul. These problems harm our health and well-being, as well as our wallets.

11. **Forgiveness is a triple blessing.** Forgiveness blesses the offender by canceling a debt owed. Forgiveness blesses us; we regain our peace and maintain our good standing before God. And forgiveness blesses God. He delights in our obedience and our likeness to His Son. He delights in our health, strength, and joyful disposition.

12. **We pray effective prayers.** Because we desire a connection with God, we want Him to hear our prayers. If we harbor unforgiveness in our hearts, we are not ready to communicate with the Father. He wants all sin and iniquity out of the way so we are restored to a place of sweet fellowship between Him and us.

    Isaiah 59:1–2 says, "*Behold, the LORD's hand is not shortened, that it cannot save; neither his ear heavy, that it cannot hear: But your iniquities have separated between you and your God, and your sins have hid his face from you, that he will not hear.*"

    He wants us to forgive, no matter who the offender is. We forgive, and we are forgiven. Mark 11:25 says, "*And when ye stand praying, forgive, if ye have ought against any: that your Father also which is in heaven may forgive you your trespasses.*"

    It is not forgiveness if we forgive others because they did some good deed. That was just a negotiated settlement—no forgiveness took place. There is only one adequate motivation to forgive others: that God, because of Christ, has forgiven us.

    Jesus ended the parable of the two servants in Matthew 18:35 with a warning against unforgiveness: "*So likewise shall my heavenly Father do also unto you, if ye from your hearts forgive not everyone his brother their trespasses."* We stand on the threshold of a whole new dimension of spiritual power, mental health, emotional strength, and relational stability. It's all summed up in the right answer to this one question: To forgive or not to forgive?

How Forgiveness Affects All of Life

We choose how to respond when someone commits an offense, or hurt, against us. We can respond God's way or man's way, and how we respond determines the attitudes both sides will carry forward after that response.

Attitudes turn into behaviors, and behaviors have consequences. Consequences produce symptoms in our lives. Whenever we are offended, God supplies grace to help us respond the right way. It's important that we act in His grace because it is given to help us forgive the offender. That is God's way. With Him, we can recover and not cause further damage to ourselves and others. We look for a solution that pursues peace with all men. We follow holiness:

> *"And make straight paths for your feet, lest that which is lame be turned out of the way; but let it rather be healed.*
>
> *Follow peace with all men, and holiness, without which no man shall see the Lord:*
>
> *Looking diligently lest any man fail of the grace of God; lest any root of bitterness springing up trouble you, and thereby many be defiled."*
>
> (Hebrews 12:13–15)

Our only *other* choice to an offense is to refuse to forgive. This choice will produce a set of attitudes leading to behaviors that will produce symptoms in our lives. So, what happens when we respond to the offender with unforgiveness? What does a heart of unforgiveness produce in our lives? Here are three consequences we want to avoid:

1. **First, we become bitter**, and bitterness poisons. If we are unforgiving, the other person will probably continue to offend us, and then we have an even bigger barrier. As the situation escalates, bad feelings develop, and each person becomes worse toward the other. Satan wants us to be unforgiving so he can take advantage of us. He will try to keep us bitter so we self-destruct on our own. In 2 Corinthians 2:9–11 Paul writes, *"For to this end also did I write, that I might know the proof of you, whether ye be obedient in all things. To whom ye forgive anything, I forgive also: for if I forgave anything, to whom I forgave it, for your sakes forgave I it in the person of Christ; Lest Satan should get an advantage of us: for we are not ignorant of his devices."*

2. **Unforgiveness produces a judgmental attitude in our hearts.** Once we become critical of the offender, it is like a magnifying glass enlarging every little offense, which extends to almost everyone else who does not suit us. A critical attitude impairs our ability to make good judgments because bitterness and unforgiveness interfere with our thinking process. If we learn to put a negative spin on everything and everyone, we become negative people. We will always look for the bad rather than the good.

3. **A heart that does not forgive will harbor a vengeful attitude.** When we retaliate, our character is reduced to the same character as our offender—we return evil for evil. In Galatians 5, Paul lists the works of the flesh: fornication, murder, envy, jealousy (at the success of another), wrath, and vengeful acts of retaliation. When we live in the flesh, we are in a constant state of anger and frustration. This will lead to anxiety and depression. When we do not know how to cope with this emotional strain, we seek relief from doctors, drugs, alcohol, and anything else that may ease our

pain. We weren't meant to live this way. Unforgiveness starts a slow self-destruction.

When we examine our two choices—to forgive or not to forgive—the *best* choice is clear. Forgiveness allows us to make godly decisions and walk in our faith. We are mentally healthy and emotionally strong when we forgive. We eliminate damaging consequences, and we see others as God sees them.

Forgiveness Leads Us to Live in a State of Grace

We also live in a state of grace as we offer grace to those who have offended us.

In broader, Christian terms, *grace* is the free and unmerited favor of God. In relation to others, *grace* can be described as the knowledge and power to do what's right—joyfully. We aren't operating in grace while moaning and groaning. We must diligently respond to and exercise grace. According to Hebrews, if we don't respond in grace, a root of bitterness will spring up.

The following are ten compelling facts about grace, which we receive when we forgive:

1. **Grace is given to all of us** at the precise moment we are offended. He hasn't deserted us. God is right there at the time of the offence—giving us knowledge, power, and grace. He promised that He is always with us— even to the end. He gives grace to every single one of us. John 1:16–17 says, *"And of his fullness have all we received, and grace for grace. For the law was given by Moses, but grace and truth came by Jesus Christ."*

2. **God's grace is always adequate.** It builds us up. When someone offends us, grace makes us strong enough to respond as God desires. We have the knowledge and power to respond in a peaceful manner. Acts 20:32 says, *"I commend you to God, and to the word of his*

grace, which is able to build you up, and to give you an inheritance among all them which are sanctified."

When someone offends us, they may appear stronger or more powerful than we feel. We are momentarily a victim of the offense. However, God says His grace is sufficient and that His strength is made perfect in our weakness. When we respond as God desires, we become strong again: *"And he said unto me, My grace is sufficient for thee: for my strength is made perfect in weakness..."* (2 Corinthians 12:9).

We are the stewards of God's grace. We must use grace wisely and appropriately, as we would manage any other gift from God. He gave us grace, and we give grace to others. It's there for us to use as we forgive. In 1 Peter 4:10, the Scripture says, *"...as good stewards of the manifold grace of God."*

3. **Grace teaches.** It gives us information as well as power. Grace teaches us to deny ungodliness and worldly lusts. We don't have to wait to figure it out. Grace is right there on the spot, so we can take care of things immediately and joyfully: *"For the grace of God that bringeth salvation hath appeared to all men, Teaching us that, denying ungodliness and worldly lusts, we should live soberly, righteously, and godly, in this present world; Looking for that blessed hope, and the glorious appearing of the great God and our Savior Jesus Christ"* (Titus 2:11–13).

4. **Grace doesn't just teach, it empowers.** Remember our definition: *grace* is the knowledge and power to do God's will with joy. Sin does not hold the power— grace does. An unforgiving attitude will not rule us because we are dealing with others by grace: *"For sin shall not have dominion over you: for ye are not under the law, but under grace"* (Romans 6:14).

Jesus Christ gives us the ability to reign in this life and the next because He gives us an abundance of grace. Jesus is called the King of Kings. He is the King, and we are the kings under His headship. We are not under our circumstances, but above them. Romans 5:17 says, *"They which receive abundance of grace and of the gift of righteousness shall reign in life by one, Jesus Christ."*

5. **Grace affects how we talk.** Forgiving people do not talk about what someone did to offend them. They don't tell themselves or others that everyone is against them. Rather than being shaken up and keeping offenses alive through gossip, we forgive and stay quiet. When we speak with grace, we spread the blessings of God. Psalm 45:2 says, *"Grace is poured into thy lips: therefore God hath blessed thee forever."*

6. **Grace is activated by faith.** We have grace because of our faith in Jesus. We stand and rejoice in the hope and the glory of God: *"By whom also we have access by faith into this grace wherein we stand, and rejoice in hope of the glory of God"* (Romans 5:2).

7. The more we concentrate on the law, the bigger the offence becomes. **Grace overcomes magnified offenses** because the grace of God is so much greater than any offense: *"Moreover the law entered, that the offence might abound. But where sin abounded, grace did much more abound"* (Romans 5:20).

8. **God gives grace to the humble.** Our wounded pride is one of the biggest reasons we find it hard to forgive. It is our pride that wants to hold others accountable and wants to retaliate. God resists the proud. To the humble, however, He gives grace, knowledge, and power to do what's right. In due time, God will exalt the humble: *"Humble yourselves therefore under the mighty hand of God, that he may exalt you in due time: Casting all your care upon him; for he careth for you"* (1 Peter 5:6–7).

9. **Grace enables us to live acceptably.** When we serve God acceptably, we receive a kingdom that cannot be moved. As a people, we cannot be fragmented or hurt. We have stability. Let us have grace so we can serve God acceptably as part of His kingdom: *"Wherefore we receiving a kingdom which cannot be moved, let us have grace, whereby we may serve God acceptably with reverence and godly fear..."* (Hebrews 12:28).

10. **Grace promotes forgiveness.** We start a root of bitterness when we don't use grace. It springs up and troubles us and tarnishes many believers. Conversely, if we *do* respond to grace, then there is no root of bitterness. That is what we want. Responding to God's grace when we're offended will reap peace, not further strife. When our responses are correct, our good attitude will produce the right behavior, leading to a positive resolution: *"Looking diligently lest any man fail of the grace of God; lest any root of bitterness springing up trouble you, and thereby many be defiled"* (Hebrews 12:15).

When contemplating forgiveness, we should conduct a self-examination. Remember, forgiveness is the most spiritual act we will ever do in our lives. It's the most God-like action a human can make. God is a forgiver. To be like Him means we are to be forgivers. Let us fully embrace this wonderful kingdom attitude by which we do for others what God has done for us. Our wonderful Father, who cancels our sins and remembers them no more, says to do for others what He has done for us.

To forgive or not to forgive? We choose to forgive.

Chapter 23

Your Eternal Future

Treasures in Heaven

Where do we place the items that mean the most to us? In our pockets? In a safe? On the dashboard of a vehicle? On a table at a restaurant? We are careful about where we place our treasures. We do not want to risk losing that which is important to us.

Jesus taught about two kinds of treasures. First are the treasures we pursue, obtain, and store on this earth. Second are the treasures we pursue on this earth but are spiritual in nature and stored in heaven. Our treasures on earth are temporary, while our treasures in heaven are eternal. Jesus said our hearts would be drawn to the place that holds our treasures. Are we drawn to heaven or to the earth?

Matthew 6:19-21 says it this way: *"Lay not up for yourselves treasures upon earth, where moth and rust doth corrupt, and where thieves break through and steal: But lay up for yourselves treasure in heaven, where neither moth nor rust doth corrupt, and where thieves do not break through nor steal: For where your treasure is, there will your heart be also."*

Two Reasons Earthly Treasures Are Temporary

There are two reasons that earthly treasures are temporary.

First, we work hard to accumulate them, and then we die. In death, we have no control over the treasures we've worked so hard to obtain. Someone else will benefit from our labors. We have no say in how they're handling our treasures. King Solomon, the wisest man of all time, faced this same worry. It troubled him to think his stockpile of stuff would end up in the hands of fools:

> *"Yea, I hated all my labour which I had taken under the sun: because I should leave it unto the man that shall be after me.*
>
> *And who knoweth whether he be a wise man or a fool? yet shall he have rule over all my labour wherein I have laboured, and wherein I have shewed myself wise under the sun. This is also vanity."* (Ecclesiastes 2:18–19)

Second, earthly treasures are temporary because after the wicked man dies, that is all he has to show for his life. No matter how much time, energy, and money the wicked man spent on treasures, he has no heaven to look forward to and no treasures there. His hopes are dissolved. Proverbs 11:7 warns, *"When a wicked man dieth, his expectation shall perish: and the hope of unjust men perisheth."*

Every person—righteous or wicked—leaves earthly treasures behind. Our earthly treasures have no effect on what awaits us in the next life. Only our *eternal treasures* accumulate and will not be taken from us. Those treasures are stored as an inheritance that is incorruptible. They cannot be damaged or stolen, and no person, system of decay, or disease can take them from us. These treasures are reserved in heaven for us:

> *"Blessed be the God and Father of our Lord Jesus Christ, which according to his abundant mercy*

hath begotten us again unto a lively hope by the
resurrection of Jesus Christ from the dead,

To an inheritance incorruptible, and undefiled, and
that fadeth not away, reserved in heaven for you,

Who are kept by the power of God through faith
unto salvation ready to be revealed in the last
time."   (1 Peter 1:3–5)

In the book of Luke, we read a parable about a man who had amassed many possessions. He was pleased with himself and thought he could sit back, relax, and enjoy his stuff. This is the same dilemma we all face. We can work hard, buy and store our stuff, and congratulate ourselves on a job well done. We can think that's all there is to life and not regard our eternal destiny as something important. This type of belief leads to the greatest loss known to man:

"And he spake a parable unto them, saying,
The ground of a certain rich man brought forth
plentifully:

And he thought within himself, saying, What shall
I do, because I have no room where to bestow my
fruits?

And he said, This will I do: I will pull down my
barns, and build greater; and there will I bestow all
my fruits and my goods.

And I will say to my soul, Soul, thou hast much
goods laid up for many years; take thine ease, eat,
drink, and be merry.

But God said unto him, Thou fool, this night thy
soul shall be required of thee: then whose shall
those things be, which thou hast provided.

So is he that layeth up treasure for himself, and is
not rich toward God."   (Luke 12:16–21)

What Matters Is the Unseen

We brought nothing with us when we entered this world, and we'll take nothing when we leave. However, living for God will benefit us in ways we cannot imagine. It's the unseen that matters most, just as the unseen spirit within each of us is our true person. How much we own does not determine our happiness and contentment, and earthly success does not determine who we are: *"But godliness with contentment is great gain. For we brought nothing into this world, and it is certain we can carry nothing out. And having food and raiment let us be therewith content"* (1 Timothy 6:6–8).

We have learned that there are two ways to judge the importance of a matter. One is by the severity of the consequences, and the other is by the magnitude of the benefits. The magnitude of benefits from storing our treasures in heaven is enormous compared to the consequences of losing our possessions in this world. Each of us has a certain amount of time on this earth. We can spend our time, talents, and energy on accumulating treasures here, but when we die, they will not matter in eternal life.

Solomon, the richest man in the history of mankind, said his labors were in vain. Even he understood all his work to accumulate wealth was for nothing, like chasing after the wind.

Jesus told us to choose the path with a magnitude of benefits. His kingdom has a whole new philosophy. It has different terms of engagement and is based on entirely different principles. He told us that we are sojourners on this planet and citizens of another world. Rather than hanging onto this *temporary* place, our time is best spent preparing for our *eternal* home. Jesus makes this simple statement: where our treasure is, there our hearts will be.

Why is the unseen so important? Here are two primary reasons:

1. **First, the unseen includes eternal life.** This life is a gift from God through Jesus Christ. We did not earn it. God gave it to us when we responded to God's grace through our repentance, faith, and baptism. If we have Jesus, we have an unseen eternal life that is of utmost importance. If we do not have the Son of God, we do

not have eternal life. And the alternative is *not* nice: *"And this is the record, that God has given to us eternal life, and this life is in his Son. He that hath the Son hath life; and he that hath not the Son of God hath not life"* (1 John 5:11–12).

Our bodies are included in our earthly treasure. When we die, our ailing, imperfect bodies are dissolved; we get new ones that never fail, and we will live without end: *"For we know that if our earthly house of this tabernacle were dissolved, we have a building of God, an house not made with hands, eternal in the heavens. For in this we groan, earnestly desiring to be clothed upon with our house which is from heaven"* (2 Corinthians 5:1–2).

He will change our vile, corruptible, declining bodies with bodies fashioned like His! Our *eternal* life is the important stuff. This is what we want the most. This life and this earth pales in comparison to what God has in store for us. He stores, and we store, and heaven awaits.

2. **Second, we enjoy eternal fruit through seeing the people we've helped into a relationship with God.** Until eternity, we may never fully know everyone whom our lives and testimonies have influenced. Most people have several encounters with the Gospel before they decide to follow Christ. You may have been the first person to tell someone about God. They may not have seemed to listen or could have even walked away, rejecting the message. Then someone else came along and watered that seed, and perhaps someone else added to that. Through several links in the chain, that individual came to Jesus in repentance. This is fruit that will never be taken away: *"And he that reapeth receiveth wages, and gathereth fruit unto life eternal: that both he that soweth and he that reapeth may rejoice together"* (John 4:36).

God will give us eternal glory, honor, and immortality according to our deeds. For every good deed we do, we have a reward in heaven. Our deeds will be tested, and the things that align with the will of God will be recognized for eternity: "*Who will render to every man according to his deeds: To them who by patient continuance in well doing seek for glory and honour and immortality, eternal life*" (Romans 2:6–7).

Our Temporary Distress Will Become Glory in Heaven

Any suffering we do here on earth secures even more treasure in heaven: "*Wherefore I beseech you, be ye followers of me. For this cause have I sent unto you Timotheus, who is my beloved son, and faithful in the Lord, who shall bring you into remembrance of my ways which be in Christ, as I teach everywhere in every church*" (1 Corinthians 4:16–17).

When we face persecution and false accusations for the sake of our Lord, we will receive eternal, nonperishable rewards in heaven. "*Blessed are ye, when men shall revile you, and persecute you, and shall say all manner of evil against you falsely for my sake. Rejoice, and be exceeding glad: for great is your reward in heaven...*" (Matthew 5:11–12).

This may come as a shock, but we aren't just teaching people; we are teaching angels. Things are happening on earth that the angels do not understand. They do not have experience with the "cause and effect" dynamic of this life. They watch us to understand the mystery of godliness: Christ in us, the hope of glory. The angels were shocked when God the Son left heaven to come to this earth. They watched Him live, die, and rise again. The cross was a mystery to them. They saw the humility of God. They saw Him value a connection with mortal man:

> "*And to make all men see what is the fellowship of the mystery, which from the beginning of the world hath been hid in God, who created all things by Jesus Christ:*

> *To the intent that now unto the principalities and*
> *powers in heavenly places might be known by the*
> *church the manifold wisdom of God,*
>
> *According to the eternal purpose which he*
> *purposed in Christ Jesus our Lord."*
>
> (Ephesians 3:9–11)

The book of Hebrews says the angels can see us, just as our brothers and sisters in Christ who have gone on before us can see us. Spiritually, we are not alone. The angels and saints witness our temptations and struggles. We are like open books, being read, studied, and analyzed. Our lives are teaching angels about the God-man relationship:

> *"Wherefore seeing we also are compassed about*
> *with so great a cloud of witnesses, let us lay aside*
> *every weight, and the sin which doth so easily*
> *beset us,*
>
> *and let us run with patience the race that is set*
> *before us, Looking unto Jesus the author and*
> *finisher of our faith; who for the joy that was set*
> *before him endured the cross, despising the shame,*
> *and is set down at the right hand of the throne of*
> *God."* (Hebrews 12:1–2)

Our character qualities are also eternal. Our lives and the characters we develop are not for nothing. The things of God are worth striving for because they carry over to eternity: *"He that is unjust, let him be unjust still: and he which is filthy, let him be filthy still: and he that is righteous, let him be righteous still: and he that is holy, let him be holy still"* (Revelation 22:11).

We gain eternal rewards based on our deeds here. This is not about our salvation. Rather, this is about what we do *after* our salvation. We need to ask ourselves if we are living for what matters here or what matters there: *"And, behold, I come quickly; and my reward is with me, to give every man according as his work shall be"* (Revelation 22:12).

The Rewards That Await Us

What are some of the rewards that await God's people? Some of them are crowns. A crown is not just an ornament or decoration; it also represents an ascribed jurisdiction. Wearing a crown shows authority over a specific area. It's not just a circular piece of gold.

The Bible speaks of several different "crowns" awarded to believers. Here are four types.

An Incorruptible Crown

In 1 Corinthians, Paul says to run the race here on earth to receive a crown in heaven. He uses an illustration from sports. Like the sportsman who works hard, trains, and prepares to do his best in his sport, he plays to win the prize. (In Greco Roman times, the prize was a crown or garland.) These crowns, of course, got dusty, decayed, or tarnished. However, Paul urged believers to train like a prize-winning athlete and to keep their eyes on the eternal crown.

In heaven, our crowns cannot decompose or lose value because they are incorruptible: "*Know ye not that they which run in a race run all, but one receiveth the prize? So run, that ye may obtain. And every man that striveth for the mastery is temperate in all things. Now they do it to obtain a corruptible crown; but we an incorruptible*" (1 Corinthians 9:24–25).

A Crown of Righteousness

Paul said he had fought a good fight. He had finished his course, and he had kept the faith. His crown was stored for him, just waiting for his arrival. The Lord Himself would give it to him, and he would be known for his righteousness, or rightness, forever.

This is the reward of all those who love the Lord: we will receive a crown of rightness. We will never again be wrong. We will be right in our jurisdiction:

> "*I have fought a good fight, I have finished my course, I have kept the faith:*

240

Henceforth there is laid up for me a crown of
righteousness, which the Lord, the righteous judge,
shall give me at that day: and not to me only, but
unto all them also that love his appearing."

(2 Timothy 4:7–8)

A Crown of Glory

By being an example to God's people, we are awarded a crown of glory. This is one reason we must know the Word of God. We can be a good example of the Word's power in our daily lives, and that is contagious. Our knowledge, attitudes, speech, and actions influence those around us: "...*being examples to the flock. And when the chief Shepherd shall appear, ye shall receive a crown of glory that fadeth not away*" (1 Peter 5:3–4).

A Crown of Life

When we remain faithful to our Lord through persecution, suffering, and even imprisonment, we will qualify for a crown of life. Through our endurance, we demonstrate we love Jesus more than temptation and more than the sin it represents. Do we love Him more than sin? Do we love Him more than the things that may seem pleasant and exciting on the surface? Do we cling to Him and choose Him above all things? Then we will receive the crown of life, which He promised to those who love Him:

"I know thy works, and tribulation, and poverty,
(but thou art rich) and I know the blasphemy of
them which say they are Jews, and are not,
but are the synagogue of Satan.

Fear none of those things which thou shalt suffer:
behold, the devil shall cast some of you into prison,
that ye may be tried; and ye shall have tribulation
ten days: be thou faithful unto death, and I will give
thee a crown of life."   (Revelation 2:9–10)

241

Jesus wants us to have a different mindset than the people around us. In His inaugural address, He laid out an entirely different way to think, believe, speak, and act. He was seeking a people who would follow Him, a people who were willing to seek a new kingdom and new way of life and that ultimately would win them an eternal place with Him. He said to lay up treasures where it counted: in heaven, not on this earth.

How to Lay Up Treasures in Heaven

Instead of focusing on treasures here on earth, we focus on the treasures we will enjoy eternally in heaven. Here are twelve ways to lay up those forever treasures.

1. **Choose the eternal over the temporary.** We consciously choose heaven and its eternal reward. Jesus said not to labor for meat that perishes but for the meat that endures. Jesus was not saying to stop working or buying food. He was making an analogy between working for what we can obtain on this earth—temporal food—and what we can obtain in heaven—eternal life: *"Labour not for the meat which perisheth, but for that meat which endureth unto everlasting life, which the Son of man shall give unto you: for him hath God the Father sealed"* (John 6:27).

2. **Seek the things above.** Christ, who is above, is whom we should seek first. Likewise, *His ways* are above our ways. Because we've made the choice to follow Jesus, our focus and priorities will have changed, too. We seek the eternal: *"If ye then be risen with Christ, seek those things which are above, where Christ sitteth on the right hand of God"* (Colossians 3:1).

3. **Set your affections.** *Set* is a primary word. It indicates purpose and intent. In our culture, most people let their affections be led along by external forces. The movie industry, advertising, and even friends can stimulate our affections. God has given us the ability to make our own decisions and to determine what our affections

will be. We must *set* our affections—choose the things to which we will commit our feelings and labors. It's our choice: "*Set your affections on things above, not on things on the earth*" (Colossians 3:2).

We have the power to set our affections because in Jesus, we are dead to this world and its controls. We are part of Him. We are in His new kingdom. We set our affections on where He is and what He starts inside us. Then we maintain those new affections, those new actions, and our new loves in Him: "*For ye are dead, and your life is hid with Christ in God*" (Colossians 3:3).

4. **Keep sight of the eternal.** If we take heaven and eternity out of our lives, there isn't much left. This eternal perspective is the difference between believers and non-believers. As followers of Christ, we know there is more than this life, and we live in the hope of an eternal reward. We know He has a place reserved for us. We can't allow ourselves to be buried with the stuff of this world and lose our focus on the eternal. We can't gather on Sunday to reconnect with heaven and then go out and forget about Christ for the rest of the week. We want to stay aware that He will appear and maintain our connection to Him: "*When Christ, who is our life, shall appear, then shall ye also appear with him in glory*" (Colossians 3:4).

5. **Destroy all opposing inclinations.** There are certain things we must purposefully destroy in our lives. If we don't, they will prevent us from being able to set our affections on things above, which are opposite to the will of God. Therefore, we must destroy them:

"Mortify therefore your members which are upon the earth; fornication, uncleanness, inordinate affection, evil concupiscence, and covetousness, which is idolatry:

> *For which things' sake the wrath of God cometh on the children of disobedience:*
>
> *In the which ye also walked some time, when ye lived in them."* (Colossians 3:5–7)

What do we destroy?

Fornication. The word "fornication" is from the Greek, *porneo*, from which we get the word "pornography." This must be destroyed. An out-of-control sex drive, whether in thought or action, keeps us focused on sexuality. Everywhere we look, everything we hear, and the way we evaluate others is based on sex. The Scripture says in the last days, men's eyes will be full of adultery. This is in opposition to the eternal.

Uncleanness. We have all heard the saying, "Cleanliness is next to godliness." Some think of this as clean surroundings, such as a clean car or kitchen, and it may include those things to a degree. Although outward cleanliness is certainly an earthly virtue, true cleanliness of heart, mind, speech, and action is an eternal virtue.

Excessive affections. There are affections within us that are misplaced, uncalculated, and out of control. "Inordinate" means out of the ordinary. Anything that we get overly affectionate about has the potential to distract us from our focus on eternity. We should not let ourselves become obsessed with anything or anyone. This could be a well-loved hobby or a sport that takes over our time, energy, and money. We end up setting aside more important things so we can feed our obsession. We can't allow excessive affections to obscure the eternal picture. Instead, we should practice moderation.

Evil sex drive. This is lust toward sexual activities that are unlawful according to God's Word. Sex within the marriage of one woman and one man is what God intended. Anything outside this is evil. Sex should be regarded as holy, undefiled, and enjoyed within the parameters outlined in Scripture.

Covetousness. The Bible calls *covetousness* "idolatry." In other words, covetousness causes us to want something so badly that it eclipses everything else. When something other than God rules us, we become a slave to that thing, and it becomes our idol.

Colossians goes on to describe other things we must cast away: **anger, wrath, malice, blasphemy, and filthy communications.** Anger and wrath act in vengeance. They work in the here and now, putting their efforts into getting even with others. Malice is hatred. It negatively focuses on the people and relationships of this earth. Blasphemy uses the Lord's name as a common or filthy word. Blasphemy is about the here and now and ignores the eternal impact of its words. It doesn't care about consequences. It doesn't store up good. Colossians 3:8 says, *"But now ye also put off all these; anger, wrath, malice, blasphemy, filthy communication out of your mouth."*

1. **Develop and maintain holy actions.** It's not enough to just stop doing bad things; we must start doing good things. Yes, we stop the attitudes and actions such as anger, wrath, and malice, and we become merciful, kind, humble, meek, and long-suffering: *"Put on therefore, as the elect of God, holy and beloved, bowels of mercies, kindness, humbleness of mind, meekness, longsuffering"* (Colossians 3:12).

   We must be diligent to develop holy actions in our daily lives. So we strive for kindness by not thinking of ourselves more highly than we should. We become meek, described as "strength" under God's control. Meekness is like steel covered with velvet. We learn to maintain holy actions through suffering well.

2. **Become tolerant.** The scriptural term for *tolerance* is to "forbear one another." We learn to dismiss things and go on with an honest heart of joy. We overlook things that may have once seemed annoying or offensive and choose to forbear with those around us in sincerity.

3. **Forgive.** We don't just forbear—we forgive. That's where our sincerity comes in. We aren't just putting up with someone through gritted teeth while hiding inner resentment. Our forbearance meets with genuine forgiveness.

4. **Develop agape love.** Our love for each other is another characteristic that allows us to keep a heavenly focus. When we love, we think as God thinks. We aren't dealing with others on this earth according to what they have said or done. When we tune into heaven, we can develop and maintain a godly attitude of love.

5. **Live in peace and gratefulness.** When we have peace, we have the mental capacity to make wise decisions, to go through life with discernment, and to enjoy it to the fullest. God wants us to be undisturbed. This is the way we function at our best within ourselves, in our relationships with others, and with God. We want and need peace all around us. We *choose* to let the peace of God rule in our hearts. With all this peace, we can naturally be thankful, even for the peace itself!

   When we live without peace with God and others, or even ourselves, that lack of peace takes away heavenly focus. We become so troubled and anxious that we're continuously stirred up inside and can't notice the good around us. The peace of God dissolves all that: "*And let the peace of God rule in your hearts, to the which also ye are called in one body; and be ye thankful*" (Colossians 3:15).

6. **Be a student of the Word of God.** We let the Word of God dwell in us. We take in its wisdom and allow it to permeate our lives. It keeps us strong, and it gives us

the power and freedom to do the right thing. The Word of God directs us to the eternal.

How do we become students of the Word? *"Let the word of Christ dwell in you richly in all wisdom; teaching and admonishing one another in psalms and hymns and spiritual songs, singing with grace in your hearts to the Lord"* (Colossians 3:16).

We memorize and meditate on the Word. We cannot overstuff ourselves with the Word of God. We let the words of Christ dwell in us richly. We live in it, and we muse upon it.

We teach it to others and use it to encourage them. The Word should be in our mouths and always on our tongues. When we talk with others, it should be in our conversation. We should share its teachings every chance we get. It should be the foundation of all our relationships and interactions. We help each other stay on track with the Word of God.

We encourage each other with psalms, hymns, and spiritual songs. We should retell the words of the psalmists and recount the doctrines, scriptural encouragements, and hopes contained in our hymns. The words in a spiritual song represent biblical ideas systematically and intelligently. Songs contain wisdom and meaning and can spark emotion.

Truth that produces such emotion is good because it moves us into action. Singing praises to the Lord helps us to always have a song in our hearts. We are then ready to speak the right words to others. A merry, worshipful heart on the inside produces blessings to those on the outside.

7. **Be thankful you can store your treasures in heaven.** We aren't just thankful for getting out of hell—we're full of gratitude to be on our way to heaven! We're thankful for the ability to store our treasures in a place that will never take it from us or allow it to decay or

fade away. This is not a selfish attitude because it is the kingdom's design.

The eternal things we do on this earth are the things that glorify God and bless others. These things last, affect the eternity of others, and bring great pleasure to God. Beyond anything that we can imagine as worthy, eternal treasures are worth keeping. Jesus said we are to store up our treasures. It's His idea, not ours. It brings Him glory. What about those crowns? We cast them at His feet. The more treasures we store, the more we can give back to Him in worship.

———

Let's set our affections. Let's destroy the things that tie us to this world. Let's develop our ability to focus on the stuff of the kingdom and to live in peace. Let's become students of the Word of God and speaking in His name. Let's store our valuables in the same place we focus our hearts—in heaven.

Chapter 24

The Benefits of Being Thankful vs. Grumbling

Thanksgiving can, for many people, be a time of gathering family to eat and celebrate. Ball games and conversations. Laughter and stories. But the overall concept of thanksgiving is more than a holiday for meals and family gatherings. It should be a lifestyle.

Why? Every motive and every attitude creates an energy in a given direction. Behaviors do the same.

The energy generated in any specific direction is a dynamic of a person's choice, motive, attitude, or behavior. The dynamic is the force that stimulates change in outcome or direction. It isn't passive or inert. Instead, it is active and has a predictable course. A *complaint*, for example, sets a dynamic in motion that is different from the dynamic a *compliment* sets in motion.

Paul, in writing to the Philippians, says to do *all* things without murmuring or disputing.

However, there's another list of things we reserve for our grumbling and strife. This is acceptable in our society and in most churches across America. From the same mouth comes thanksgiving and grumbling, joy and gladness, complaining and disputes. This is not what Paul had in mind. He said to do *all* things, not just some things, without complaining. Philippians 2:14–15 instructs, *"Do all things without murmurings and disputings: That ye may be blameless and harmless, the sons of God, without rebuke, in the midst of a crooked and perverse nation, among whom ye shine as lights in the world. ..."*

When we are unhappy and grumbling over things, we set a dynamic into motion. It will cause controversy—or argument—with others, and we will be at fault. We begin to do harm with our negativity, and often we will need someone to speak against our grumbling to get us back on track. Biblical rebuke is merciful when it is done with meekness and gentleness. It guides us back to the right path and keeps us safe, productive, and in our position of hope. We give and receive biblical rebuke for the good of all.

We stay blameless, above rebuke, and shining like lights when we become "thanks-givers." When we "err in spirit," or go astray, instruction in God's Word is the quickest way to get back on track. So, when we understand and learn doctrine, we will stop grumbling and become givers of thanks: *"They also that erred in spirit shall come to understand, and they that murmured shall learn doctrine"* (Isaiah 29:24).

We gain wisdom and understanding from the Scriptures. Understanding leads us to *know* the cause–effect relationship between an attitude and its result, between a motive and its result, and between a behavior and its result. Understanding enables us to know *why* a thing happened—the dynamics.

People who murmur need to learn doctrine. Scriptural doctrines are designed to help us achieve maximum health—mentally, emotionally, physically, spiritually, and socially. One example of a doctrine in Scripture is *eschatology*, which concerns future events. When we understand what is going to happen in the future, as it is given in prophecy, we will no longer grumble about future events. As Christians, we can give thanks for the future. We get a bigger picture, and as our grumbling and complaining gives way to the Truth, we are thankful.

The Dynamics of Thanksgiving

When we engage in thanksgiving, it elevates us and others, and it glorifies God. Here are thirteen ways powerful dynamics are associated with thanksgiving:

1. **Thankfulness causes us to acknowledge benefits.** The "grumbler" cannot see the benefits. His glass is always half-empty. Because grumbling is a condition of the heart and mind, a dynamic is produced that virtually scales the eyes to seeing anything positive. People who grumble can't even see God correctly. Only thanksgiving will give us a new and right perspective: *"And they sang together by course in praising and giving thanks unto the LORD; because he is good, for his mercy endureth for ever..."* (Ezra 3:11).

2. **Thankfulness creates a positive response: celebration.** In the book of Nehemiah, they were celebrating by singing and playing cymbals, psalteries, and harps. They were celebrating the rebuilding of the wall in Jerusalem, and their joy spread around them. They had reason to rejoice, and their rejoicing produced even more rejoicing: *"And at the dedication of the wall of Jerusalem they sought the Levites out of all their places, to bring them to Jerusalem, to keep the dedication with gladness, both with thanksgivings, and with singing, with cymbals, psalteries, and with harps. And the sons of the singers gathered themselves together, both out of the plain country round about Jerusalem, and from the villages of Netophathi"* (Nehemiah 12:27–28).

3. **Thankfulness enables us to joyfully see God clearly.** Singing helps us all to be joyful, and we don't have to be on a worship team to feel uplifted when giving thanks to God in song. When we magnify something, we make it bigger. Through song, we magnify God. We make Him bigger and bigger before our eyes, and

we see Him more clearly. Worship can change our entire perception of God. He dwells in our praises, and that alone is cause for rejoicing. Our thanksgiving magnifies Him: *"I will praise the name of God with a song, and will magnify him with thanksgiving"* (Psalm 69:30).

4. **Thankfulness is a means of demonstrating God's goodness.** Many times, Jesus refers to His followers as sheep in His pasture. He is our *Good* Shepherd, and He tends us and cares for us. This picture of care and safety should spark our thanksgiving and inspire us to show our praise for Him. Show me a father and mother who show thankfulness to the Lord, and I'll show you children who have a better chance in life than anyone else. How will our children learn to love God if all we do is grumble and complain? Will they be inclined to love Him? Our example to our children teaches them how to know God, to love Him, to respond to Him, and to be emotionally and spiritually sensitive to Him. Parents have the power to raise generations of "thanks-givers." Psalm 79:13 says, *"So we thy people and sheep of thy pasture will give thee thanks for ever: we will shew forth thy praise to all generations."*

5. **God inhabits the praises of Israel.** He's right in the middle of them. He loves to receive our praise and He gives us joy, gladness, hope, and assurance as we bask in His presence. Psalm 22:3 says, *"But thou art holy, O thou that inhabitest the praises of Israel."*

6. **Thankfulness prepares us to receive in the sanctuary.** When we enter God's house, we should come prepared with thanksgiving and praise. We are thankful for Him and bless His name. We come ready and expecting, as a thankful people prepared to worship our Lord. Our ability to receive from Him is affected by our attitude. Grumblers will not get much, if anything, from times of worship. Thanks-givers open themselves fully for

great deposits to take place. The Lord is good, His mercy is everlasting, and His Truth endures for all generations. We come into the sanctuary with this awareness and this dynamic set in motion: *"Enter into his gates with thanksgiving, and into his courts with praise: be thankful unto him, and bless his name. For the Lord is good; his mercy is everlasting; and his truth endureth to all generations"* (Psalm 100:4–5).

7. **Thankfulness reduces discontent.** What happens when people know God but decide not to worship Him as God? What happens when they aren't thankful? What if a person knows Him and then stops worshiping and stops being thankful? What happens when they do not glorify Him? The Bible says they become evil in their imaginations, and they become vain in their thinking. They literally can't think straight. Not only have their brains become damaged; their hearts are darkened.

When hearts are darkened and all that can be seen is the negative in this world, people become discontent. They grumble. They change their thinking and start worshiping the wrong things. Finally, God gives them over to their imaginations. When God lets go of someone, that is the worst spiritual condition anyone can experience. It is a frightening and devastating thing. All this loss started because the person didn't glorify God with a thankful heart: *"Because that, when they know God, they glorified him not as God, neither were thankful; but became vain in their imaginations, and their foolish heart was darkened"* (Romans 1:21).

We are full of thanksgiving when we are rooted and built up in Him and established in positive faith.

Colossians 2:7 says it this way: *"Rooted and built up in Him, and stablished in the faith, as ye have been taught, abounding therein with thanksgiving."*

8. **Thankfulness enables us to realize hidden benefits.** People who grumble about everything misses out on

hidden benefits. They are ready to point out the bad, the negative, the way something will *not* work out, or how a thing will end in disaster. They do not hold on to the Scriptures that tell us all things will work together for the good for those who love God. Their faith is based on his imagination. They lack a God-sized perspective, so they don't expect positive things to happen.

When we are thankful, we get the hidden benefit of contentment. When we trust in God's power and perspective, we realize the hidden benefit of peace in all circumstances: "*And we know that all things work together for the good to them that love God, to them who are called according to His purpose*" (Romans 8:28). "*Giving thanks always for all things unto God and the Father in the name of our Lord Jesus Christ*" (Ephesians 5:20).

When we are thankful, we are sure that all things will work according to His plan of perfect love toward those called by Him. Only those who give thanks can peer into even the darkest situations and know that God is at work, causing the unknown and unseen to work out for the best: "*In every thing give thanks: for this is the will of God in Christ Jesus concerning you*" (1 Thessalonians 5:18).

We can trust God in all things; therefore, we can give thanks in everything and for all things. He is faithful. He will bring the best result. It is His will that we give thanks.

9. **Thankfulness produces unimaginable peace.** We can relax and worry about nothing. We give thanks in everything and for all things. We pray about everything and know all things will work out for our good. These are absolutes. *All* things. Everything. When we pray and give thanks, making our requests known to God, we receive a peace we cannot describe.

It surpasses all human understanding. That's why I call it "unimaginable."

This peace of God will calm our hearts and minds. We have no need to worry or stress. We want to keep our minds in a world that is going mad without God. He guarantees that He'll care for us—we need only to pray, give thanks, and request His care:

> *"Be careful for nothing; but in every thing by prayer and supplication with thanksgiving let your requests be made known unto God.*
>
> *And the peace of God, which passeth all understanding, shall keep your hearts and minds through Christ Jesus."* (Philippians 4:6–7)

10. **Thankfulness affects every area of life in a positive way.** Thanksgiving will affect each area of our lives— grumbling will, too. Thanksgiving doesn't mean we ignore the troubles around us or that we bury our heads in the sand. Yes, we are very aware of this world's decline and the real, tangible hurts in our lives. Yet, rather than focus on the problems, we choose to focus on God. We take our concerns to Him and trust Him with the outcomes. We joyfully, thankfully, hopefully, and expectantly trust in Him. We don't ask for His help because we believe we will get our way. Instead, we ask because we know with absolute assurance that His ways are best. Grumblers have no such hope. They are left helpless in their own understanding and misery.

11. **Thanksgiving affects the way we pray.** When we have a thankful heart, we approach prayer in a different way. When we set aside any incorrect thinking, we are more receptive to God's voice and can focus on praising Him. Colossians 4:2 instructs, *"Continue in prayer, and watch in the same with thanksgiving."*

12. **Thanksgiving affects our relationships.** How can we not be thankful for each other? We are blessed to stand with our brothers and sisters in prayer, thanksgiving, service, and fellowship. In 2 Thessalonians 1:3, we are told, *"We are bound to thank God always for you, brethren...."*

13. **Thanksgiving affects the food we eat.** When something affects the food we eat, it also affects our health. We thank God for our food before consuming it. We receive it with thanksgiving. Some people tell us to abstain from meat, or other foods, that God created for our use and enjoyment. The Word of God and prayer sanctify the food He created. In 1 Timothy 4:3–5, we are told, *"Commanding to abstain from meats, which God hath created to be received with thanksgiving of them which believe and know the truth. For every creature of God is good, and nothing to be refused, if it be received with thanksgiving: For it is sanctified by the word of God and prayer."*

God tells us to give thanks, and we have every reason to give thanks. The grumbler can grumble on and miss the abundant life our Lord has come to give us. Instead, we choose to remain blameless, harmless, without rebuke, and shining like lights in this new kingdom. In our new way of living, God receives all the glory and thanks. So begin now. Right now. Take time to give God thanks.

Chapter 25

Overcoming the Consequences of Being Judgmental

Judge Not

When we notice someone behaving a particular way, we quickly critique their motives. A facial expression might look angry, so we assume that person is mad. A tone of voice might sound harsh, so we guess that person is mean. But we do not know the story. We can quickly conclude incorrectly. He might be sad instead of mad. She might have just heard devastating news.

In His inaugural address, Jesus taught the multitudes how to live their personal lives. He told them how to respond when they were persecuted or mistreated by others. He taught them the model of prayer and warned of the consequences of not forgiving. He warns us not to judge in Matthew 7:1: *"Judge not, that ye be not judged."* It's like the command to "forgive, so that you may be forgiven."

Here Jesus offers us a warning against judging others. Just like the positive and uplifting things we do for others are returned to us, so do the negative and destructive things come back to us. If we judge, we'll be judged. We'll be judged for the very same things we judge others for, and we will get the same amount of judgment as we allotted to them: "*Judge not, that ye be not judged. For with what judgment ye judge, ye shall be judged: and with what measure ye mete, it shall be measured to you again*" (Matthew 7:1–2).

People in today's culture—including Christians—can be extremely judgmental. We judge other parents on how they parent. We judge the way people choose to spend their money. We judge world leaders and their policies. We judge people on the clothes they wear, their hair color, and the size of their waistline. We judge "how Christian" someone is acting or how many ministries they support. We judge the world, and we judge the church. We talk about what we see in ways that are unproductive and condemning.

However, in this new kingdom, or grouping of people, Jesus said there was to be *no* judging. He did not come to judge the world, so why should we? The church should be a judgment-free zone—and not just when we're in the church building! We are not to judge…ever. People should find sanctuary within our congregations. Churches should be the safest place in the whole world.

We need to understand judging others is wrong because *judgment belongs to God.* God, even with His perfect knowledge of our failures and how far we miss the mark, is merciful toward us. We should extend the same mercy to others. He alone is holy and perfect, and He alone can rightfully judge. When fellow imperfect humans go around judging one another, their judgment is not from perfect knowledge and an understanding of what they judge.

Not only does judgment come back to us by the people we judge; also God says He will judge us for being judgmental. He is the only one who has the right to do so: "*Be ye therefore merciful, as your Father also is merciful. Judge not, and ye shall not be judged: condemn not, and ye shall not be condemned: forgive, and ye shall be forgiven*" (Luke 6:36–37). Only God's judgment is true. Judgment is His job, not ours: "*But we are sure that the judgment of God is according to truth against them which commit such things*" (Romans 2:2).

We will escape the curse of the law (death), but we do not escape the demands of the law. The law demands that we obey it. There are both natural consequences for disregarding the law on this earth and eternal consequences when we face the judgment seat of Christ. We will be held accountable for disobedience to it. It safeguards our lives when we follow it. Romans 2:3 says, *"And thinkest thou this, O man, that judgest them which do such things, and doest the same, that thou shalt escape the judgment of God?"*

Satan Judged Others

Judging others invades the responsibility, office, position, and right of God. When we put ourselves in the position of judge, we are playing God and usurping His authority. In fact, this is exactly what Satan did. Satan wanted to be like the Most High God, so he exalted himself to God's position. When we judge, we not only move ourselves from common humanity and presume we have the competence and authority to judge our fellow man, we act like Satan! We let our ego and pride take over. We can't be me-ruling and God-ruling at the same time.

Paul said Jesus will do the judging at the right time, and not before. No one else has the right to step in: *"Who art thou that judgest another man's servant? to his own master he standeth or falleth. Yea, he shall be holden up: for God is able to make him stand"* (Romans 14:4).

There are two ways we can judge ourselves. We can judge another person's actions and reveal our own actions because we do the same things we speak against. We can also misjudge ourselves. We can self-destruct as we pick apart our thoughts, words, and actions with impossible scrutiny. Then Satan can go to work on someone else because he's won the victory in our lives.

We can become so afraid of what others think of us that we become enslaved to their opinions and condemn ourselves for not meeting *their* expectations. Paul said he doesn't judge himself or others but leaves it up to the right person at the right time—Jesus. There can only be one master:

"For I know nothing by myself; yet am I not hereby justified: but he that judgeth me is the Lord.

Therefore judge nothing before the time, until the Lord come, who both will bring to light the hidden things of darkness, and will make manifest the counsels of the hearts: and then shall every man have praise of God."   (1 Corinthians 4:4–5)

Ways Judging Damages Us

The fact that Jesus warned us against judging others should be reason enough not to do it. But there are additional reasons to avoid judging because it negatively impacts our everyday lives. Here are nine.

1. **Judging escalates to more judging.** This mandate tells us not to judge people. We do judge things. We judge the difference between right and wrong. However, we do not judge people: *"But he that is spiritual judgeth all things, yet he himself is judged of no man"* (1 Corinthians 2:15).

   When we judge, it magnifies judgment. If we judge our spouse, he or she will judge us back. If we judge our children, they will judge us back. This is the law of sowing and reaping. We can have whole families judging each other all day long. Once someone starts, it comes right back. Our churches can function the same way. If we point out another person's moral failures, criticize them, or argue about everything we disagree with, we set up the atmosphere for more judgment. This kind of atmosphere is toxic, and a church will not thrive or survive under those conditions.

   Likewise, families who judge everything in the culture around them will also live in judgment of each other and pass this on to future generations: *"Woe unto them that call evil good, and good evil; that put darkness for light, and light for darkness; that put bitter for sweet, and sweet for bitter"* (Isaiah 5:20).

2. **Judging destroys a merciful disposition.** We cannot judge people and love them at the same time. Likewise, we cannot be judgmental and merciful toward a person at the same time. (Mercy is born out of love.) We've already learned that the merciful will receive mercy. When we judge, we destroy our merciful disposition toward others and forfeit God's merciful disposition toward us.

3. **When we judge, we condemn.** There's a direct relationship between judging and condemning. Both find fault, accuse, and go looking for ways to point the finger. Yet God is not out to get people, or He would have gotten us a long time ago. When we think *we* are God's representation of judgment, we are hindering others from coming to salvation *and* discouraging our fellow Christians. Satan is the accuser of the brethren, and he would like to see us condemned forever.

   If we are like Christ, we will not do as Satan does. Jesus came to save us, not to accuse and condemn us: *"For God sent not his Son into the world to condemn the world; but that the world through him might be saved"* (John 3:17).

   One of the most powerful examples of Jesus's mercy is in the account of the adulterous woman. We looked at this story earlier, but it bears repeating. Some Pharisees (the most religious Jews in New Testament times) brought a woman to Jesus. She was sexually involved with a man who was not her husband. They were ready to stone her. The Pharisees wanted to force Jesus into judging the woman and then condemning her to death. Many would have jumped at the chance to pronounce a verdict on the woman, but Jesus took His time. He had a point to make. He didn't overreact. In fact, He didn't react at all.

He said, "Let him that is without sin, cast the first stone." Then He stooped down and began to write in the sand. I suspect He started writing the name of one of the accusers and then a woman's name next to it. Then another accuser's name and a name next to it. One by one, they walked away. When Jesus stood up, they were all gone. From the oldest to the youngest, they had to face their own sins. Jesus taught, "No judging!"

> *"When Jesus had lifted up himself, and saw none but the woman, he said unto her, Woman, where are those thine accusers? hath no man condemned thee?*
>
> *She said, No man, Lord. And Jesus said unto her, Neither do I condemn thee: go, and sin no more."* (John 8:10–11)

Jesus told her to stop sinning and go on her way. It's not that He condoned her adultery. He wanted it to stop, but He was kind to her. Likewise, we will never get people to stop sinning by condemning them. It's not God's strategy. Judging always interferes with the agenda of Jesus.

Many times, we judge out of a knee-jerk reaction. We may think we see something improper. When we make assumptions and act on them, then we condemn the ones we suspect, whether they are guilty or not. When we are too quick to step in and act as judge, we are usurping Jesus and the way He would handle situations. We should stop and think before we judge an action. We need to have mercy for people, even though their deeds may be evil. Remember, Jesus was judged and condemned, when He came to condemn no one.

4. **We have no excuse.** Jesus came to save, and He delights in saving. Conversely, people who judge and condemn others delight in judging and condemning.

The truth is, if any of us had been present when they brought the adulterous woman to Jesus, we could not have lifted a single stone against her. We are all like sheep gone astray. None of us is righteous—no, not even one. We are disqualified from passing judgment. We have no excuse: "*Therefore thou art inexcusable, O man, whosoever thou art that judgest: for wherein thou judgest another, thou condemnest thyself; for thou that judgest doest the same things*" (Romans 2:1).

5. **Judgment destroys the incentive to repent.** Are we jealous of God's goodness and mercy for others? Do we wish He'd agree with us on how to handle the sins of others? Would we want Him to agree with the people who would design *our* punishment? In 1 Corinthians 13, it says that love suffers long. People come to God because He is good and loving, not because He's a condemning judge. He wants us to live. He does not want anyone to perish. His kindness leads us, and everyone else, to repent. Romans 2:4 says, "*Or despisest thou the riches of his goodness and forbearance and longsuffering; not knowing that the goodness of God leadeth thee to repentance?*"

6. **Judging shows a hardness of heart.** Hardness of heart shows a lack of compassion toward others. We have no mercy for the offender; instead, we feel wrath. Unfortunately, we are storing up our wrath against the day of wrath when God will judge us. Judging others indicates we are asking to be judged. In His kingdom, Jesus banned judgment for the good of each of us: "*But after thy hardness and impenitent heart treasurest up unto thyself wrath against the day of wrath and revelation of the righteous judgment of God; Who will render to every man according to his deeds*" (Romans 2:5–6).

7. **Judging abuses and misuses the law.** When we gossip about someone, even if it's true, we are judging that

person. When we do so, we judge the law. We speak evil of the law and determine that the law justifies our condemnation of others. When we use the law to judge others, we set ourselves up illegally as judges. We are to follow the law just like anyone else, not presume to be the judges of it. James 4:11–12 says, "*Speak not evil one of another, brethren. He that speaketh evil of his brother, and judgeth his brother, speaketh evil of the law, and judgeth the law: but if thou judge the law, thou art not a doer of the law, but a judge. There is one lawgiver, who is able to save and to destroy: who art thou that judgest another?*"

8. **Judging destroys discernment.** Discernment is an alternative to judgment. Discernment considers an *action* and determines whether it's correct or incorrect. However, judgment always negatively affects the *person*: "*But strong meat belongeth to them that are of full age, even those who by reason of use have their senses exercised to discern both good and evil*" (Hebrews 5:14).

9. **As Jesus warned, judging others will bring judgment upon our own heads.** Judging usurps God's natural design, and it will destroy relationships. Jesus, our example, shows mercy. It's clear that, as believers, we should have nothing to do with passing judgments. When we participate in judging others, we are in dangerous territory and reflect the deceiver (Satan) more than our Father.

The Evils of Judging

Not only does judging others damage our walk with Him and create havoc in our everyday lives; it emanates from evil. Here are eight ways judging is evil.

1. **Judging comes out of an evil spirit.** Some people get a devilish pleasure in sharing evil reports. They delight in finding, retelling, and harshly rebuking others.

2. **Judging cultivates a condemning disposition.** Habitual judging alters people's disposition. They become bitter, negative, fault-finding, and condemning.

3. **Judging exalts self and displays a sense of superiority.** Judging comes from self-righteousness. It looks down on others. Sometimes people judge to pull others down and lift themselves up.

4. **Judging makes an accusatory posture.** It allies with Satan, the accuser, and does not resemble the meekness of Christ.

5. **Judging involves sinful words.** Judging involves hate, gossip, and ridicule. It bashes our brothers and sisters, launching attacks on the people we *should* hold dearest. It insults and humiliates others and dissolves unity.

6. **Judging holds grudges.** It spreads bitterness and grudges among the church, personally, and in other groups.

7. **Judging robs us of mercy.** Judging keeps mercy from you and from others. It disregards forgiveness and reconciliation.

8. **Judging usurps God's role.** Worst of all, judging is a demonstration of iniquity and an indication of a sinful nature. It usurps God's role and places us at the head.

Judging others is contagious. It spreads, leaving destruction behind it. We can rightly discern and cautiously and lovingly confront, but judgment is not for us to give. *Confrontation* and *condemnation* are two different things. We aren't out to offend others and push them away, but to gracefully restore them. We cannot judge others and touch their souls at the same time.

We should show the way so others can respond to this wonderful grace of God. Judge not!

Love is the greatest force, and it, too, is contagious. Genuine love proves that we are Christ's followers. He said it would show the world that we are His disciples. Christians should be the nicest people in the whole world. We should be the most loving and forgiving. If we are to win the world for Christ, we will win it with love.

Chapter 26

The Positive Alternative to Judging

Judging, Discerning, and a Meek Approach

F ame. Fortune. Finances. Big businesses and large churches. Being known. Being seen. Those are examples of selfish ambitions. People pursue power. They desire, demand, perform, and push.

Look at the fall of Satan. That is just what he did.

At the heart of his fall, Satan wanted God's role. He wanted to make the decisions, call the shots, and receive the praise. He wanted to be the master. He wanted to take over a throne that was not his, to rule over things and people he did not create or love. That is the essence of "iniquity," the Bible's word for narcissism. However, he could not rule over people who didn't belong to him. Instead, he is the accuser of the brethren, and he has proven to be merciless.

How Judgment Differs from Discernment

We've learned that God is the only righteous authority, and He alone judges the people He has made. We belong to Him, and we are accountable to Him alone.

Let's compare a judgmental spirit with that of Christ-like discernment:

1. Judgment accepts hearsay and doesn't vet the facts. Discernment is based on intellectual honesty and does not accept hearsay as evidence.

2. Judgment makes conclusions and condemns. Discernment looks for causes. Why is the person in this situation?

3. Judgment avoids self-evaluation because it's busy evaluating others. With discernment, people compare other people's experiences with their own.

4. Judgment is hostile to the one being judged. Discernment conveys genuine concern.

5. Judgmental people usually have the same or similar issues as the people they judge. A discerning person is looking for a solution and overcomes the errors in his or her own life to help others.

6. Judgment is careless and makes outlandish accusations with a pointed finger. Discernment is tender, careful, sensitive, and understanding.

7. Judgment rejects the person. Discernment rejects the sin.

8. Judgment points out the wrong. Discernment points toward the solution.

9. Judgment gives no direction but condemns and abandons the person to their fate. Discernment helps to restore the person and assists them as they go forward.

10. Judgment discourages the people being judged because it is focused on reaction. Discernment encourages

people to move toward victory, leaving them room to respond.

11. Judgment is proud and assumes a high position over others. Discernment is humble, with people viewing others as fellow sinners saved by grace.

12. Judgment is self-exalting and seeks to be served. Discernment has the heart of a servant who comes to help, not to harm.

13. Judgment is cold and harsh. Discernment is gentle.

14. Judgment is motivated by anger and malice. Discernment is motivated by love—which chooses the highest good for others without personal benefit.

15. Judgment is mean. Discernment is merciful.

16. Judgment is indifferent to the other person. Discernment compassionately considers the other person.

17. Judgment is destructive. Discernment is constructive.

18. Judgment is thoughtless and doesn't calculate any unintended consequences. Discernment is thoughtful and weighs the outcomes. Other people are aware that they have been considered.

19. Judgment is personally blaming. Discernment acknowledges that no one is perfect.

20. Judgment is negative. Discernment is positive.

21. Judgment is worldly and world-like. Discernment is Christ-like.

22. Judgment is evil. Discernment is righteous.

One of the biggest complaints against the church today is that it's composed of hypocritical, judgmental people. *Ouch.* When we spend our time judging others, we are not fulfilling our purpose. We can see from this extensive list why we aren't winning the world for Christ. Judgment puts people down, while discernment lifts people up. Judgment is cold and destructive, while discernment is brokenhearted and redemptive. Discernment uses the situation to demonstrate the love of God, not the judgment of man. The church must exercise discernment and must not get caught up in the demonic pleasure of pointing out the sins of others.

Judging prevents self-evaluation. Jesus rebuked a group of Pharisees for always finding fault in others when they themselves were full of sin and iniquity. He called them hypocrites.

We Must Not Be Pharisees

If the church in America is going to succeed in its mission for Christ, we need to get rid of the judgment and exercise sincerity, honesty, and love. We cannot draw others to the cross by bashing them for every fault we find or by displaying our own righteousness or pretentiousness. We cannot judge others while we remain sinful ourselves. We cannot be Pharisees:

> *"Judge not, that ye be not judged.*
>
> *For with what judgment ye judge, ye shall be judged: and with what measure ye mete, it shall be measured to you again.*
>
> *And why beholdest thou the mote that is in thy brother's eye, but considerest not the beam that is in thine own eye?*
>
> *Or how wilt thou say to thy brother, Let me pull out the mote out of thine eye; and, behold, a beam is in thine own eye?*
>
> *Thou hypocrite, first cast out the beam out of thine own eye; and then shalt thou see clearly to cast out the mote out of thy brother's eye."* (Matthew 7:1–5)

How does "Phariseeism" work? A Pharisee beholds the "motes." A *mote* is an imperfection, and in the context of Matthew 7, also very small. It's interesting that Jesus uses the word *beholdest*, which means to concentrate on something and to stare at it with intensity. We know how hard it is to find a speck of dust or debris in another person's eye. We must look hard.

The Pharisees would go around trying to find some little blemish. They wanted to blow it out of proportion. They had their magnifying glass on the world around them, self-appointed to judge wrongs. They considered themselves experts, and they had to watch closely. They were ever-ready to point out an inconsistency or slip-up, and they judged it all the same. They overlooked the good in a person and instead condemned them for the parts they got wrong. They looked at everyone with unfriendly eyes.

At the same time, the Pharisees disregarded their own state of being. They were so set on finding the faults in others that they did not take the magnifying glass to their own thoughts, words, and deeds. Their lack of attention to their own faults made them spiritually blind to other people's needs.

Hypocrites are not fit to judge. We cannot disguise, cover up, overlook, or excuse our own sins. We must first cast the beam out of our own eyes. We must turn the concentration off others and back on ourselves. We are not only to examine ourselves for sin; we are to also take the proper actions. We must acknowledge, confess, repent, and perform restitution for our sins. With an experienced heart focused on resolution, restoration, and healing, we can *then* help someone else do the same. How can we help our brothers and sisters if we're trying to see around a plank stuck in our own eyes?

We Must Search Ourselves before Helping Others

The Scriptures instruct us to search and test our ways and turn to the Lord. We must determine our status in the faith and prove ourselves. We must acknowledge and then resolve our own failings if we ever hope to help others with theirs: *"Let us search and try our ways, and turn again to the LORD"* (Lamentations 3:40). And 2 Corinthians 13:5 says, *"Examine yourselves, whether ye be in the faith; prove your own selves. Know ye not your own selves, how that Jesus Christ is in you, except ye be reprobates?"*

Until our own hearts are broken with our conditions, we don't get to touch anyone else's eyes. Otherwise, we can do great damage to them. Psalm 139 instructs believers to ask God to search their hearts. Sometimes we are unable to search ourselves, and we need His help to find our hidden motives, attitudes, or wrongs. We ask Him to check us out and then to lead in the everlasting way: *"Search me, O God, and know my heart: try me, and know my thoughts: And see if there be any wicked way in me, and lead me in the way everlasting"* (Psalm 139:23–24).

The psalmist David asked God to create in him a pure heart and to renew a right spirit within him. We all need a right spirit, a spirit that does not judge or condemn. Life and death are in the power of the tongue. We can use discernment to speak life to those around us, and when we speak with love, our words lead to resolution. David went on to say that once he had a renewed spirit and purified heart, he would teach others in God's ways. This is the way Jesus taught. This is the way He desires for His kingdom to function. We get ourselves right first. Then, in mercy, we reach out to others: *"Create in me a clean heart, O God; and renew a right spirit within me"* (Psalm 51:10).

If we are going to remove something from someone else's eye, we must be close to them and be very careful as we remove the problem. We come close to them slowly and with tenderness, and then we examine the problem. Trust is built when we gently point out what we see and offer help to them. This requires spiritual maturity.

Spiritual maturity deals honestly with oneself before it helps others. If we do not intend to deal with ourselves, we cannot deal with others. Even if we see legitimate sins in others, we should not address them if we are not addressing our own faults. We must be qualified.

Restoration requires a spirit of meekness. Meekness knows that, but for the grace of God, we are the same as that person. That's what he or she needs – the grace of God, shown through our loving approach, words, and actions. Galatians 6:1 says, *"Brethren, if a man be overtaken in a fault, ye which are spiritual, restore such one in the spirit of meekness; considering thyself, lest thou also be tempted."*

Christianity has devolved to the point that it often has little resemblance to the kingdom Jesus spoke of in His inaugural address. The fundamental intention of God is for us to be like His Son. We are to walk in meekness and remember how hopeless we would be if it weren't for the grace of God.

My hope is that we will return to the Lord as a sweet-smelling fragrance as we properly touch the lives of others.

Chapter 27

Watching Out for Dogs and Swine

I n the 1957 classic film *Old Yeller*, we see a glimpse of a once-loyal and loved dog turning on his master after contracting rabies. As his master brings him food, Old Yeller growls, snarls, and attacks the very one he once followed. The grieving master, Travis, is forced to shoot the dog. Jesus warns us that we should expect the same response from the dogs and swine that have rejected the Truth. If we bring something holy to them, they're going to tear us to pieces. They will speak evil of the things we hold so dear, treasured, and holy.

Jesus modeled for us how to lovingly and, without judgment, confront the faults of others. As followers of Christ, we must understand the difference between *judgment* and *meek discernment*. All reconciliation starts as we take care of our own sins first, so we can see to help others.

However, Jesus warns believers of people *of the world*. A sad truth is that we will encounter those who are more like animals in their thoughts and behaviors. The Scripture compares them to dogs or swine: "*Give not that which is holy unto the dogs, neither cast ye your pearls before swine, lest they trample them under their feet, and turn again and rend you*" (Matthew 7:6).

At first glance, this verse is odd. However, Jesus tells us we must discern who the dogs and swine are so we don't give them what is holy.

Five Characteristics of People to Avoid

The people Jesus warns us about have some general characteristics in common. Here are five of them:

1. **They are compared to animals.** There are people in our lives who are driven by their carnal nature and instincts. In this way, they are more like animals because they are not in control of their own bodies.

2. **They are compared to *dirty* animals.** They are not only referred to as animals, but as *dirty* animals. The Scripture is not referring to the trained puppy you have in your house, but to dogs in ancient times. They were wild. They fed off the garbage heaps and were mangy mutts. Likewise, swine will eat *anything*. That includes urine, excrement, decaying flesh or vegetables, and even cancerous growths off other pigs.

3. **They will not appreciate the precious things.** Jesus knew that we cannot entrust some people with the things of God. Our meekness, gentleness, and discernment will not help them. They will not respect or appreciate holy things. Swine do not know what to do with pearls, and neither will some people receive God's graciousness with gladness. Swine will trample pearls, and some people will trample the things of God.

4. **They will hatefully twist our words.** They will try to use our good words against us. They will accuse us of being hateful if we speak to them about being righteous. If we speak with them about holiness, they will ridicule us and say we are being "holier than thou." If we tell them a certain sin is not appropriate, they even may file a lawsuit against us.

5. **They will tear us to pieces.** They will respond with anger, hatred, and wrath as we attempt to share with them from honesty and sincerity. They may spread rumors about us and try to discredit our reputation. Jesus warns they will turn on us and rend us. In the

Greek, *rend* means to reduce to fragments. There will be no reasonable interaction and no calm observation of the facts.

How We Discern Dogs and Swine

Obviously, identifying the "dogs and swine" in our lives is critical to protecting the holiness of Scripture. There are many ways we can discern dogs and swine among us; here are thirteen:

1. **They are not sheep that have gone astray.** We are not talking about followers of Christ who fell away from Him but are now returned. The sheep are not the dogs or swine. 1 Peter 2:25 says, *"For ye were as sheep going astray; but are now returned unto the Shepherd and Bishop of your souls."*

2. **Dogs are workers of evil that are outside the city walls.** The Scripture warns of evil workers, those who divide. Philippians 3:2 says, *"Beware of dogs, beware of evil workers, beware of the concision."* In Revelation, we find that these scavengers, these devourers, are not allowed in Jerusalem. They are outside the city walls. They keep company with lovers of evil: *"For without are dogs, and sorcerers, and whoremongers, and murderers, and idolaters, and whosoever loveth and maketh a lie"* (Revelation 22:15).

3. **Dogs were with Jesus to nail Him to the cross and are greedy for their own fill.** Psalm 22 speaks prophetically about Jesus and the scene at Calvary, and around Him were dogs. This is an analogy referring to a group of people with certain character deficiencies. He said dogs encompassed Him. The assembly of the wicked had circled Him and pierced His hands and feet: *"For dogs have compassed me: the assembly of the wicked have inclosed me: they pierced my hands and my feet"* (Psalm 22:16).

In Isaiah, he speaks of greedy dogs that never have enough. They come seeking their own agendas. They have an insatiable desire to destroy for their own gain. These people will always put you down, try to one-up you, and outdo you. They are *full* of themselves:

> *"All ye beasts of the field, come to devour, yea, all ye beasts in the forest.*
>
> *His watchmen are blind: they are all ignorant, they are all dumb dogs, they cannot bark; sleeping, lying down, loving to slumber.*
>
> *Yea, they are greedy dogs which can never have enough, and they are shepherds that cannot understand: they all look to their own way, everyone for his gain, from his quarter."*

(Isaiah 56:9–11)

4. **Swine are committed to moral uncleanness.** There was a man possessed by demons. Jesus delivered him of the unclean spirits and sent the spirits into the pigs nearby. The pigs ran violently down into the sea: "*And forthwith Jesus gave them leave. And the unclean spirits went out, and entered into the swine: and the herd ran violently down a steep place into the sea, (they were about two thousand;) and were choked in the sea*" (Mark 5:13).

Pigs are omnivores; they'll eat anything—even things that aren't even food! They are scavengers all over the world. I've been in places in where there are no toilets. The people excrete in public, and the pigs are right there to clean it up. They enjoy their own excrement and that of other animals and humans. They host an incredible number of parasites, worms, toxins, and latent diseases. Some of these are passed to humans. Jesus used swine as receptacles for the demons.

278

Like a clean pig is drawn back to the mud, Peter says the dog returns to his own vomit. Neither can help themselves, and they return to the pit they left. We learn in 2 Peter 2:22, *"But it is happened unto them according to the true proverb, The dog is turned to his own vomit again; and the sow that was washed to her wallowing in the mire."*

5. **Both dogs and pigs are those in deliberate, willful disobedience.** This isn't talking about people who have never heard the truth. These are people who have exchanged truth for a lie. The Scriptures say it would be better for them if they had never known the truth: *"For it had been better for them not to have known the way of righteousness, than, after they have known it, to turn from the holy commandment delivered unto them"* (2 Peter 2:21).

It would be better if they had never known Jesus. Wow, what a sad reality!

In 2 Peter 2:20, we are told, *"For if after they have escaped the pollutions of the world through the knowledge of the Lord and Saviour Jesus Christ, they are again entangled therein, and overcome, the latter end is worse with them than the beginning."* They escaped the pollution of the world through the knowledge of the Lord and Savior Jesus Christ and then returned to their former lives of sin. Their latter state is worse than their first. Then they become "as natural brute beasts."

This is not just backsliding. They are not content in just "unbelief"—they are motivated to destroy the faith of others and God himself. They actively want to tear down, ridicule, mock, and live in filth and moral degradation: *"But these, as natural brute beasts, made to be taken and destroyed, speak evil of the things that they understand not; and shall utterly perish in their own corruption..."* (2 Peter 2:12).

6. **Such people choose corruption over sanctification.** They choose evil over righteousness. They will perish for what they have chosen. They are hedonists and seek the reward of the unrighteous. What God says does not concern them, and they do not respect His Word. They don't care about God or anyone else: "*And shall receive the reward of unrighteousness, as they that count it pleasure to riot in the day time. Spots they are and blemishes, sporting themselves with their own deceivings while they feast with you*" (2 Peter 2:13).

7. **They glory in the things they do wrong.** They will tell us all about their exploits, as if there's nothing wrong with them. We should not associate with people like this. They pull us toward the things that have deceived them. They are shameless and proud of their actions and beliefs.

8. **They look for ways to increase their evil.** They have devouring, insatiable appetites and eyes full of adultery. They look at everyone and everything with a filter of immorality and cannot cease from such sin. They are seducers, wishing to include us in their evil. Although they are often charming, they are mentally and emotionally unstable.

9. **They have no substance.** They have left the way of truth and abandoned what they once knew. They didn't happen to wander out of the way; they purposely and deliberately left. These people are overcome by their desires. They are slaves to such cravings. They are blown about by lusts and untethered to reality. They act without consequence and are in bondage and out of control. In 2 Peter 2:17, they are described as "*wells without water, clouds that are carried with a tempest; to whom the mist of darkness is reserved for ever.*"

10. **They love to speak of their immoral lifestyle.** Often, these types of people will attempt to lure other believers away. They will speak of the rules of the church

lifestyle and compare it to the "freedom" and fun of living for self. They exaggerate their evil behavior, trying to attract others. Self-centeredness is at the core of their iniquity: *"For when they speak great swelling words of vanity, they allure through the lusts of the flesh, through much wantonness, those that were clean escaped from them who live in error"* (2 Peter 2:18).

11. **They speak of being free, but they are in bondage.** For a train, freedom doesn't mean running off the track. A train off the track isn't going *anywhere*. Its forward progress and purpose of being are stopped as long as it remains off track. Humankind is the same. Our Creator designed us to live by a certain code of ethics, standards, values, and paths—certain tracks. If we get off the tracks, we lose our freedom and purpose. *Freedom* is not the ability to do whatever we wish; it is the *power* to do what we should. People who stray lose their true freedoms. They become slaves. They talk a big talk, yet they are in bondage: *"While they promise them liberty, they themselves are the servants of corruption: for of whom a man is overcome, of the same is he brought in bondage"* (2 Peter 2:19).

   Jesus instructed believers in the path of righteousness. We will know if we are on the right path or not: *"Enter through the narrow gate. For wide is the gate and broad is the road that leads to destruction, and many enter through it. But small is the gate and narrow the road that leads to life, and only a few find it"* (Matthew 7:13–14 NIV).

How to Deal with Incurable Ungodliness

Dogs and swine no longer share the things of God with you, and we no longer try to reach them with His Word. The best strategy is to leave them alone and walk away. The *only way* they return to the fold is if they learn from the consequences of their own behavior and return in repentance: *"Let them alone: they be blind leaders of the blind. And if the blind lead the blind, both shall fall into the ditch"* (Matthew 15:14).

We remove ourselves from the presence of a fool. When we perceive that he doesn't care about the facts, we leave him alone: *"Go from the presence of a foolish man, when thou perceivest not in him the lips of knowledge"* (Proverbs 14:7).

We do not engage in his folly. We do not respond to his vain arguments or speak on his level. He will not listen to us or turn from his deception. He will only despise us: *"Answer not a fool according to his folly, lest thou also be like unto him"* (Proverbs 26:4). And Proverbs 23:9 says, *"Speak not in the ears of a fool: for he will despise the wisdom of thy words."*

Some people are past all feeling. We cannot reach them to bring them back. They are happy where they are in their lust and greed. We are to leave them there: *"Who being past feeling have given themselves over unto lasciviousness, to work all uncleanness with greediness"* (Ephesians 4:19).

Jesus tells us that we will encounter these types of people. He does not want them to be this way, and He is not telling us to be cold and uncaring. Instead, He is warning us that they will not listen to us, and we are wasting our time. He is *not* talking about refraining from preaching the Gospel to unbelievers. He's referring to the people who are devourers and destroyers, who knew the truth and left it behind. These people cannot be reached by preaching, arguments, debates, or compassion. Because our time and treasure are precious, we must share the Gospel with those who are receptive.

Is there hope for these people? Yes, but it's not going to come through us. Their own depravity will teach them. It will get hard. If they learn from that, they may be redeemed. It should be our hope and prayer that they return to the truth. Until then, they are dogs and swine. We should not try to present holy things to them, which they already know and despise. Do not allow them to trample and devour you.

So, what should we do? Two words: let go. Thank God for His instruction that keeps us from throwing our pearls before people who will not receive them. Thank God for His protection and guidance. As you thank Him, let go.

Chapter 28

How to Receive from God

Think of a time when you gave something to someone. Maybe a person expected a gift but wasn't sure what was inside the box. Maybe a person opened a box covered with birthday wrapping paper and cried because of the love he or she felt from what was received. A stranger didn't expect a gift card. A coworker didn't know you would purchase lunch.

Gifts make statements. Receiving gifts, though often difficult, is a way of realizing others meet a need or offer a statement of appreciation.

That takes us to God. He is a giver. We know that because He tells us *how* to receive from Him. It is His pleasure to give to His children.

Jesus spoke of an entirely new way of thinking, believing, speaking, and acting. In His wisdom and understanding, He showed us a new kingdom in which its members were strikingly different from all others. He wanted to draw mankind to God in an entirely new way. He taught about the God-to-man and man-to-God relationship that brings peace, joy, rewards, and eternal blessings.

He showed us the way we receive from God—we ask, seek, and knock: *"Ask, and it shall be given you; seek, and ye shall find; knock, and it shall be opened unto you"* (Matthew 7:7).

Six Ways to Prepare Ourselves to Receive from God

We are blessed to receive gifts from God, and our hearts and minds must be prepared to do so. Here are six ways we can prepare to receive gifts from God:

1. **We acknowledge the "in-between" man.** There is one God and one mediator between God and man—Jesus Christ. Through His death on the cross, Jesus acts as the bridge between sinful man and a perfect God. He is our "in-between" man, so to speak. This role is important for us to understand. Through Jesus Christ, we can receive from the Father, and He has voluntarily put Himself in that role: "*For there is one God, and one mediator between God and men, the man Christ Jesus; Who gave himself a ransom for all, to be testified in due time*" (1 Timothy 2:5–6).

    Scripture says Jesus makes intercession for us before the Father. He's our mediator. He takes our needs to the Father and demonstrates to the Father why a need or request should indeed be met. There is only one mediator. There is no one else between God and us. There is no pastor, priest, rabbi, husband, or anyone else. We have direct access to the Father only though Jesus.

    This point cannot be over-emphasized. For believers today, access to God through Jesus is our reality. This has not always been the case. This direct access to God would have been a radical shift in thinking for the Jews of Jesus's time.

    The temple was the center of Jewish religious life. Until Jesus's death on the cross, animal sacrifices were made to atone for sin, and worship consisted of following the laws passed down from Moses. Hebrews 9:1–9 describes a veil that separated the temple area from the Holy of Holies—which was the earthly dwelling place of God's very presence. Only the high priest was permitted to pass the veil. He would enter God's presence *once a year* to make atonement for *all* of Israel. This veil—estimated to be about 60 feet high and 4 inches thick—was physical in nature, but it figuratively represented our access to God.

Matthew 27:50–51 says, *"Jesus, when he had cried again with a loud voice, yielded up the ghost. And, behold, the veil of the temple was rent in twain from the top to the bottom...."* Jesus ripped the veil, both physically and figuratively. He paid, once and for all, for our sins. The law was completed, and we now have access directly to the Father through Jesus.

2. **We realize the "in-between" man's nature**. Jesus gave Himself as a ransom for all. Because He has already given Himself up for us, we can trust Him. He isn't running interference to *stop* our prayers. He's running interference to make sure they get to the Father. He's on our side.

Jesus is called "the High Priest." All the priests in the Old Testament have been canceled. We do not have to wait for an earthly high priest to make atonement for our sin once a year. We can access our High Priest every moment of the day and night. He is in tune with everything that touches us. He understands what we face and how we feel: *"For we have not a high priest which cannot be touched with the feeling of our infirmities; but was in all points tempted like as we are, yet without sin"* (Hebrews 4:15).

He knows our inadequacies, our self-doubts, and our fears. He's touched with our infirmities. How could He be that way? Because He was in all ways tempted like we are, yet He didn't sin. So, when He was here—the Creator entering creation, the Creator becoming one of His created—He experienced the same things we do. And then He conquered them.

Because the first covenant (the law) was imperfect, another one was needed. Jesus became the mediator of a better covenant, which is established on better promises:

> *"But now hath he obtained a more excellent ministry, by how much also he is the mediator of a better covenant, which was established upon better promises.*
>
> *For if that first covenant had been faultless, then should no place have been sought for the second."* (Hebrews 8:6–7)

3. **We realize we have the right to receive.** The result of His intercession in this new covenant is a simple one. We can come boldly before the throne of grace and obtain mercy. We don't have to come to God with a spirit of timidity, and there is no need to shy away. Hebrews 4:16 instructs, *"Let us therefore come boldly unto the throne of grace, that we may obtain mercy, and find grace to help in time of need."*

We are invited to come right into the throne room of the Almighty. This does not mean we are arrogant in our approach to God. Think, instead, of a child entering his or her parent's bedroom. There is a sense of comfort and "belongingness" as children approach their parents for help, advice, or just relational interaction. Children should know they can speak boldly—honestly—with their parents.

It is the same with our relationship to our heavenly Father. We come boldly because we know we are in relationship with the Father and that He loves us. He gives us grace, love, direction, and comfort in our time of need. That is why it's so important that we learn to pray.

4. **We need to ask properly.** Jesus gave us a model for prayer called the Lord's Prayer. Then He told us to ask because it will be given. I have heard parents tell their children, "I can't help you if you don't tell me what you need." Matthew 7:11 says, "*If ye then, being evil, know how to give good gifts unto your children, how much more shall your Father which is in heaven give good things to them that ask him?*"

But many people don't ask. They complain that God doesn't help them, yet they haven't asked. Some people complain that God will give the same "stuff" to the lost when they haven't asked for it. We must understand that some of God's blessings are for all His creation, and others are reserved only for His children. The Bible says He sends rain on the just and the unjust.

As believers, we are in another category. He's not just our Creator—He is our Father. What He gives us is above and beyond what He gives everyone else who is part of His creation. We ask our Father. We seek our Father. We knock at our Father's door. Like a Father, He is there to always answer us: "*Ask, and it shall be given you; seek, and ye shall find; knock, and it shall be opened unto you*" (Matthew 7:7).

To ask is to put a question to, to request, to inquire, to solicit from. So, if you have a question, a request, need additional wisdom, or need additional help in any way, you are to ask! Once we ask, however, we need to realize that God is not a magic genie granting every request exactly as it is asked.

When you were young, did you ever ask for something that wasn't good for you? Most parents don't let their children eat cookies every time they ask! Later, you realized how kind and loving a "no" might be. Sometimes it might be the right request but at the wrong time. Sometimes we ask and don't receive because we ask for the wrong things or with the wrong motives. Some things are not wise or loving for God to give us. Our motives need to align with Scripture, or the request is not what's best for us: "*Ye lust, and have not: ye kill, and desire to have, and cannot obtain: ye fight and war, yet ye have not, because ye ask not. Ye ask, and receive not, because ye ask amiss, that ye may consume it upon your lusts*" (James 4:2–3).

Jesus says if we live our lives in Him, let His words come alive in us, and then live His words out, we can ask, and it will be done: "*If ye abide in me, and my words abide in you, ye shall ask what ye will, and it shall be done unto you*" (John 15:7).

If our hearts do not condemn us (or our consciences do not convict us), then we have confidence toward God. We keep our hearts attuned to Him, and then we will receive whatever we ask of Him. He will answer us because we keep His commandments and do what pleases Him. Would a father give his car keys to a disobedient son? If he knows his son breaks the law, a wise and loving father will not give him the keys: "*Beloved, if our heart condemn us not, then have we confidence toward God. And whatsoever we ask, we receive of him, because we keep his commandments, and do those things that are pleasing in his sight*" (1 John 3:21–22).

Jesus told His disciples to ask in His name, and they would receive. The purpose of asking and receiving was to bring complete joy. God wants us to be happy. How great is our God? He is worthy of praise! He creates us, sustains us, and wants us to be happy: "*Hitherto have ye asked nothing in my name: ask, and ye shall receive, that your joy may be full*" (John 16:24).

God is able. He can give more than what we think we need or want and surprise us with the very best things. He accomplishes this through His power working within us: "*Now to him that is able to do exceeding abundantly above all that we ask or think, according to the power that worketh in us*" (Ephesians 3:20).

5. **We need to ask for some things.** We need to start
    asking our heavenly Father instead of running around
    trying to solve, gather, and control every area of our
    lives apart from Him: "*Ask, and it shall be given you;
    seek, and ye shall find; knock, and it shall be opened
    unto you: For every one that asketh receiveth; and he
    that seeketh findeth; and to him that knocketh it shall
    be opened*" (Matthew 7:7–8).

    There are three levels to inquiring of the Lord:
    asking, seeking, and knocking. Seeking is the step
    beyond asking. Some things only come by seeking.
    When we come to God as a seeker, we are seeking His
    wisdom. We search for it like silver and gold.

    Job knew firsthand that God does great things
    because he sought Him. Job describes God as
    unsearchable, marvelous, without end, an exalter, and
    a helper! These things (and more) come from seeking
    the Lord:

    > "*I would seek unto God, and unto God would I
    > commit my cause:
    > Which doeth great things and unsearchable;
    > marvellous things without number:
    > Who giveth rain upon the earth, and sendeth
    > waters upon the fields:
    > To set up on high those that be low; that those
    > which mourn may be exalted to safety.*"
    >
    > (Job 5:8–11)

    The wicked do not seek the Lord. ("Wicked"
    doesn't refer to those who sin—*everyone* sins.) The
    words "wicked" and "sinful" are not interchangeable.
    Wickedness is a state of being, while *sinfulness* is a
    state of doing. Because of pride, wicked people will not
    seek God. Pride doesn't need God for anything. Pride
    does its own thing. When ego rules, it prevents us from
    doing one of the most wonderful activities that could

ever be done—to seek God: *"The wicked, through the pride of his countenance, will not seek after God: God is not in all his thoughts"* (Psalm 10:4).

We are now living in what's described as the post-Christian era in America. This does not mean it's the end of true Christianity started by Jesus. Rather, it means the end of legalism handed down through Constantine, who started Christendom in 300 AD. In America and all over the world, churches are jammed with people who admire the sacraments and rituals but do not seek God. This is rampant in our country—people who have a form of religion but do not follow God. David said he would seek the Lord. His heart was inclined to do so. Psalm 27:8 says, *"When thou saidst, Seek my face; my heart said unto thee, Thy face, LORD, will I seek."*

We must crave the Lord. We should pursue Him so much that He is as important to us as food and water. We should make seeking God a top priority in our lives: *"O God, thou art my God; early will I seek thee: my soul thirsteth for thee, my flesh longeth for thee in a dry and thirsty land, where no water is"* (Psalm 63:1).

People who seek the Lord with their whole hearts are blessed. Actively *seeking* is the key. Psalm 119:2 says, *"Blessed are they that keep his testimonies, and that seek him with the whole heart."*

As we seek God, we get a clear picture. We'll understand the condition of the people and culture around us. We'll know why people act the way they do. This does not come to the casual observer of Christianity; it comes from seeking the Lord: *"Evil men understand not judgment: but they that seek the LORD understand all things"* (Proverbs 28:5).

The Bible holds the key to seeking the Lord. None of what we see within its pages will ever fail. We should make it our goal to seek God's wisdom as we read it, meditate on it, and make it ours. The Word of God is the best place to invest our academic energy because we will find true understanding:

> *"Seek ye out the book of the LORD, and read;*
> *no one of those shall fail, none shall want her*
> *mate: for my mouth it hath commanded, and*
> *his spirit it hath gathered them."* (Isaiah 34:16)

God says to seek Him—He is ready to be found. Like the child's game of "hide and seek," there is joy in being found. God is waiting to see if we truly want Him and if we'll put our hearts into it. He promises to be found, and then He will set us free. Jeremiah 29:13–14 promises, *"And ye shall seek me, and find me, when ye shall search for me with all your heart. And I will be found of you, saith the LORD: and I will turn away your captivity, and I will gather you from all the nations, and from all the places whither I have driven you, saith the LORD; and I will bring you again into the place whence I caused you to be carried away captive."*

Again, this knowledge of God is not casual. It's deliberate, serious, focused, and true. We ask, and we receive. We seek, and we will find. He rewards all who diligently seek Him. We don't seek Him casually. We mean it with all diligence: *"But without faith it is impossible to please him: for he that cometh to God must believe that he is, and that he is a rewarder of them that diligently seek him"* (Hebrews 11:6).

We ask. We seek. Everyone who asks receives, and anyone who seeks will find: *"For every one that askesth receiveth; and he that seeketh findeth; and to him that knocketh it shall be opened"* (Matthew 7:8).

6. **We need to knock.** God tells us to knock. To illustrate this point, Luke's account recounts a story Jesus gave to His followers. At the heart of the illustration is the principle of persistence. We are not to knock once and

give up. We are to persist in our knocking and not take "no" for an answer. When we knock, God will answer:

> *"And he said unto them, Which of you shall have a friend, and shall go unto him at midnight, and say unto him, Friend, lend me three loaves;*
>
> *For a friend of mine in his journey is come to me, and I have nothing to set before him?*
>
> *And he from within shall answer and say, Trouble me not: the door is now shut, and my children are with me in bed; I cannot rise and give thee.*
>
> *I say unto you, Though he will not rise and give him, because he is his friend, yet because of his importunity he will rise and give him as many as he needeth.*
>
> *And I say unto you, Ask, and it shall be given you; seek, and ye shall find; knock, and it shall be opened unto you.*
>
> *For every one that asketh receiveth; and he that seeketh findeth; and to him that knocketh it shall be opened."*   (Luke 11:5–10)

How do we know all this asking, seeking, and knocking really works? In Matthew 7:9–11, Jesus made a comparison to the earthly father and son relationship. He said if a son asked his father for some bread, would the father give him a stone? If a son asked his dad for a fish, would his father give him a snake? If a son asks for something to eat, would a father give him something inedible or harmful? Jesus said if we, being evil, sinful humanity, know how to give good gifts to our children, how much more shall our Father in heaven give good things to those who ask Him?

In this example of Scripture, if the first thing is true, the next thing is even truer. If the oldest brother is too young to get a driver's license, his younger brother is that much more too young to get a driver's license. If we who are evil give good things to our children, how much more will the Father in heaven give good things to those who ask Him?

The Jews did not call God their Father. In fact, when Jesus referred to God as His Father, they wanted to stone Him for blasphemy. However, they did use the word *Abba* when referring to their earthly fathers. *Abba* means "daddy" in Greek. The scriptures tell us we can call God *Abba-Daddy*, Father. Our relationship with Him is real. It's close, personal, and enduring.

What will we ask of our Father? Will we seek Him? Will we knock to gain the benefits only He can give to His children?

Whoever asks will receive. He who seeks will find. He who knocks, the door will be opened to him.

God *always* answers. He may say, *"No, I love you too much to give you that."* Or *"No, not right now—you need to wait."* Or He may answer, *"Yes, I've been waiting for you to ask. And here's more."*

It is not for us to decide the answer, but it *is* our responsibility to *ask.*

Chapter 29

What's So Golden about the Golden Rule

I magine a world in which people lined up to do nice things for their fellow men just like they line up to buy the newest iPhone. This is the reason Jesus should be listened to worldwide. He is the only one with such skill, wisdom, love, and power to transform humankind. Imagine if all men followed His teachings: "*Therefore all things whatsoever ye would that men should do to you, do ye even so to them: for this is the law and the prophets*" (Matthew 7:12).

On the side of the mountain, as thousands of people from a mixed multitude were gathered to listen to His Sermon on the Mount, Jesus taught one of the greatest truths about human exchange. Most people—believers and nonbelievers—know this principle as the Golden Rule, but this teaching was not called "the Golden Rule" until the seventeenth century. Theologians thought it would be a good name for this portion of Scripture.

What makes the Golden Rule so golden? It's a simple, direct, all-inclusive truth. It's so simple that we could miss its message. Yet it carries the weight of the law and the prophets.

Religions Are Missing the Essence of the Golden Rule

Every religion *claims* to have this rule, but they do not. First, in Judaism, the Talmud says, "Whatever is hateful to you do not do to your neighbor." The Bahá'í faith says, "Lay not on any soul a load that you would not wish laid upon you. And desire not for anyone the things you would not desire for yourself." Confucianism says, "One word sums up the basis of all good conduct. Loving kindness. Do not do to others what you do not want done to you." Next is Hinduism: "This is the sum of the duty. Do not do to others what would cause pain if it were done to you." Every religion on the face of this earth has some of the parts of the Golden Rule but does not have the *essence* of the Golden Rule.

All other religions focus on what *not* to do to others, or what they would *not* want done to them. Jesus's instructions, instead, are a rule of action—of *doing*. This is the fundamental difference between the Christ-taught Golden Rule and all world religions or philosophies. No one in history said it like Jesus. He made it a rule of positive action toward others instead of one of abstaining.

It's revolutionary. It can change our lives.

Notice the progression in Jesus's teaching. First, He instructs believers not to judge. Then He teaches us to deal with the beam in our own eye rather than going after the mote in our brother's eye. Then He instructs us not to give holy things to dogs or cast pearls before swine. This is followed with the instruction to ask, seek, and knock and the promise that God will answer. Up until this point, Jesus has focused on our relationship with Him. Now He's talking about our *relationship with others*—man to man. Jesus is teaching that there is a right way to conduct these important interactions with our fellow man. Each has its own results.

What's So Golden about the Golden Rule?

The Golden Rule is a strong foundation for your ultimate life management system. Here are seventeen reasons why it will always provide effective guidance for the way we interact with others:

1. **Gold represents the highest standard.** The Golden Rule is brief, simple, and straight to the point—*do* to others. As mentioned, other religions teach a more passive rule—to *not* do to others—which lowers the standard. So, basically, a person would be able to fulfill the "not" command by doing nothing. Jesus expects more. He expects action that will change human behavior. Its simplicity makes it golden.

2. **It makes clear how we should act.** Suddenly, our doubts and questions are cleared up by His simple statement. Nobody can plead ignorance, and no one can say they didn't know.

3. **It covers every behavior and leaves no guesswork.** Instead of having a rule for every little thing, the Golden Rule covers behaviors of every kind—every situation, circumstance, and relationship.

4. **It is the basis of measurement for all behavior.** It's the standard for how we measure our behavior.

5. **It is the rule of conduct that has no specific command.** When there are no definite instructions governing the situation, this rule applies. It gives us the answer.

6. **It is the ultimate basis for social regulation.** We can apply the Golden Rule to any political, international, or family situation. It works one-on-one, in groups, and with entire countries. It is never outdated. It is the basis for regulating all social behaviors. If a society followed this one rule, it would rarely need a court system, and it could do away with thousands of statutes.

7. **It is not treating others as they treat us.** People have mocked this rule. Some say, "I know the Golden Rule: he who has the gold sets the rules." Others say, "Do to others before they do to you." Probably the biggest temptation is to treat others the way they have

(wrongly) treated us. However, treating others as they have treated us puts *them* in the driver's seat of our lives. It gives them the controlling position.

8. **It is not treating people according to their merits.** We have been taught to treat others according to their merits. Aren't you glad God doesn't do that with us? He gave us His grace rather than treating us based on our merit—or lack thereof.

9. **We put ourselves in their position.** What if we were in the condition or position of the other person? If we were in their shoes, how would we like to be treated? We need to ask ourselves these questions frequently. Would we like to be told we're a mess or no good? Would we like it if we were ridiculed or scorned? Would we rather be forgiven and receive a helping hand? The Golden Rule forces us to think outside ourselves and for the good of the other person.

10. **It is the secret to preserving a good conscience.** Paul told Timothy, a young preacher, that he was sending him into battle for God, armed only with faith and a clear conscience. Paul knew the importance of having a conscience void of offense before God and men.

    There is an old illustration that depicts a fight between a good dog and an evil dog. The grandson asks his grandfather which will win the fight. The grandfather replies, "The one that's been fed."

    The conscience is much like that. If you do unto others as we would have them do unto us, we "feed" our conscience. However, 1 Timothy refers to a "seared conscience." This means it has stopped working. We clear our conscience by confessing the sin and stopping the sinful action. Then we will find mercy, and our conscience will be clear again. The Golden Rule will not let us justify our actions based on what the other guy did. By following this rule, we can actively keep a clear conscience between God and others.

11. **It is an active form of love that fulfills the law.** The Golden Rule brings the concept of "loving our neighbor as ourselves" into greater focus. We lovingly do for them as we do for ourselves. We *actively* love them. The Golden Rule is love in action, motive, and behavior. It is the way love conducts itself. Love is not legalistic—following a set of rules. Instead, love considers what is best for the other person. The letter of the law kills, but the Spirit gives life.

12. **It is, in a nutshell, God's will for mankind.** If you wanted to reduce God's will to its simplest form of instruction, it is to treat others the way you want to be treated in their situation. This summarizes all the laws of God and the entirety of the will of God for my life and yours.

13. **It is not a sacrifice but an investment.** To treat others the way we wish to be treated is not a sacrifice; it's sowing for a great harvest. We won't lose anything by practicing the Golden Rule. We may not see the rewards in the moment, but we are doing the best thing for ourselves as well as the other person. We walk away with a clear conscience, and Jesus will reward our obedience.

14. **It's the key to a successful business.** If we are to apply the Golden Rule to our businesses, then we (as the leadership of our companies) should put ourselves in the customer's place. Just as in our personal lives, there is no limit to the application of this rule in business. As Christians, we should be the best businesspeople out there. We should reflect forward-moving, positive action to all we serve or supply.

15. **It is the standard by which we will be judged either righteous or not.** Somewhere we've gotten the mistaken notion that we can love God yet treat other people any way we want. This is wrong! Remember when Jesus taught the concept of serving the least of

His brethren? Jesus said that by doing so, it was as if they had done it directly for Him. We can't treat Jesus one way and people another. Our duty is to treat everyone as if Christ died for them—because He *did*.

16. **It is the sum of the law and the prophets.** This rule is golden because it culminates everything taught by the law and prophets and sets the standard for mankind.

17. **It is the definition of the narrow way.** It covers every behavior, person, and relationship. It covers every encounter and circumstance. It directs and instructs us in one short sentence. It leaves no room for chance or interpretation. It defines the way and guides the path. It is the straight gate—the narrow way—that leads to life, and few find it. We don't take the broad way. The crowds who do not follow the rule and lordship of Jesus take the easy way. Followers take the narrow way to life.

————————

Most of us have committed the Golden Rule to memory, but have you committed it to your way of life? Don't just follow this rule when you *think* it will work in your favor. It always works in our relationships with spouses, children, friends, extended family, coworkers, neighbors, strangers, and in the church. It has no limits. It's always appropriate, always godly, and always correct.

Matthew 7:12 sums up the essence of the Golden Rule simply yet profoundly:

> *"Therefore all things whatsoever ye would that men should do to you, do ye even so to them ... We do not do some things but do **all** things to all men at all times."* (Matthew 7:12, bold emphasis mine)

This is the kingdom.
This is God's way.
The Golden Rule always works.

Chapter 30

The Benefits of the Straight and Narrow vs. the Crooked

H ave you entered a cave? The entrance might be small. The tunnel might be so tiny you can hardly breathe as you crawl through. Fear might bombard you. But when you endure and arrive in a larger room, you notice the wonder around you. You reflect on the history. You are glad you endured the narrow path.

Jesus taught about a straight and narrow path. He taught that we should do for others the same thing we would have them do for us. Isn't that a wonderful principle? Wouldn't that change the world if we actually lived according to His instructions?

In His next phrase after that, Jesus says to enter through the straight gate. This way of life, the one before us as we enter the straight gate, is living out the Golden Rule. It puts us on a narrow path. Most people desire the wide, broad, easy gate. It gives them lots of room to do as they please without interference from God. However, that way leads to destruction. Few will walk as Jesus instructs; only a few will find the way:

> *"Enter ye in at the strait gate: for wide is the gate, and broad is the way, that leadeth to destruction, and many there be which go in threat:*
>
> *Because strait is the gate, and narrow is the way, which leadeth unto life, and few there be that find it."*
> (Matthew 7:13–14)

In this passage are several concepts that are said simply but are extremely important. First, we are told to "enter the straight gate," which signifies an action. We aren't already inside this gate naturally. By an act of our will, we must *enter* the straight gate. Matthew 7 also warns us that there is a second gate. This gate is wide and may appear the easier of the two paths, but the broad gate leads to destruction.

There are three purposes of these gates: to allow in, to keep out, and to give access to whatever is on the other side of the gate (a road, a path, a dwelling, etc.).

Jesus said there were only two paths: the narrow and the broad. There are a few people on the straight and narrow path and many on the crooked and broad one. This is a metaphor for the two choices we face today: follow God's way or Satan's way. We can accept Jesus as Lord, or we can stay on the throne of our own hearts. These two choices have two very different outcomes. One leads to life, and one leads to destruction.

Benefits of Living the Straight and Narrow Way of Life

Although choosing the straight and narrow path can be difficult at times, it is the most rewarding. Here are fifteen benefits we can reap by taking this route:

1. **The path is simple because it's straight.** Truth is always narrow. Two times two is four. It's always four and never anything else. That's narrow and specific.

2. **It's simple because it's narrow.** There is only one way to go down a narrow path. You are hedged in,

protected, and do not have to navigate complicated turns.

3. **It's well defined by Divine commands.** God's commands hem us in by keeping a steady pressure on each side. This keeps us straight on the path ahead. He sets and defines the course, and all we must do is follow. David, in Psalm 119:32, describes it this way: *"I will run the way of thy commandments, when thou shalt enlarge my heart."*

4. **The way is well lit.** God's Word, His ways, and His commands are like a light on our path. There's no ambiguity and no room for discussion. Things are well defined, and we can see exactly where to put our feet. Psalm 119:105 says, *"Thy word is a lamp unto my feet, and a light unto my path."* So we do not fear stumbling in the dark. Jesus said whoever followed Him would have the light of life and not walk in darkness. On this narrow path, we will always know the right decision. We'll always have the right direction and the right attitude. We'll always have the emotional strength because it's so plain—we just walk in the well-lit path.

5. **The narrow path is well-established.** It's not like walking through the woods, trying to cut your own way through the brush. It is a ready-made, well-marked, and well-traveled path. Jeremiah 6:16 (NIV) says, *"This is what the LORD says: 'Stand at the crossroads and look; ask for the ancient paths, ask where the good way is, and walk in it, and you will find rest for your souls. ... '"* Some people think it's difficult to follow God, but Jesus says the way of the *transgressor* is hard. When we walk in the ancient paths, we find rest for our souls because His way is easy, and His burden is light.

6. **The path is a "high way."** I do not mean the narrow path is like the road we call a "highway" today. Instead, it is the *high way*—an elevated way, a higher path. It is the way of holiness. God is holy, and holiness involves

precision. We can trust the way He set for those He loves. This path doesn't work for everyone. The unclean cannot use it. It will not work for them. Only the redeemed will be found there:

> *"And an highway shall be there, and a way,*
> *and it shall be called The way of holiness; the*
> *unclean shall not pass over it; but it shall be for*
> *those: the wayfaring men, though fools, shall*
> *not err therein.*
>
> *No lion shall be there, nor any ravenous beast*
> *shall go up thereon, it shall not be found there;*
> *but the redeemed shall walk there."*
>
> (Isaiah 35:8–9)

7. **It's an easily understood way.** The narrow way is so simple, anyone can walk it. It's not complicated or confusing. Even a fool knows one thing—God's path is easy to understand. The fool knows immediately he wants no part of it. For us, however, the simplicity of this way is very good.

8. **It's a safe way.** There is nothing to harm us on this path. There are no wild beasts, and the people are trustworthy. The redeemed are there. If some people are called redeemed, yet they are not safe and trustworthy, they are not truly on the path: *"No lion shall be there, nor any ravenous beast shall go up thereon, it shall not be found there; but the redeemed shall walk there"* (Isaiah 35:9).

   It's also a safe way because God is leading us, and of course He is trustworthy. In her famous poem "God Knows," Minnie Louise Haskins paints a beautiful image of trusting in the safety of God. She writes:

> And I said to the man who stood at the gate
> of the year: "Give me a light that I may tread
> safely into the unknown."

And he replied: "Go out into the darkness and put your hand into the Hand of God. That shall be to you better than light and safer than a known way."

9. **Blessings are strewn along the way.** God blesses His people. When we walk in His ways, He intends to bless us. His blessings cover every area of life: health, family, business, and everything else. The psalmist said, blessed is *everyone*. These blessings come automatically: "*Blessed is every one that feareth the Lord; that walketh in his ways*" (Psalm 128:1).

10. **There is no destruction on the path.** In Matthew 7, Jesus compares the two paths. The narrow path is straight, and sojourners are protected by God's ways. We will not be destroyed on this narrow path. Jesus, however, warns us of the broad way, which leads to destruction. The wide path is embedded with harmful, precarious, and evil events. It is so lethal, even the people on the broad path become self-destructive: "*Enter ye in at the strait gate: for wide is the gate, and broad is the way, that leadeth to destruction, and many there be which go in thereat*" (Matthew 7:13).

God turns the way of the wicked upside down. Those on the right path stand firm: "*The Lord preserveth the strangers; he relieveth the fatherless and widow: but the way of the wicked he turneth upside down*" (Psalm 146:9).

The lifestyle of the broad path kills the people who walk it. However, God knows the way of the righteous. He made the way, and He will keep it. There is nothing unholy, ungodly, destructive, or worldly on His path: "*For the Lord knoweth the way of the righteous: but the way of the ungodly shall perish*" (Psalm 1:6).

11. **There is guidance along the way.** The Holy Spirit gives us guidance on His path. As we walk, we hear

His voice telling us how to walk. The path is well lit by the Word of God. It's so easy that even a stubborn person can understand it. The Holy Spirit whispers in our hearts, showing us how to walk it: *"And thine ears shall hear a word behind thee, saying, This is the way, walk ye in it, when ye turn to the right hand, and when ye turn to the left"* (Isaiah 30:21).

Jesus said His sheep hear His voice, and they follow Him. As we travel the path, His voice is clear. It is a securely guided route: *"My sheep hear my voice, and I know them, and they follow me: And I give unto them eternal life; and they shall never perish, neither shall any man pluck them out of my hand"* (John 10:27–28).

12. It's a path of thoughtfulness, not thoughtlessness. Most people don't think about what they think about. They don't exercise any self-monitoring: "Am I doing the right thing? Am I speaking the right thing? Am I treating people the right way?" People often live thoughtless lives. On the broad way, it doesn't matter much. In fact, most people are there *because* they are thoughtless.

But following Jesus doesn't mean committing intellectual suicide and never thinking for oneself again. Mankind is not an animal. Animals don't reason; they are programmed by God to live according to instinct. Beavers build dams, cows moo, dogs bark, horses neigh…and man was created to think. In fact, most of us think twenty-four hours a day, even when we're sleeping. Dreams and nightmares indicate thought, even when we are not aware of it. Mankind was meant to think, think, think.

God made us for brilliance. We should stop letting the broad way and the broad thinkers rule our lives. God has personally crafted us, and we were made to contemplate, not to live a thoughtless life. He made us to walk the narrow path and to exercise all that He put in us. Those on the narrow path know where they are going. People on the broad path don't think about the future consequences of their actions or where they're headed.

We look straight ahead and consider our way. We ponder our path and let all our ways become established. We make decisions we never have to reverse. So many people are headed to dead ends and cul-de-sacs. They will spend their entire lives rerouting and recalculating and never know why:

> *"Let thine eyes look right on, and let thine eyelids look straight before thee.*
>
> *Ponder the path of thy feet, and let all thy ways be established.*
>
> *Turn not to the right hand nor to the left: remove thy foot from evil."*   (Proverbs 4:25–27)

13. **It's not crowded.** God desires all people to follow His narrow path. He doesn't want anyone to perish, but for all people to come to repentance. Unfortunately, the broad way is crowded with many, many people. Some think they are on the narrow path because they go to church or have said a prayer or were born into a Christian home. Yet they live the same self-directed, godless life of the people on the broad path. They are self-deceived. Yes, they believe God exists, and they know sin exists. Yet neither makes an impact on their lives, and they are not living on the narrow path.

Watch out if something is popular with the masses. It is usually an indicator of the broad path:

> *"Woe to the multitude of many people, which make a noise like the noise of the seas; and to the rushing of nations, that make a rushing like the rushing of mighty waters."*
>
> (Isaiah 17:12)

"Thou shalt not follow a multitude to do evil;
neither shalt thou speak in a cause to decline
after many to wrest judgment."   (Exodus 23:2)

A man at a restaurant changed his order from a menu because no one else in his group placed that same order. A friend asked him, "Why?"

He said, "Nobody else got it, so I wasn't going to be the only one."

People often change their beliefs and opinions based on popular opinion. Don't follow the crowd. Jesus said we are a *little* flock and a *remnant* of people. There is no rush to the narrow gate. There are only a few travelers here, but the rewards are great: *"Fear not, little flock; for it is your Father's good pleasure to give you the kingdom"* (Luke 12:32).

14. **We keep moving along the way.** One of the great benefits of the narrow way is that we keep improving as we proceed. We progress. We learn. We get smarter. We develop more power and more light: *"But the path of the just is as the shining light, that shineth more and more unto the perfect day"* (Proverbs 4:18). Job 17:9 put it this way: *"The righteous also shall hold on his way, and he that hath clean hands shall be stronger and stronger."*

Job went on to say, *"But he knoweth the way that I take: when he hath tried me, I shall come forth as gold. My foot hath held his steps, his way have I kept, and not declined. Neither have I gone back from the commandment of his lips; I have esteemed the words of his mouth more than my necessary food"* (Job 23:10–12).

We produce fruit as we travel along the narrow path. This is also known as the law of accumulation. We *accumulate* intelligence, emotional power, spiritual insight, wisdom, knowledge, and discernment. When we stick to the narrow road, we will become like gold. (This is one reason we do not judge. What we see in a person now is not who they will become. We need to realize their *potential*.)

15. **It leads to life.** This narrow path leads to abundant life while we are here on this earth, and it yields eternal life with God. When He said to enter through the straight gate and to proceed onto the narrow way, His intention was to give us life, fullness, and joy. On this road we have nothing to fear and everything to gain.

How to Access the Narrow Way

How do we get on the narrow way, the godly path that is so desirable? Here are three steps we must take:

1. **First, we enter the narrow way when we come to Jesus properly.** We need the Lord's mercy and pardon. Jesus is the door to the Father. In Him is the way of salvation. When we come to Jesus to be saved, we are choosing the narrow way. We are saying His ways are best and we trust Him. We are taken care of and enjoy great peace as all our needs are met. We need not worry: "*I am the door: by me if any man enter in, he shall be saved, and shall go in and out, and find pasture*" (John 10:9).

    Jesus says He is the only way—the gate, the door—to eternal, abundant life: "*Jesus saith unto him, I am the way, the truth, and the life: no man cometh unto the Father, but by me*" (John 14:6).

2. **Next, we reject the broad way and change our thinking.** When we accept Christ, we exchange our ways for His. He is now on the throne of our hearts, and He is leading us in His Truth. Also, we change our thoughts. This happens by renewing our minds (changing our thinking). We must reject the broad way and enter the narrow gate. Romans 12:2 says, "*And be not conformed to this world: but be ye transformed by the renewing of your mind, that ye may prove what is that good, and acceptable, and perfect, will of God.*"

God will have mercy on us and abundantly pardon us: "*Let the wicked forsake his way, and the unrighteous man his thoughts: and let him return unto the LORD, and he will have mercy upon him; and to our God, for he will abundantly pardon*" (Isaiah 55:7).

God says His ways and His thoughts are not our ways and our thoughts. As high as the heavens are above the earth, so are His thoughts higher than ours and His ways higher than ours. Glance at the sky in the morning or evening. Stare at the trees. Gaze at the waves of an ocean. Our Creator has crafted captivating artwork. His work is gripping. We can trust His ways.

God also says the Word He sends from His mouth will not return void. It will accomplish exactly what He sent it out to do. What does He desire to accomplish? He wants us to go with joy and to be led with peace. Even the hills, the mountains, and the trees will rejoice for us. This is the God we serve. He set the straight and narrow way for our highest good. It is His pleasure to give us the kingdom.

3. **Finally, we acknowledge Jesus as prophet, priest, and King.** He is our priest before God. There is no other mediator between God and man. He is the Prophet, the one who gives us instruction. He is our King, the one who rules over us. People on the broad way do not want Him to be prophet, priest, or the king of their lives. They do not want His instruction or His headship as a king.

Choose the narrow way.

There are fewer on that path, but they are the winners.

We properly pursue that ultimate life management system. We win the best there is, for now and forever. We get abundant and eternal life!

Chapter 31

Beware of Wolves in Sheep's Clothing

I don't know which type of animal you consider your favorite. I don't know what type of pet you have. I don't know your preferred meal, weather, time of year, or ball team. But I know this: Jesus mentioned familiar creatures in unexpected ways to make some powerful points. Wolves in sheep's clothing? That had to get attention.

He didn't talk about the obvious. He brought out the obscure and taught us to be cautious of things that bring subtle and sometimes sudden harm. He was talking about things that damage us from the inside out. We hear about this concept even in politics. It's the idea that we should not fear the enemy outside our walls; rather, it's the enemies within who will bring down a country.

Along these same lines, Jesus taught about wolves posing as sheep. He used those as illustrations to make clear His case. These wolves in sheep's clothing that mingle with God's flock are false prophets who bring false messages. They may appear to be sheep, but their messages are not from God:

> *"Beware of false prophets, which come to you in sheep's clothing, but inwardly they are ravening wolves.*
>
> *Ye shall know them by their fruits. Do men gather grapes of thorns, or figs of thistles?*

Even so every good tree bringeth forth good fruit;
but a corrupt tree bringeth forth evil fruit.

A good tree cannot bring forth evil fruit, neither
can a corrupt tree bring forth good fruit.

Every tree that bringeth not forth good fruit is hewn
down, and cast into the fire.

Wherefore by their fruits ye shall know them."

(Matthew 7:15–20)

It is essential that we know what we believe and that it's true. False teachers and prophets are dangerous. Jesus describes these people as "ravening wolves." This image is of a predatory, bloodthirsty creature seeking to harm. Then, 1 Peter 5:8 tells us to be sober and alert because Satan (and his false prophets) are looking for someone to devour.

Here are five important facts about our beliefs:

1. **What we believe always matters.** There are always results to whatever we believe. That's why we must believe the truth, the whole truth, and nothing but the truth. If we make decisions based on false beliefs, we will get catastrophic results. That is why our theology is so important. *Theology*, our religious doctrine of belief, is like a compass by which we discern the words, actions, and intentions of those seeking to influence us. What we believe has consequences. The truth of God's Word always trumps our experiences or personal preferences. False prophets will lead us away from God, while the Holy Spirit will always lead us to Him.

2. **What we believe about God is the most important thing about us.** What we believe about God is the biggest issue of life. Eternity is at stake.

   Jesus told the parable of the talents in Matthew 25 to illustrate that what we believe about God is important. The parable tells of a master who gave a different number of talents to each of his servants. (A *talent*

314

refers to money in biblical times.) One servant used his talents and gained more, while a second man did the same. The third man, however, buried his talents. When the master came to see what each man did with the talents he gave them, he was pleased with the men who produced more than what they'd been given. The third man, however, believed his master was a hard man. Out of fear, he did not sow what he had been given.

Likewise, if we believe God is hard, our attitude toward Him will also be hard and harsh. We operate in fear rather than in love. When we know what our Master is truly like, we will have the right attitude toward Him. We will desire to serve Him, and we will take the gifts He gives us and multiply the return back to Him. So what we believe about God is important. It can change our lives.

3. **Satan is more effective by counterfeiting the truth than by openly denying it.** Satan has been counterfeiting Truth since the fall of man. When he spoke to Eve in the garden, he did not come out and contradict God's instructions. Instead, he casted doubt by asking, *"Did God actually say..."* (see Genesis 3:1 ESV). If Satan can get us to think *slightly* contrary to God's Word, or even pose as one of God's messengers to confuse us, we can be led astray. If he poses as an angel of light and redefines God's Truth, he is much more effective than trying to get us to flatly deny it. This is an effective strategy.

4. **False messengers give direction under the pretense of the Divine.** False messengers will say they have heard from God and have been given authority to share His words. This is a precarious position. It is dangerous to give false advice. The Scriptures say teachers will be judged at a much higher standard than the average person. Because a teacher or a prophet can

misrepresent the truth and lead thousands or tens of thousands astray, he or she must know God's truth and relay it so that others will also understand it.

Not all false teachers are intentionally so. Some are sincere—but sincerely wrong. One might think he or she is taking the right medicine, but if it is poison, all the sincerity in the world will not prevent the tragedy.

False messengers have been around for a long time. The book of Jeremiah talks about people who tell lies in God's name. They used His name to promote their authenticity, their authority, and the weight of their arguments for selfish financial gain. However, God did not send them.

But even with all the false representation throughout the centuries, God's Word remains. Salvation through Jesus Christ is alive and active. Liars have done a great deal of damage, but the way to eternity with God has endured it all:

> *"Then the LORD said unto me, The prophets prophesy lies in my name: I sent them not, neither have I commanded them, neither spake unto them: they prophesy unto you a false vision and divination, and a thing of nought, and the deceit of their heart."* (Jeremiah 14:14)

5. **False ideas can seem attractive.** In the time of Jeremiah, a wonderful and horrible thing was happening in the land. The prophets were giving false prophecies, and the people loved it. Unfortunately, people can get excited about falsehood. It can seem attractive and pleasant. What will you do when you have learned to love the lies? Jeremiah 5:30–31 says, *"A wonderful and horrible thing is committed in the land; The prophets prophesy falsely, and the priests bear rule by their means; and my people love to have it so: and what will ye do in the end thereof?"*

Jesus and His Disciples
Warned Us about False Prophets

God's Word is filled with warnings to us from Jesus and His disciples, admonishing us to watch for false prophets. Here are five:

1. **Paul warned us** that wolves would enter the congregations and would not spare the flock. Why would this happen after he left rather than while he was still there? Because he would not allow it. He would not let them get away with their lies, hypocrisy, and deceptions that would destroy the church. However, he knew they were coming, and his warning was firm. They would appear with their own agendas, speaking evil things to draw followers to themselves: *"For I know this, that after my departing shall grievous wolves enter in among you, not sparing the flock. Also of your own selves shall men arise, speaking perverse things, to draw away disciples after them"* (Acts 20:29–30).

2. **Peter also warned us** of false prophets and teachers living among us. Their heresy would have the ability to damn people who believe in it. It would destroy heart, mind, soul, body, eternity, the future, the family, marriages, and businesses—all destroyed by false teachings. These false teachers would even deny the Lord within His own congregations. Unfortunately, many will follow them as they speak evil about God's truth:

   > *"But there were false prophets also among the people, even as there shall be false teachers among you, who privily shall bring in damnable heresies, even denying the Lord that bought them, and bring upon themselves swift destruction.*

317

And many shall follow their pernicious ways;
by reason of whom the way of truth shall be
evil spoken of."   (2 Peter 2:1–2)

3. **David warned us.** In Psalm 41, David said it would be fine if his enemies were from someplace else—if they were down the street or from across the country. However, his enemies were the people with whom he had walked to the house of God. His enemies were close, in his inner circle. They were people he had called friends. The wolves appear as sheep. We must vet each person according to his or her fruit.

4. **John warned us.** John warned us not to believe everything we hear or witness. We must test the spirits. Many did not come from God, and false prophets spread their lies in word and deed: "*Beloved, believe not every spirit, but try the spirits whether they are of God: because many false prophets are gone out into the world*" (1 John 4:1).

5. **Jesus warned us.** In His address, Jesus warned that false prophets would come as wolves in sheep's clothing. He told us they did not look like wolves or smell like wolves. In fact, outwardly, there was nothing unusual about them to give them away: "*Beware of false prophets, which come to you in sheep's clothing, but inwardly they are ravening wolves*" (Matthew 7:15).

How Can We Tell
Who the False Prophets Are?

In Old Testament times, many of the prophets went about in hairy, animal garb. A false prophet could put on the same clothes and look as if he were a legitimate prophet of God, then go give false guidance. Paul, Peter, John, and Jesus Himself warned us. Beware! False prophets and teachers are all around us. Are we hearing the warning? Are we aware of this dangerous reality?

False prophets pose as if they're from God. False prophets and teachers may have a form of godliness, but they don't have the inward power of a godly life. Because they lack the true power of God, they tend to prey on the weak, shallow, or vulnerable of society:

> *"Having a form of godliness, but denying the*
> *power thereof: from such turn away.*
>
> *For of this sort are they which creep into houses,*
> *and lead captive silly women laden with sins, led*
> *away with divers lusts,*
>
> *ever learning, and never able to come to the*
> *knowledge of the truth."* (2 Timothy 3:5–7)

Here, Paul says these wolves go to weak women and lead them astray. It's important that women, as well as men, study and know the Scriptures. Women are not weaker than men in any intellectual or spiritual sense. They have an enduring impact on their children and a great influence on their husbands. Women are not intellectually weak, so their spiritual education is very important. False teachers look for women who have not learned the Word.

Paul also warns that false apostles will transform themselves into the appearance of an apostle of Christ. We should not be surprised by this since Satan himself transforms into an angel of light. If he came dressed in a red costume and horns, we'd know who he was right away! Instead, he comes dressed as a saint. Because he poses as an angel of light, his ministers will, too:

> *"For such are false apostles, deceitful workers,*
> *transforming themselves into the apostles of Christ.*
>
> *And no marvel; for Satan himself is transformed*
> *into an angel of light.*
>
> *Therefore it is no great thing if his ministers also*
> *be transformed as the ministers of righteousness;*
> *whose end shall be according to their works."*
>
> (2 Corinthians 11:13–15)

The word "beware" is used throughout the Scriptures as a warning to believers. When we see "beware" used, we should take special note. Whatever follows this warning is of great importance!

Jesus warned us to watch out for false prophets. We will need to discern what is true and what is a lie when we are receiving teaching. How can we be sure who is who? He said we would know them by their fruits:

> *"Beware of false prophets, which come to you in sheep's clothing, but inwardly they are ravening wolves.*
>
> *Ye shall know them by their fruits. Do men gather grapes of thorns, or figs of thistles?*
>
> *Even so every good tree bringeth forth good fruit; but a corrupt tree bringeth forth evil fruit.*
>
> *A good tree cannot bring forth evil fruit, neither can a corrupt tree bring forth good fruit.*
>
> *Every tree that bringeth not forth good fruit is hewn down, and cast into the fire.*
>
> *Wherefore by their fruits ye shall know them."*
>
> (Matthew 7:15–20)

In Matthew 16, Jesus told the parable of a man who went out at night and sowed tares, or weeds, into a field of wheat. No one saw him do it, and the tares and the wheat looked similar as they grew. In the parable, He warned if the tares were pulled up too soon, they would also pull up the wheat, so both must grow together until the time of harvest. In this story, the harvest represented the Judgment. At that time, angels will be sent to the four corners of the earth to gather up the tares and burn them. The wheat will be spared.

The Traits of Authentic Believers

For now, however, we must be careful, as weeds have been planted around us. They may not be easily recognized for what they truly are—weeds. Besides the "truth test," we are to test and examine the fruit of people claiming to be a part of us.

We can't tell much about people based on their outer appearance. Anyone can look good, but their actions reveal the truth. Jesus told the Pharisees that they looked good on the outside; however, on the inside, they were dead. Jesus compared them to white-washed tombs, in that they were clean and fresh on the outside but contained a dead, stinking corpse on the inside. So we must look past the exterior of a person and watch what fruit is born from the inner man or woman.

By what standard do we examine them? Jesus tells us to examine the fruit. Galatians 5:22–23 lists the fruits produced by an authentic believer: *"But the fruit of the Spirit is love, joy, peace, longsuffering, gentleness, goodness, faith, meekness, temperance: against such there is no law."*

The following nine fruits of the right spirit should reside in every true believer in Christ. When we notice these traits in followers of Christ, we see Him at work in their lives. These characteristics, or fruits, provide believers with clear indicators of how to recognize people with the right Spirit.

1. **Are they loving?** Do they speak with love? Does their message demonstrate affection for all mankind? Or is it selective love? Authentic followers of Jesus Christ operate in love. A false message will not direct love toward others; it will censor, criticize, condemn, and point the finger. Is the messenger loving? *"By this shall all men know that ye are my disciples, if ye have love one to another"* (John 13:35).

2. **Are they joyful?** *Joy* is the exultation of the spirit that comes from genuine harmony with God and others. Are they joyful or sour? Are they mean or angry? How do they treat others? Do they pay attention to those around them at all? Romans 15:13 says, *"Now the God of hope fill you with all joy and peace in believing, that ye may abound in hope, through the power of the Holy Ghost."*

3. **Are they peaceful?** *Peace* is inward tranquility. A peaceful person is not upset and does not hold onto animosity, hatred, or condemnation. A true messenger of Jesus is loving, joyful, and peaceful. Jesus was called the Prince of Peace, and His followers are peaceful: *"Depart from evil, and do good; seek peace, and pursue it"* (Psalm 34:14).

4. **Are they longsuffering?** Are they tolerant toward others, and do they possess an enduring, uncomplaining attitude? Are they quick to jump on people, or are they patient? *"And we exhort you, brethren, admonish the disorderly, encourage the faint-hearted, support the weak, be longsuffering toward all"* (1 Thessalonians 5:14 ESV).

5. **Are they gentle?** Somehow, we have an image of a "real man" as tough, rough, macho, loud, and vulgar. The true spirit of a man of God is gentle. He is kind with men, women, and children. He is never rude, coarse, uncaring, or rough. In fact, Jesus, the greatest man to ever live, was extremely tender toward children. Jesus said in Matthew 18:3 we are to *"become as little children"* or we will not enter the kingdom of heaven. This is hardly the image we have of a prophet today.

6. **Are they full of goodness?** Or are they conniving? Do they lie, cheat, and try to get the best of others? Jesus's messengers desire a win–win. They are full of goodness and goodwill toward others.

   American TV personality and Presbyterian minister Fred Rogers dedicated his life to spreading goodness to those around him, especially toward children. He said, "Imagine what our real neighborhoods would be like if each of us offered, as a matter of course, just one kind word to another person."

   Romans 12:21 tells us we won't overcome evil with evil. Instead, we are to cling to good because the Lord is good. True believers will be like Him.

7. **Are they full of faith?** True believers have faith in God and see the potential for good in others. They help bring others to saving faith because they know how good God is: *"Now faith is the assurance of things hoped for, the conviction of things not seen"* (Hebrews 11:1 ESV).

8. **Are they meek?** Meekness does not mean weakness. Instead, it is strength under control. Meekness implies a spirit of humility and deference instead of an attitude of self-reliance.

   Author and pastor Andrew Murray said this of Jesus: "Christ is the humility of God embodied in human nature; the Eternal Love humbling itself, clothing itself in the garb of meekness and gentleness, to win and serve and save us."

   Jesus was the perfect example of meekness—power under control. His true disciples will also possess this fruit of the Spirit.

9. **Are they temperate?** Temperance is identified by the ability to self-regulate in all circumstances. Those who bear the fruit of temperance do not go overboard, do not swing from one emotional extreme to the next, and they always practice constraint. First Thessalonians 5:22 says, *"Abstain from all appearance of evil."*

Be Diligent to Spot the Wolves

It is important to spot counterfeits. Even earthly governments take counterfeiting seriously. In America, for example, it is illegal to produce, spend, and even possess counterfeit money. In fact, if a prosecutor can prove intent to defraud, federal law can punish the offender for up to twenty years in prison.

If counterfeiting pieces of paper holds such strict penalties, how much more harshly will the Judge punish those who seek to defraud His sheep?

We are to watch and be aware. We are to test the people who say they are from God. We must test their message to see to if it aligns with Scripture and watch to see if they deliver it while demonstrating the fruits of the spirit. We have been warned that wolves would come up among us. Now we must be diligent to spot them.

As we do our part, we are making a difference. Lives are being saved.

Chapter 32

Overcoming Fake Christianity

Through these pages, we have listened to the words of Jesus. His encouraging words. His firm words. His beatitudes. His illustrations. His instructions.

Each part, though varying in style and tone, has this in common: Jesus spoke the truth. And He does not want us accepting anything that is not part of that truth.

When you seek to enter a room and the door is locked, you need the correct key or code. Not just any key. Not just any numbers to hit. The *right* key can unlock the door. Deceptive teaching declares just any key will open the door. That is not what Jesus said.

Antinomianism
Spoils the Church in America

Jesus warned that false teachers and prophets would come to us, like wolves in sheep's clothing. Their messages are not from God, and we would know them by studying the fruit of their lives. Over time, false prophets and teachers have promoted false messages until they have become widely accepted. These seemingly "Christian" messages have been passed down without further investigation of the message or messenger. Today, many of these messages plague the church.

One of these false teachings is called "antinomianism" or "the No-Lordship Gospel." This means someone can make a confession of belief in Jesus as his or her savior. Perhaps they sign a card and say a prayer, but that's the full extent of their relationship with Christ. They believe the endowment of grace releases them of the obligation of fulfilling the moral tenets of the law. They believe their place in heaven is secure because their salvation is through faith and grace alone. He is Savior, yes, but never Lord. This teaching has spoiled the church in America.

The idea that we can become Christians and not obey Christ is the essence of antinomianism. Jesus grants eternal salvation to those who obey Him, not to the people who do their own thing: *"And being made perfect, he became the author of eternal salvation unto all them that obey him"* (Hebrews 5:9).

If we say we have fellowship with Him but still walk in darkness, we are lying and do not know the truth. The core proof of who He is and who we are is shown in our obedience: *"If we say that we have fellowship with him, and walk in darkness, we lie, and do not the truth"* (1 John 1:6).

The trap is offering the profession of our lips as an alternative to obedience. For approximately the past seventy-five years in America, antinomianism has asserted the erroneous idea that we can be hearers and not doers. If we say the right words, then we're okay. In fact, that is what Jesus came to teach against. The Pharisee's lips did not save them, and neither will we be saved by our words. We must do—obey—with a heart that desires Him as Lord.

We were never meant to take the management position in our lives. That has always been, and always will be, God's position. Like sheep, we have gone astray. We've turned to our way. Self-rule and self-love have taken the place of God's rule in our lives.

Jesus taught us that not everyone who says, "Lord, Lord," will enter the kingdom of heaven. Saying the right words does not ensure the right heart. Merely repeating words—even religious words—does not mean we get our ticket to heaven punched without further effort from us. Jesus said the person to whom Christ is truly Lord is the person who does the will of His Father in heaven: *"Not everyone that saith unto me, Lord, Lord, shall enter into the kingdom of heaven; but he that doeth the will of my Father which is in heaven"* (Matthew 7:21).

Romans 10: 9 says, *"That if thou shalt confess with thy mouth the Lord Jesus, and shalt believe in thine heart that God hath raised him from the dead, thou shalt be saved."* We are saved because our confession and belief are true and real. Confession is not lying—it's an acknowledgment that something is true. Lip service gets no one into the kingdom. If you lie and say that Jesus is in your heart, you will *not* be saved.

Five Categories of People

In my estimation, there are five categories of people: those who are not Christian and don't pretend to be, those who say they are Christians but aren't, "formal Christians," hypocrites, and authentic Christians. Let's look at these five groups:

1. **Non-Christians**—The first group is easily understood. They are not Christians, and they don't act, think, believe, or speak like Christians.

2. **"Nominal Christians"**—These people say they are Christians but aren't. *Nominal* means they are Christian in name only. Maybe they are born in a Christian nation like America. They say, "Of course I'm a Christian." Others may have been sprinkled as babies. Their parents told them they were Christians based on an infant baptism. They may show up at church for Christmas and Easter and "try to do good things" in between, and they believe they are part of the kingdom. Still others may have parents who attend church, so they feel like they are Christians via proxy.

   These people are deceived. Proverbs 30:12 says, *"There is a generation that are pure in their own eyes, and yet is not washed from their filthiness."*

3. **"Formal Christians"**—They have gone through classes and learned a catechism. They adhere to a system of rules, regulations, and functions within a

specific church. They follow rituals and give mental assent to the Bible. They see God as a nice guy and Jesus as a great teacher. They'll speak flattering words about both and follow some formalities that honor them. But there is nothing inside. It's outward religion.

This is rampant in Romanism or Catholicism, but there are many Protestant denominations that are also as formal. They specialize in keeping external observances, special holidays, and special days of the year. We would say they have a form of godliness, but they deny its power: *"Having a form of godliness, but denying the power thereof: from such turn away"* (2 Timothy 3:5).

4. **Hypocrites**—This group is perhaps the largest group who professes to be Christian, yet are not. They are pretenders. They attend church on Sundays, and then they go out into the world, following its ways rather the God's. However, because they attend church regularly, we have hope that they will turn to the Truth and follow it. We probably sit with them in the pews each week: *"In the meantime, when there were gathered together an innumerable multitude of people, insomuch that they trode one upon another, he began to say unto his disciples first of all, Beware ye of the leaven of the Pharisees, which is hypocrisy"* (Luke 12:1).

5. **Authentic Christians**—In this group are those who desire for Christ to rule and reign over them.

True Christians, the true servants of Christ, do the will of God from their hearts. They're authentic in their faith because their motive is all about pleasing God, not man: *"Not with eyeservice, as menpleasers; but as the servants of Christ, doing the will of God from the heart"* (Ephesians 6:6).

Saying we're Christian doesn't make it so. Not everyone who says, "Lord, Lord," will enter the kingdom of heaven. What makes Jesus Lord in our lives is when we purposefully get off the throne of our hearts and *establish* Him as Lord. The proof of His Lordship in us is in the fruit we bear as we obey Him.

In Luke 6, Jesus asks why people would call Him Lord if they do not plan to do the things He says. What's the point of calling Him Lord if He has no management of our lives?

Jesus said many people would claim they did many works in His name, but they are strangers who never knew Him. These people may be involved in ministries and do things that appear to be godly. Remember, Satan appears as an angel of light; so will his messengers. Jesus will tell them to leave, for they are workers of iniquity. Matthew 7:22 says, "*Many will say to me in that day, Lord, Lord, have we not prophesied in thy name? and in thy name have cast out devils? and in thy name done many wonderful works?*"

Jesus said His sheep hear His voice and follow Him. They follow because He leads every aspect of their lives. His true sheep follow because following is the essence of obedience: "*My sheep hear my voice, and I know them, and they follow me*" (John 10:27).

If we are authentic Christians and Jesus is our Lord, things go *His* way. We don't have an option on how to treat our spouses or children. We don't have an option to commit adultery, lie, steal, kill, or anything else He has outlawed in His Word. An authentic Christian has Jesus in the Master position of his or her life. We give up self-assertion and follow what He says. When Jesus is Lord, we cease to have an opinion on any matter on which He has already spoken in His Word!

The safest, smartest, wisest thing any human being can do is to bring Jesus into the management position of his or her heart and life. Can we trust Him? Yes, we can trust Him because He loves us, and He has all wisdom. The religious trap, the Christian deception, that says just speak the right words and you're in is a lie. The profession of our lips cannot replace obedience.

Characteristics of a Genuine Christian

Here are three characteristics of a genuine Christian:

1. **A genuine Christian establishes Jesus as Lord.** Jesus died for all people so we could live abundant lives for Him who died and rose for us. When we accept Christ, our lives are no longer ours. We've been bought with a price. We belong to the Redeemer: "*And that he died for all, that they which live should not henceforth live unto themselves, but unto him which died for them, and rose again*" (2 Corinthians 5:15).

   There's a story about a missionary in India who was walking along the river. He saw a woman with her two sons. One was a strong, young man. The other was weak and sickly. She was about to offer a son to the crocodile gods of the Nile, as her religion dictated. When the missionary saw what she about to do, he rushed over to her. He explained that such a sacrifice was not needed because Jesus died as the permanent sacrifice for everyone.

   The missionary went on his way and came back later that day. When he returned, the woman was still there. This time, she just had her sickly son by her side. With great sadness, the missionary walked over, crying. He asked, "Why, why, why, did you sacrifice to the false crocodile gods? And why did you throw your stronger son in instead of the sickly one who may not live anyway?"

   The woman looked at him and said, "Sir, we give our gods the best."

   This is a tragic story, but what about its converse? Sadly, many modern false teachers advocate we offer to God whatever we can, whatever is convenient, or whatever doesn't cost us much. If Jesus requires too much of our time, energy, thoughts, or money, we'd rather not establish Him as Lord. We may be okay with giving God our leftovers, but we are mistaken if we believe He is also okay with it. He isn't. We should not be.

Years ago, I was challenged with the question, "If God is such a loving God, why does He send people to hell?" The truth is that it's not God who sends people to hell, but our own choices that condemn us. Imagine what the universe would be like if God gave eternal life to selfishness. We would do in the heavens what we have done on earth. Instead of nation against nation, ethnos against ethnos, and man against man, we would have a war in the universe...galaxy pitted against galaxy. The whole universe would become a hell. Selfishness must be confined. It is unsustainable.

Others ask, "Why doesn't God just force us to be Christians?" Even the most secular person would not want to be forced into a marriage union with someone they didn't like, let alone love. So why would God force anyone to love, to live a philosophy opposite to that which they have chosen? Forcing people to become Christian, to live by the rule of love...forever? Heaven would be a very sad place filled with prisoners forced to love. This is precisely why so many have gravitated toward the no-lordship gospel—because it lets them think they're going to heaven while they continue to do as they please. If one does not enjoy praising God now, why would he or she want to do it for eternity?

2. **A genuine Christian will produce good works after he or she is saved.** We become Christians because of what Jesus did on the cross of Calvary, and that alone. Nothing we *do* can make God love us more, and nothing we *do* can make God love us any less. It's not about what we *do*. Good works do not proceed or earn our salvation. They do not make us Christians.

    However, good works will naturally follow our true confession of faith. We are God's workmanship, created in Christ Jesus to do good works. That will happen. We will do the works God has planned for us after we have been saved. We are not saved *by* good works, but *for* good works: *"For we are his workmanship, created in Christ Jesus unto good works, which God hath before ordained that we should walk in them"* (Ephesians 2:10).

3. **A genuine Christian will weather the storms of life without losing faith.** It was common for Jesus to tell stories, or parables, to make a point. In Matthew 7:24–27, Jesus told the parable of the wise and foolish builders:

> *"Therefore whosoever heareth these sayings of mine, and doeth them, I will liken him unto a wise man, which built his house upon a rock:*
>
> *And the rain descended, and the floods came, and the winds blew, and beat upon that house; and it fell not: for it was founded upon a rock.*
>
> *And every one that heareth these sayings of mine, and doeth them not, shall be likened unto a foolish man, which built his house upon the sand:*
>
> *And the rain descended, and the floods came, and the winds blew, and beat upon that house; and it fell: and great was the fall of it."*
>
> (Matthew 7:24–27)

The point of the parable was to illustrate the importance of our foundation. Jesus explained that the storms of life will test us and reveal the truth about us. He said whoever hears His words and does them is like a wise man who built his house on a rock. Although the rain descends, the water rises, and the winds blow and beat on the house, it remains standing because it is built on a rock. Next, He said if anyone hears His words but does not do them, he is like a foolish man who built his house on the sand. When the same storm descends, the same amount of water rises, and the same winds blow and beat upon the second house, it falls because it was built on the sand. It did not have a firm foundation.

The two men who built these homes used the same materials but different foundations. To the casual observer, the houses may have looked the same. When the storm came, it was obvious who was the better builder. The house built on the rock stood firm, while the one built on sand was destroyed.

Likewise, the wise man hears Jesus's words and follows them. His life is built on the Solid Rock. The foolish man hears Jesus's words and does not follow them. His life is built on the sand. It will not endure the tests of this life. The wise man made Jesus the foundation, or Lord, of his life. The foolish man did things his own way and cut corners. This is not just a temporal thing—eternity lies in the balance. If we are not wise and do not build on the Rock, according to Matthew 7:27, our fall will be "great."

Are you willing to risk your eternal soul for earthly comforts?

The storms of life will come. They are blowing wind all around us. They will prove if we have the correct foundation. They will reveal our true purpose for living. The right management system of life must depend on the Rock, not the things of this world.

How to Claim This Ultimate Life Management System

T he government and religious leaders at the time wanted Jesus arrested, tried, and convicted for teaching the Life Management System you just learned. The arresting officers refused, and they, in turn, were brought to account and asked why they had not arrested this Teacher. Here was their response: *"The officers answered, Never a man spake like this man"* (John 7:46). Then the religious leaders asked the officers, "Are you also deceived?"

Indeed, no one had ever spoken like this. And still, to this day, no philosophy of life can be compared with His. It is certain that anyone who has learned what you have learned from Him will understand the superlative, the pinnacle, the highest degree and respect for His acme, excellence, accuracy, and truthfulness. He is incomparable, unequalled in manner, kind or degree; matchless, peerless, and transcendent. By now you have listened to His message, discovered His philosophy, read His words, and understood His manner of management.

May I tell you a bit more about Him, descriptions I have preserved over my lifetime?

- Who like Jesus can pity the homeless orphan?
- Who like Jesus can welcome a prodigal back home?
- Who like Jesus can make a drunkard sober?
- Who like Jesus can take a lost woman of the streets and make her a queen unto God?
- Who like Jesus can catch the tears of human sorrow in His bowl?
- Who like Jesus can kiss away our sorrow?

- To the one in sorrow, He is their comfort.
- To the aged, He is the light of hope on the hills of tomorrow.
- To the lonely, He is the friend that sticketh closer than a brother.
- To the thirsty, He is the oasis in the desert.

- He is not like the bursting forth of an orchestra that is too loud and might be out of tune.
- He is not like the seas when lashed into a rage by a storm that is too boisterous.
- He is not like a mountain wreathed in lightning, canopied with snow that is too solitary and remote.
- He is the Lily of the Valley, the Rose of Sharon, a gale of spices from heaven.

There is no singular metaphor to describe Jesus; He is your Life Manager in all situations:

- In every want, He is your friend.
- In every danger, He is your defense.
- In every sorrow, He is your joy.
- In every pain, He is your peace.
- In poverty, He is your provider.
- In sickness, He is your health.
- In hunger, He is your bread.
- In trouble, He is your consolation.

- In perplexity, He is your counselor.
- In the furnace, He is your refiner.
- In the floods, He is your rock.
- In assaults, He is your refuge.
- In accusation, He is your advocate.
- In debt, He is your surety.
- In slavery, He is your ransom.
- In captivity, He is your deliverer.
- In daylight, He is your sun.
- At night time, He is your keeper.
- In the desert, He is your Shepherd.
- In life, He is your hope.
- In death, He is your life.

- He died to save us; He rose again to prove it; He ever lives to guarantee it; He's coming back again to demonstrate it.
- He became the Son of Man that we might become Sons of God.
- He became sin that we might be made the Righteousness of God.
- He became exceedingly sorrowful that we might have exceedingly great joy.
- He became poor that we might become rich.
- He became a partaker of our human nature that we might become partakers of His Divine Nature.
- He became weary that we might have rest.
- He became the companion of sinners and publicans that we might know the companionship of God.
- He was born in a manger that we might live in a mansion.
- He was homeless that we might have an eternal habitation.
- He was condemned that we might not be condemned.

- He became a servant that we might be made kings and priests unto God.

- He bore our chastisement that we might have peace with God.

- He was wounded for our transgressions that we might have eternal forgiveness.

- He bore our stripes on His Own Body on the tree that we might be healed.

- He was stripped that we might be clothed.

- He was cut off that we might be brought nigh.

- He was made a curse that we might be redeemed from the curse.

- He was forsaken that we might be embraced.

- He died that we might live.

- He entered the realm of darkness that we might dwell in the Kingdom of Light.

- He was silent that we might speak.

- He was humbled that we might be exalted.

- He was rejected that we might be accepted.

- He was strong and had His hands transfixed in helplessness to the accursed tree that our hands might wave the palms of victory.

- The light of the world was shrouded in darkness that we might not go into outer darkness.

- He who came to give Living Water cried that we might have our thirst quenched.

- He became an outcast that we might never be cast out.

- He was crucified for us that we might reign with Him.

- He wore a crown of thorns that we might wear a crown of glory.

- He was abused, tempted, persecuted, despised, derided, betrayed, denied, smitten, scourged, buffeted, taunted, blasphemed, frowned upon by pride, and oppressed by power.

- He gave up all things that we might receive all things.
- He is our all in all.

But all this means nothing if He is not the manager of your life, personally and directly.

How to Make Jesus's Ultimate Life Management System Yours

1. Recognize that there must be a change of management, a change of managers. Anything with two heads is a monster. There can be no dual presidencies, no duplicity of leadership—no more than one Chief Shepherd.

2. Understand that by "manager," we mean the Ultimate Authority, one who has been given the "right to rule," unchallenged by anyone or anything else.

3. To change management requires replacement of previous usurpers.

4. Recognize that the new Manager of your life must be fully qualified to do so.

5. The new Manager must love you which means to desire and implement the highest good for your life without His own personal benefit as a motive. The new Manager must be smart—very smart, the smartest, the one with ultimate wisdom; able to provide, control, regulate, lead, empower, and inspire. And the new Manager must be trustworthy and reliable and never quit on you.

6. The new Manager must be followed, obeyed, and adhered to, or He will be no manager to you at all. You would be left to shift for yourself, albeit religiously.

You already know that Jesus has many names. Such is the height, breadth, diversity, and infinity of His person. Most have already told you that you need a Savior. That would be partly true. The whole truth is, you and I need the Life Manager! The name "Savior" is used thirty-seven times in Scripture. The Manager's name is "Lord," used 7,979 times in Scripture. Beware! Much of modern Christianity in America is based on marketing. I refer to it as "the industrialized church." Its goal is to attract the world, but without transformation. Remember, God formed us; sin deformed us; man tries to reform us; but Christ transforms us!

If the Gospel is diminished and does not require change, we will perpetuate antinomianism, the "no-lordship Gospel." The modern Gospel presented throughout Christianity in America doesn't require us to give up what is wrong; it accommodates it. Jesus has become tolerable because of a fake Gospel that doesn't interfere with our selfishness. The present culture has redefined sin or ignored it altogether.

Charles Spurgeon, England's best-known preacher for most of the second half of the nineteenth century, said, "That very church which the world likes best is sure to be that which God abhors…A time will come when instead of shepherds feeding the sheep, the church will have clowns entertaining the goats." Ouch!

It has been said, "At first we overlook evil. Then we permit evil. Then we legalize evil. Then we promote evil. Then we celebrate evil. Then we persecute those who still call it evil." Be careful, my friend. Right is still right, even if nobody is doing it. Wrong is still wrong, even if everyone is doing it. Perhaps this is why Jesus said, *"Broad is the way that leadeth to destruction, and many there be which go in thereat…narrow is the way, which leadeth unto life, and few there be that find it"* (Matt. 7:13–14).

The biblical word for "manager" is Lord. "Lord" means leader, ruler, master, sovereign, one who has ultimate authority and dominion to whom service and obedience are due. It means "boss" (but He's not a bossy boss, if you know what I mean).

In essence, *genuine* Christianity is not merely a *belief* in Jesus; even the devils believe. (See James 2:19.) Real faith is belief that is sufficient to trust implicitly and explicitly on Jesus, to receive Him as Lord. And the proof of His Lordship is our obedience to

His leadership. As Dietrick Bonhoeffer said, "Only those who really believe obey. And only those who obey really believe."

So now comes the question, my dear friend: If you haven't, will you, right now, welcome the Lord Jesus Christ into your life, your heart, the management position of your life, not to merely manage some of the pieces but the whole of you?

Is it easy or difficult? It's easy because it is simple. It's difficult because we have to give up the management position and remove ourselves from the throne of our hearts, from usurping God's rightful place. We play God! We have been going our own way, making all the calls, following our own whims and often, even the expectations of others. All it takes is surrender! Absolute surrender! No parts held back!

It is difficult if we attempt to hold on to any known sin. Dropping any one or more known sins is like chopping off the limb of a tree when the whole tree needs to come down. To come to Jesus, we must come properly. Imagine a guy saying to his girlfriend, "I love you so much, I'm going to give up three of my other ten girlfriends." It's not going to work, right?

It is difficult because of the contest of wills. We must end the contest!

It's easy because you are coming to love. There are three kinds of love. First, there are those who have "*if* love"—they will love you "if." Then there is "*because* love"—people will love you "because." The third kind of love is the only one that is genuine. It's "*in spite of* love." He loves us "in spite of" (you name it).

It's the "Come as you are" to Jesus that it makes it easy. If something is dirty, the new Manager will clean it up. He specializes in that. Some stains can only be removed by blood, and only His blood has that power. "*Without the shedding of blood is no remission of sins*" (Hebr. 9:22). "*Unto Him that loved us, and washed us from our sins in His own blood*" (Rev. 1:5). Theologians call this "repentance and faith."

If something or some things in your life are broken, the new Manager knows how to fix it—all of it. He will show you the way. Being a genuine Christian is a change of management, a change of government, from self-rule to Christ's rule! From self-management to Christ's management! From self-government to Christ's government. Remember it well: *"The government shall be upon his shoulder: and his name shall be called Wonderful, Counsellor, The mighty God, The everlasting Father, The Prince of Peace. Of the increase of his government and peace there shall be no end..."* (Isa. 9:6–7).

The other thing that makes it easy to come to Him properly is His very welcoming, loving nature. Of all the descriptions and depictions of Him in Scripture, I personally like that He is the Chief Shepherd that gives His life for the sheep. Read this, believe this, feel this, respond to this.

> *"I am the good shepherd: the good shepherd giveth his life for the sheep. But he that is an hireling, and not the shepherd, whose own the sheep are not, seeth the wolf coming, and leaveth the sheep, and fleeth: and the wolf catcheth them, and scattereth the sheep. The hireling fleeth, because he is an hireling, and careth not for the sheep. I am the good shepherd, and know my sheep, and am known of mine. As the Father knoweth me, even so know I the Father: and I lay down my life for the sheep."*
>
> (John 10:11–15)

Knowing the Shepherd Changes Our Lives

I will close with a story that I hope demonstrates the incomparable power of Jesus's leadership and salvation to transform our lives.

As a boy in my father's church, I listened with bated breath to an evangelist who told this story. Here it is, exactly as I heard it:

A number of years ago, a very eminent lady in the city of London, England, invited to her home some of the finest people who could be found in all the British Isles. These were a cross-section from the arts and sciences, and their individual accomplishments had made them to be revered at home and across the seas.

For the entertainment of this prestigious company, the hostess had brought from the stage one of England's finest actors. This remarkable man was the professor of an outstanding memory. Once he committed something to his mind, it was seldom ever forgotten.

On this memorable afternoon, the audience listened with bated breath as he quoted continually those beloved passages of English literature. In closing, he astounded his little group as he allowed them to ask for specific passages and promised to quote them verbatim. One after the other, men and women stood to their feet and asked for the beloved passages of yesteryear.

The last person to stand was an elderly clergyman. Every eye in the room was fastened on his beloved face as he said, "Sir, would you be so kind as to quote for me the twenty-third Psalm?"

The actor's face went ashen, and then he said, "Yes, sir, I will if, when I am finished, you, too, will do the same."

The actor began, and his voice and intonation were perfect. As he quoted that psalm, the beauty, the tender, the pitch of his voice, and the melody of his diction were of such a caliber that the recitation stirred every heart. The last of the words had scarcely died in the air when wave after wave of applause rang across the drawing room. The actor sat in his chair, and the aging clergyman rose to stand behind the rostrum. He lifted his eyes heavenward, and in a voice that was worn by more than five decades of preaching, he began that beautiful psalm: "The Lord is my Shepherd, I shall not want. He maketh me to lie down in green pastures ... Yea though I walk through the valley of the shadow of death, I will fear no evil."

As he came to these words, his head bowed on his chest, and big tears began to tumble down his cheeks. A great sob broke from the depths of his heart, and instantly everyone was greatly concerned for the aged man. Many thought him to be ill. Others felt he must have had a loss of memory, but such was not the case.

As the old man came to those words of that fourth verse, his mind had, in a moment of time, skipped back across the span of forty years. He stood again as a young man by the side of his equally youthful wife. Before them was a mound of earth that marked the resting place of their darling little girl, and for them, there seemed to be no light on the hills of tomorrow. How could there ever be a day of joy when their wee girly would play no more around their home?

He remembered how he and his wife, in silence, had walked hand in hand to the old church on the hill. They bowed in tears and asked the Christ who walks every road to dry their tears, open their eyes, and give them a vision of the Beloved Shepherd that will someday make all things new. He saw in bold relief every thrilling aspect as his spiritual ears heard the stately steppings of Jesus Christ, who is the King of Kings, the Great Captain of all conquerors, and the Lord of Lords. Once more across the span of a lifetime, he caught a vision of the Master who had picked them up and folded them to His bosom, even as He did to the lambs of long ago.

This vision had come in a moment, and instantly, the old preacher straightened his tired shoulders and began once more to quote the eternal promise for those who walk in the dark valleys. His voice became more dynamic; his enlightened soul was ablaze with heaven's light. His face shone like Steven's on the morning when the curtains of heaven were pulled back and he recognized his lovely Lord. He moved once more across the plains of light, hand in hand with a friend who sticks closer than a brother, and came to the closing words with ringing and triumphant declaration of dwelling in the House of the Lord forever.

The old man sat down, but there was no applause. Every head was bowed, and tears stained every eye. The actor, the great man he was, rose and put his arm around the shaking shoulder of the old clergyman. He said, "Friends, today you have heard two men quote the same piece of poetry, but there is a tremendous difference, for I merely know the twenty-third Psalm, but this old gentleman knows the Shepherd."

Here is my final question for you, dear reader: Do you know the Shepherd, the Life Manager?

Here's how you can know. Jesus, the Shepard, said, "My sheep hear My voice, and I know them, and they follow Me" (John 10:27). Do you hear His voice? If so, follow Him! Follow His Ultimate Life Management System!

If not, get to Him now. The stakes have never been higher. He is tenderly waiting for you! Oh, how He loves you!

If You Enjoyed This Book, Please Tell Others!

- Post a 5-star review on Amazon.

- Write about the book on your Facebook, Twitter, Instagram, LinkedIn, or any social media platforms you regularly use.

- If you blog, consider referencing the book or publishing an excerpt from it with a link back to our website. You have permission to do this as long as you provide proper credit and backlinks.

- Recommend the book to friends, family, and caregivers. Word-of-mouth is still the most effective form of advertising.

- Purchase additional copies to give away to others or for use by your church or other groups.

Learn more about the authors or contact them at
www.NothingButTheTruth.org

Enjoy These Other Books by David Johnston

Why You Were Born -
A Blueprint for Discovering
Your Life Potential

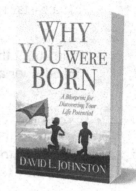

Why are you here on planet earth? Once you know why you were born you will have a new appreciation for your true self, have a known purpose in life and know why you matter. Then, and only then, can you choose a life path, a course of action and eventually a fulfilled life... no disappointments, no pressure to conform to the ideas and expectations of others. You will be free to be you, the real you.

In the second part of this book you will learn how to discover your ENA, your Embedded Natural Abilities. How tragic that some will cross the stage of time, be standing at the exit sign, and look back only to see a wasted life of insignificance. None of us can run a good race on the wrong track. "My Way," only counts if it's the right way.

Read and apply the truths of this book and you will never be a prisoner to your past or the false notions imposed upon you by others. Joy, satisfaction, and fulfillment in life will be yours.

How to Have Peace in Difficult Times -
Staying Calm No Matter What's Going
on Around You

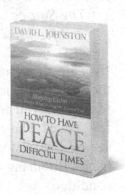

We live in turbulent times. Society sometimes
seems like it is teetering on the brink of chaos.

Too often we look towards our circumstances
to bring us a sense of peace and calm.
Unfortunately, you simply can't control your
surroundings and the events that happen to
you. All too often they are beyond your control.

This powerful book will give you keys to experiencing peace and
staying calm no matter what may be happening to you or around
you.

Pastor Johnston uses Scripture to show how God can bring you
true and lasting peace.

For example, discover:

- How your words can not only speak peace to others but to
  your own heart and mind

- The secret to cultivating a lasting peace that cannot be shaken
  when bad things happen

- The mystical connection between your heart and your mind

- The authority you have to become a "peacemaker"

- How to start making better and wiser decisions

- Beating back anger, resentment, bitterness and strife

When everyone around you is leaning into fear, panic, tension
and worry – YOU have the power to walk in peace, even in difficult
times.

How You See Yourself -
The Source of Your Struggle
and How to Conquer It

Ever go to a carnival and look into one of those distorted mirrors, you know, the ones that make you look three feet tall and five feet wide? The image of yourself that you see back is distorted. It can produce a good laugh. But many of us struggle with a similar condition – we don't see ourselves accurately. We are hindered from being the best version of ourselves, the version God intended. We are prevented by this insidious thing called iniquity.

Iniquity is mentioned 334 times in the Bible, yet so many remain oblivious to its significant and negative impact on everyday living. Iniquity is the ancient term for narcissism. It's one of the four reason Jesus went to the cross… "He was bruised for our iniquities" (Isa. 53:5). As you journey through the pages of this book you will not only identify the problems iniquity imposes upon us, but you will also discover the solutions.

This book will help you discover:
- How iniquity contributes to mental illness

- How iniquity causes divorce and destroys households

- How conquering iniquity will cause your prayer life to flourish

- How you can finally live without fear and regret

- How to embrace the benefits that come from being free from iniquity and the way it robs you of your God-given potential!

- How iniquity is different from sin

Nothing But The Truth Ministries

Dedicated to the single task of explaining the truth in its simplest and purest form to all peoples of the world.

People matter. YOU matter! Truth is the substance of all wise decision-making. So it's important to know the truth – about you, about why you were born, about every aspect of your life. Truth is wonderful, even when sometimes it may not seem comfortable.

This site is dedicated to sharing God's truth with you – truth that you can apply to your daily life, your relationships, your finances, your choices, your future.

Visit our website at
www.NothingButTheTruth.org and
www.KingofKingsChurch.us